ACTION,
SYMBOLISM,
AND
ORDER

# ACTION,
# SYMBOLISM,
# AND
# ORDER

*The Existential
Dimensions of
Politics in
Modern Citizenship*

## ROBERT J. PRANGER

Vanderbilt University Press 1968

For Charlotte

# *Preface*

THE world of politics is often pictured as an arena of trans-
actional conflicts and resolutions of conflicts, a kind of field of
systemic relationships involving competition for social authority.
At the same time, politics does embrace the actions of living
actors who, much like stones thrown into a pond, generate
ripples that stir the surface of life. Amid clamorous bargain-
ings in the political marketplace move real persons.

This book is an attempt to look at personal politics. My intention is to focus on personality and on the politics that develops
in the wake of individual action. This focus limits my perspective to one of looking from the "inside out," rather than seeing
actors from more general political contexts.

If the study of politics is complicated when viewed from a
general context, it is equally difficult when approached from the
individual's position. Few conceptions in the modern sciences
of man evoke as many controversies as does "personality," and
few words in everyday speech seem as curious as "person." For
"person" at once signifies a true identity and an evasive one: an

viii    PREFACE

identifiable individual and an enigmatic one. When personalities act in politics, both attributes—authenticity and evasion—contribute to action, and both must be understood to make sense of politics. "Personality" somehow involves the labyrinthine relationships between individual and mask. At work are the enormously subtle, complicated, and mysterious forces of both self-fulfillment and social disguise.

A reliable political language that focuses on persons active in politics must be equally subtle. I have attempted here to specify some of the requirements I think necessary for such a language, though my conclusions may not be very encouraging for those who demand a simple, unambiguous vocabulary for political analysis. It has been said that in political science one ought to simplify wherever possible, but beware of simplification. This book is excessively conservative about simplification, perhaps—especially about the formalizations toward which the behavioral sciences seem headed—but for good reason. The rush to systematize in political science has not always proceeded from a careful discussion about what it is that requires systematization.

This book grows out of a long period of gestation and revision dating back to graduate work. For his encouragement in the earlier phases, I would like to thank Professor Sheldon S. Wolin. For his support during the final stages, I express my gratitude to Robert P. Emmitt of Vanderbilt University Press. Generous financial aid for this book has been supplied by the Social Science Research Council and the University of Illinois Research Board.

ROBERT J. PRANGER

*University of Washington*

# Contents

ACTION,
SYMBOLISM,
AND
ORDER

# Citizenship and Political Science Method

IF political theory, dealing with that area of consent and co-ercion which arranges persons into polities and transforms them from private individuals into citizens, has been traditionally concerned with a "life of common involvements,"[1] its task in the twentieth century is far more complicated than ever before. Today we possess greater self-consciousness about our common involvements, or lack of them, in the sense that we know more about what makes the other fellow "tick," but such knowledge is diffused through the vast complexity of contemporary societies, compared with the rather simple structures in the ancient and primitive worlds. True, the ancient world was well acquainted with urban life, bureaucratic organization, and industry, but it did not experience that urbanization, bureaucratization, and industrialization common to modern polities (though the *relative* impact of these three developments on ancient society would make a fascinating study). But, while

1. Sheldon S. Wolin, *Politics and Vision* (Boston: Little, Brown, 1960), p. 434.

3

simpler in its social structure, antiquity required perhaps greater dedication of citizens to their community; at least this was so in two ancient cities, Athens and Rome. The Ionian citizenship ideal, exemplified by brilliant Athens, sharply distinguished between "idiotic" man (his own) and "politic" man (communal).[2] Cicero, on the other hand, apotheosized the Roman republican notion that "a people is not any collection of human beings brought together in any sort of way, but an assemblage of people in larger numbers associated in an agreement with respect to justice and a partnership for the common good."[3] Naturally, class warfare and other divisions plagued Greece and Rome, so that these sentiments remained ideals only. Yet there is evidence that such ideals suffused the two communities in a way unknown today, though we still employ the terminology of "community" and the "common good." Even among professional students of contemporary sociopolitical phenomena, a declining interest in community has been observed.[4]

We can say, therefore, that men once knew less about their fellows in psychological and sociological terms, yet they were forced by the nature of their governments, the intimacy of their states, the urgencies of their political creeds, and perhaps their own ignorance, into more profound political involvements with their fellow citizens. Cicero wrote, many centuries before nationalism gave men easy civic stimulation,

I hold that all members of boroughs have two fatherlands, one in nature, one in the state. Even as the great Cato was born at Tusculum and received into the community of the Roman people, so, though he was a Tusculan by origin, he was yet a Roman and had one local and one legal fatherland. . . . We must prefer in affection

2. Werner Jaeger, *Paideia*, 3 vols., 1933–1943 (Oxford: Basil Blackwell, 1954), fourth English edition, I, 111.

3. "Populus autem non omnis hominum coetus quoquo modo congregatus, sed coetus multitudinis iuris consensu et utilitatis communione sociatus." *De Re Publica*, translated by Clinton Walker Keyes (Cambridge, Mass., and London: The Loeb Classical Library, Harvard University Press, and William Heinemann, 1928), pp. 64–65.

4. See Maurice Stein, *The Eclipse of Community* (1960) (New York: Harper Torchbooks, 1964), p. 96.

that one which is called the state and the whole community, for which we must be ready to die, and to which we must surrender our whole being and in which we must place all our hopes, and to which we must consecrate all that is ours. But the fatherland which begot us is not much less beloved by us than that which adopted us.[5]

It would be a mistake, however, to equate intimacy or common involvements with the physical size of any social unit, including the state, thereby establishing some inverse ratio between size and enthusiasms. There is more to it than this. The family represents a small group, but estrangement often develops within it. On the other hand, our present means of communication and transportation have conquered the problems of great distance. And what technics have not accomplished, the increased birth rate has. Indeed, it has been the consensus of thinkers since Malthus and Fichte that our planet is becoming not less but more crowded. The phenomenon of "crowding" precisely illustrates where the real problem of community and common involvements rests today: sheer physical density, the pressing together of one body against another, does not create intimacy or sharing. Crowding, as contrasted to community, manifests characteristics of aggression, fear, insecurity, and loneliness. Love becomes hatred. Commonwealth converts into mass. *Gemeinschaft* metamorphoses into *Ersatzgemeinschaft*. So the feature least connected with common involvement is physical space. Modern politics, with the technical means at its disposal, can conquer simple physical distance.

Such crowding together, however, has been accompanied by one of history's greatest paradoxes. Our knowledge of the human being has increased many-fold from the time when Europe was fissured into feudal domains. Yet Medieval Europe was united in its spiritual orientation toward human existence, even while it was split into contending fiefdoms (fiefdoms which included the Pope's own). Precisely the opposite holds true today: every economist points out the increasing material inter-

5. *De Legibus* II, 2. 5. Quoted and translated by A. N. Sherwin-White, *The Roman Citizenship* (Oxford: Clarendon Press, 1939), p. 134, n. 5.

dependence of men, yet nearly every intellectual historian laments the profound fragmentation of the human intellect with its psychological and sociological fundaments. And who has not read convincing arguments against national sovereignty in today's internationalized world? That such syntheses as Marxism and Freudianism exert great influence in modern life only illustrates the magnitude of this alienation in every corner of the human self. Here is the area where common involvements have broken down—in the realm of intellection and spirit. Hannah Arendt has carefully recorded how the ancient polis was not primarily physical at all: "it is the organization of the people as it arises out of acting and speaking together, and its true space lies between people living together for this purpose, no matter where they happen to be."[6]

If political life is determined by how people act and speak together, then we can readily see in our contemporary situation some corruption of a sense of common involvements. Liberalism's self-reliant individual was politically apathetic, if not a-political, because he presumed the state would simply provide him a necessary neutral peace and order for pursuing his private goals. This contextual theory of politics was best stated by Adam Smith. In such a view, politics has functions but no purposes separate from the individuals who engage in political action. To this neutralizing of the state was added the current "war of ideas," dating back to the French Revolution, which further disrupted intellectual communication. Today we witness both competitive action and competitive thought together with that symbiosis between them which creates and reflects our general situation of fragmentary disorganization. Max Scheler's observation has relevance in this context.

In no other period of human knowledge has man ever become more problematic to himself than in our own days. We have a scientific, a philosophical, and a theological anthropology that know nothing of each other. Therefore we no longer possess any clear and consistent idea of man. The ever-growing multiplicity of the particular sciences

6. *The Human Condition* (Garden City, N.Y.: Doubleday Anchor Books, 1959) (Originally published by the University of Chicago Press, copyright © 1958), p. 177.

that are engaged in the study of men has much more confused and obscured than elucidated our concept of man.[7]

Ernst Cassirer once noted how the nineteenth century became the era of "autonomous sciences," each seeking to prove "the unity and homogeneity of human nature," yet each ironically proving just the opposite.[8]

A second irony, perhaps causally connected with the first paradox of fragmentation, is the rise, since the eighteenth century, of a humanism inspired by respect for and exaltation of vital life forces. This secular humanism is magnificently stated in the works of Goethe, Nietzsche, and others. Surely, modern existentialism itself represents such a "humanism," as Sartre has observed.[9] But this same humanism infuses modern social science as well, with its concerns for progress toward more rational, self-conscious controls over society. Both social science and existentialism—indeed the whole intellectual community of the West—seems to lust for life, value self-consciousness, and support both in the face of political and other persecutions.

Yet this irony is not yet complete. On the other side there is the plain fact that life today is cheap, in spite of our vaunted humanistic advances. This has great importance for citizenship, because it is precisely the citizen role, not the military, the legislative, nor the judicial role, that is most affected by this fact. It was true of the ancient world that certain large groups of persons such as slaves had no right to life at all. Others lived under the constant threat of cruel despotisms. But citizens, contrasted to slaves, were truly human beings, and their lives had high premium.

Today nearly every person is a citizen: destruction and mutilation of life must affect citizens with greater force. Hitler moved to denationalize Jews before he gassed them, though not because

7. *Die Stellung des Menschen im Kosmos* (Darmstadt: Reichl, 1928), pp. 13 f.; quoted in Ernst Cassirer, *An Essay on Man* (1944) (Garden City, N.Y.: Doubleday Anchor Books), p. 40.

8. *Ibid.*, p. 39.

9. *Existentialism and Humanism* (New York: Philosophical Library, 1948).

he valued citizenship. But stategic bombing during the Second World War and after was aimed deliberately at civilian, citizen populations, to say nothing of the present threat posed by thermonuclear war. Even in peacetime the average citizen is nowadays constantly subjected to more threats against his life. Statistics make abstractions from individual fatalities on the highway and in the home, while the present population explosion renders each individual person less in relation to the whole.

Last, but not least, ideologies such as communism classify human beings into worthy and unworthy, characteristically promoting a certain carelessness toward the lives of the unworthy. Indeed, our only hope for locating ourselves in a complex world is to organize people into abstract groups. Life's prevailing abstractness and cheapness easily leads to apathy, despair, and pessimism—attitudes which dominate important segments of Western intellectual life as well as the actual behavior of Western man. Small wonder this proves true, given the dimunition of citizen status.

The second irony is therefore this: we hear an increasing demand and witness a mounting effort for the protection and prolongation of human life, while simultaneously the life of the *average* citizen becomes the life of the *ordinary* citizen who is given only *ordinary* protection. The actual content of contemporary societies does not sustain contemporary humanism, and the result is a kind of despair over the future of humankind. This also explains why so much tragedy in modern dramatic art takes the form of social protest rather than universal pathos. Without social support, intellectual protestations—both existentialist and social-scientific—seem more specialized, less universal.

One need not, however, take existentialism and social science less seriously on this account. The opposite has more truth: whereas it is relatively easy to appreciate a philosophy and science in tune with a particular environment—Oriental societies once presented such wonderful paradigms of equilibrium—it is more difficult to balance intellectual criticism against actual social behavior. Western man is presented with the spectacle of almost unanimous intellectual protest from the *avant garde* against "the bomb," "statelessness," and "totalitarianism," which are, nonetheless, three of the twentieth century's genuinely unique inventions. Citizens today face at least two sets of social standards—those of the more advanced intelligentsia in the humanities and sciences, and those given them by their political and social leaders.

Representing the human tradition, existentialism and social science are allies on a plane that transcends mere epistemological and methodological disputes. They still occasionally speak of "man" as opposed to "men." My book attempts to demonstrate a division of labor within this modern intellectual life, which may aid us in charting man's common involvements. Political theory, so concerned with common involvement, can learn much from these movements of thought. What we shall attempt here is to widen the circumferences of our thinking in order to view modern citizenship from *multiple* viewpoints. Symbolically, and this method will be covered more fully in Chapter Five, this means placing ourselves in several different situations and operating with several different vocabularies in order to see citizenship in various dimensions.

The brilliant critic, Kenneth Burke, once pictured the ways in which we circumscribe things when we define them linguistically. Among other things, this suggests that there are various modes of definition relevant to various problems and that questions as complex as citizenship require multiple angles of vision, if we aim to be general in our approach, operations, and conclusions. Citizenship, as one of society's most general roles, provides us with an opportunity to test the relevance of social science, existential philosophy, certain areas of psychology, as well as theories of symbolism relating to political theory. As noted above, each of these approaches provides a different circumference or position from which to view a single consideration—citizenship.

My chief concern will be to present a way in which political theory might solve its age-old problem of citizenship's common obligations within a contemporary context. Faced with the imperative of citizenship, which is to reconcile individual person and polity, it seemed to me that the dimensions of action, symbolism, and asymptotic order between private and public proved a kind of nexus within which the central problem of citizen obligation might be studied fruitfully. These dimensions open a few very tentative hypotheses for future inquiry. First, political action, in all its forms including citizenship, is purposive and vocational (or creative) as well as functional. Hence, it has unpredictable, irreversible, and anonymous consequences, as Arendt argues in her book, *The Human Condition.* As does all action, political action exemplifies that constant "going-beyond" which existential philosophy refers to when speaking of living, acting human beings. Second, private attitude also exhibits protean forms, made so by the uniqueness of individual symbolizations. Third, the private attitudes and public actions of any single individual do not quite fall together with social order; that is, these attitudes and actions are "asymptotic" to any social system. Even a sociological theorist such as Talcott Parsons, dedicated to finding continuities in social structure, admits this drift or wandering from fixed norms by social actors. In fact, Parsons has incorporated such drift into his social theory.

These three hypotheses, if they merit the title of hypotheses, together with subsidiary questions raised in the following essay, may aid political theory's quest for a life of common involvements in our age of diversity. At the same time, however, they stand as caution signs along the way toward such a quest. Men are not merely functional ciphers in the group struggles of politics. They are something more than integers in a political system. These assertions are not only testimonies of faith, though they are that too; they form purposive and occasionally metaphysical emendations to a well-rounded view of man in his multiple political activities as citizen and leader, or in Aristotle's words, in his actions as both ruler and ruled.

But the present book not only deals with citizenship; it is about methods of political analysis. To widen circumferences of political thought by viewing citizenship from various angles, I hope to expand our ideas of what is "meaningful" in the way of political knowledge. Perhaps this wider understanding verges on a "metapolitics" that uses political ideas to move beyond myriads of apparently unrelated studies toward an open-ended synthesis. This procedure is not necessarily "unscientific"; on the contrary, a metapolitics can be a valuable tool for expanding research.

Expanded meanings desired by science are never just a matter of building one small block on top of another until some final general theory emerges. But the other extreme is also unwise—that of constructing a general theory with no research support. While research and theory obviously go hand in hand in science, theory's function is to open new avenues for research, to point out new directions through systematic explanations of phenomena. Theory can perform this task only if it keeps a certain distance from research, which means that theory is never produced simply by generalizations one makes as conclusions to a piece of empirical research. The test of good theoretical work in science is twofold: does it accord with research being *accepted somewhere* in science? and does it provide explanation that is productive of *new* research? The present attempt to grapple with citizenship as a threefold problem in action, symbolism, and order is designed to meet these two criteria.[10]

A controversial methodological argument developed in this book asserts that every science must tailor its methods and aims to fit its subject matter. Max Weber argued that science, as the analytical ordering of empirical materials, is quite variegated according to the special subject matters involved.[11] One could take a more "unified science" position with regard to political science, of course, and with considerable profit. Such a view would argue that every science seeks to investigate its subject matter with substantially the same aim in mind, the building of general laws. Weber, on the other hand, was much concerned about the separate identity of scientific disciplines in terms of their subject matters, a point still vigorously debated in the social sciences and elsewhere.

10. For a prescient view of relations between theory and empirical fact in science see Stephen Toulmin, *Foresight and Understanding* (New York: Harper Torchbooks, 1961), Chapter 5.

11. " 'Objectivity' in Social Science and Social Policy" (1904), in Max Weber, *The Methodology of the Social Sciences*, translated and edited by E. A. Shils and H. A. Finch (Glencoe, Illinois: The Free Press, 1949), pp. 49–112.

The preceding methodological point grows out of my conviction that political science has still not faced certain problems of complex space and time within politics, especially the thorny question of how specialized languages of analysis "fit" ordinary political situations. One obvious problem is how the development of a "political system" relates to the development of an individual "self" within politics.[12] Another question concerns the highly symbolic nature of time in all its dimensions—a symbolism complicated by variegated cultures and by pluralistic activities.[13] One regulates one's life on the basis of many different time periods or rhythms, not all of which are congruent. And of course political forces in various parts of the world tend to understand even calendar time in different ways and to interpret the significance of action differently within any given time span.

When we face the kinds of problems mentioned above in terms of action within political situations, we find that languages of explanation about such matters tend to be complicated and by no means homogeneous, at least in contemporary political science. These complications may result from the youthfulness of political science as a science, but under these circumstances it would be a mistake to press analysis prematurely into any single mold. As I shall try to point out, however, such difficulties are not just a matter of the youth of political science. Human experience proves to be multidimensional and even ambiguous, not because this or that philosopher asserts that it is, but because the cultural sciences demonstrate that it is by their profusion and mixed languages. I am interested in how the social sciences and

12. See Paul Kress, "Self, System, and Significance: Reflections on Professor Easton's Political Science," *Ethics*, LXVII (October 1966), 1–14.
13. On the importance of clock time in Western civilization see Lewis Mumford, *Technics and Civilization* (New York: Harbinger Book, 1963), pp. 12–18. But Mumford exaggerates the central importance of this one kind of time. See also Stephen Toulmin and June Goodfield, *The Discovery of Time* (New York: Harper Torchbooks, 1965); and the notable encounter in 1922 between Henri Bergson and Albert Einstein on the subject of ordinary time versus scientific time, as related by Maurice Merleau-Ponty in "Einstein and the Crisis in Reason," in his *Signs*, translated by Richard C. McCleary (Evanston: Northwestern University Press, 1964), pp. 195–197.

modern philosophies of human experience, particularly existential philosophies, view this multidimensionality.[14]

Citizenship has various dimensions—action, symbolism, and order—but each of these can be approached at various levels of analysis and significance. My interest here is in those writers who do not adopt a simplistic, purely objectivist view of human experience, in those who argue for openness in human experience as the ultimate problem with which the human sciences must reckon—but an openness not to be coerced into abstract categories of analysis. The title of the book refers to this question of openness in the expression, "existential dimensions." "Existential" denotes the daily, whole experience, involving action, thought, and feeling, that a person has when he is in "asymptotic congruence" with other persons and larger systems, including his relations with the state.[15] Yet the idea that such experiences are "dimensions" indicates that these experiences are linked together in meaningful, total biographies lived by real persons. There is both continuity and creativity in this enterprise of the real, existing "individual."[16] Our point of departure, citizenship, proves to be that political role most general

14. Maurice Merleau-Ponty speaks of "*dimensions* of history" as "that formula which sums up some unique manner of behaviour toward others, towards Nature, time and death." *The Phenomenology of Perception*, translated by Colin Smith (London: Routledge & Kegan Paul, 1962), p. xviii. In spite of his reliance on *Gestalt* psychology, however, Merleau-Ponty is quite dogmatic about multidimensionality. See also Paul Ricoeur's idea of "the pluralization of the order of truth" in our cultural history, as well as his reference to Emmanuel Mounier's interest in multidimensionality, in *History and Truth*, translated by Charles A. Kelbley (Evanston: Northwestern University Press, 1965), pp. 161, 166.

15. See the discussion of these three dimensions, from the viewpoint of an existential phenomenology, by Paul Ricoeur, *Fallible Man*, translated by Charles Kelbley (Chicago: Henry Regnery Co., 1965).

16. "Individual" will be used throughout this book more in the sense of "person" than the "individualism" associated with liberalism. This usage accords somewhat with Mounier's treatment of the person in his book, *Personalism*, translated by Philip Mairet (London: Routledge & Kegan Paul, 1952). Other sources dealing with the individual-as-person have been used here, but these sources in existential philosophy parallel to some extent Mounier, whose all-pervasive influence on a generation Ricoeur likens to Péguy's.

in scope but least generalizable because of the vast numbers involved. At the same time, citizenship provides the most occasions for political tension between self and world; in fact, citizenship represents a "given" status to which the self *must* adjust, with all the tensions latent in any such mandatory adjustment. Thus, citizenship provides an excellent case study in the personal, tension-filled politics of daily experience.

While this book says something about political analysis, it also tries to say something about political action—especially contemporary political action. Weber argued that the social sciences ought to deal with matters of cultural significance, and as these matters shift, so do relevant fields of analysis. This significance, which involves the discernment of meaning as well as behavior, separated the social sciences from the natural sciences in Weber's mind.[17] Contemporary investigations of alienation, and the commentaries such investigations have evoked, are partly responsible for the idea of asymptotic congruence developed in Chapter Six. Such a concern also stems from modern literature and theology. Likewise, existential philosophy says something important about contemporary politics and is, therefore, relevant here. Existential analysis has cultural significance, both in terms of how it pierces to the core of modern existence and also as a manifestation of modern life, even though its methods of analysis do not jibe with many practices in the social sciences at this point.[18]

17. The problem of "meaning" in social interactions has not been discovered by existentialists and phenomenologists, as if contemporary social science neglected this question, though they often give this impression. On the contrary, Weber considered meaning the core problem for the social *sciences* (not just for social *philosophy*).

18. A similar point is made by Henry S. Kariel, "The Political Relevance of Behavioral and Existential Psychology," *American Political Science Review*, LXI (June 1967), 334–342. I do not entirely accept, as I hope this book demonstrates, Kariel's declaration that, while the existential persuasion is committed to freedom as the highest public value, it evades the *political* problem of reconciling conflicting claims to power and the *empirical* problem of weighing such claims (p. 341). Of course, like all other sciences, the social sciences are culturally significant in themselves, as well as being vehicles by which culture is analyzed.

Contemporary political science evinces little interest in existential or other social and political philosophies (phenomenology, for example) which have relevance to human issues but do not use familiar empirical data-gathering techniques. To the extent that political science is interested only in general cultural laws, existential philosophy ought to be ignored, *if* one believes that empirical research leads to discovery of general laws.[19] But in the measure that political science is concerned with matters of cultural significance, the object of social science investigation in Weber's mind, it ought to be interested in existential philosophy. This is not meant as a criticism of political science. Apart from the pretentiousness of such criticism, the fact of all scholarly life is the division of labor, and a division of labor within certain conventions. Some persons think about more empirical matters, while others worry about questions of scope and direction. Also, the conventions of political science preclude at this time much concern about existentialism, since the discipline is much more in the mode of "scientific philosophy" even on matters of direction.[20]

Yet political science *is* concerned today about its direction and at least this book fits into a *genre* of books on "political theory" and "scope and method." Also, political scientists do think about questions of what *ought* to be done in public policy, so the present book touches another area of political science called "political thought" or "political philosophy" or "value theory."

In summary, the present book deals with ordinary citizenship. Within this general area a multidimensional approach to self and others within typical political contexts is used—an approach employing the existential dimensions of action, symbolism, and order. We shall relate thought to action by focusing our vocabularies on matters of everyday political experience for citizens, on the "tension of citizenship" between "private man and public

19. For some problems concerning this assumption see Quentin Gibson, *The Logic of Social Enquiry* (London: Routledge & Kegan Paul, 1960), pp. 120–124.
20. See Eugene J. Meehan, *The Theory and Method of Political Analysis* (Homewood, Ill.: Dorsey Press, 1965), pp. 14–20.

duty."[21] Although the strategy to be adopted and methods to be proposed may not fall within the usual approaches to behavior in political science, this book does belong to two streams within political science's over-all tradition, one dealing with scope and direction and the other with values.

21. The expressions form the basis of a much different approach to citizenship by H. Mark Roelof, *The Tension of Citizenship, Private Man and Public Duty* (New York: Holt, Rinehart and Winston, 1957).

# II | The Institutional Setting for Citizen Action

## Institutional Theories of Citizenship

CITIZENSHIP denotes both an ascribed status and a certain complex political activity. Hence it may be analyzed by two kinds of political theory; first, that concerned with institutions and the ways legal obligations and statuses are assigned individuals and groups in a polity, and, second, that interested in the actions of individuals and groups and the relationships between them in politics. Both institutional theory and action theory are important for analyzing citizenship, although only the latter will be examined and used extensively here. In order to provide a more comprehensive theoretical background for citizenship, however, a brief consideration of institutional theory and its relation to the analysis of citizenship is mandatory. The present chapter supplies this need.

Citizenship means "doing" something—citizens voting, soldiering, and the like. Other political action terms include "legislator," "judge," "administrator"; that is, one "is" a citizen, one "is" a legislator, just as one "is" a father. If it appears that the ground has slipped suddenly from a purely descriptive one (citizens "do" something) to an ontological one (citizens "are" something), the change is intentional. Action and existence are closely related when it comes to the particular style any individual adopts when playing his social roles, and this fact necessitates an expansion of purely descriptive action theory, and its applications to politics to include ontological matters—an expansion discussed in the next chapter. Kenneth Burke's statement is apposite in this context: "action is not merely a means of doing but a way of being."[1] One elementary qualification seems necessary: the discussion here centers on *political* action and *political* existence. How this type differs from other forms of action and existence will be expanded in the second section of this chapter.

At the same time, while citizens act and interact, their activity, like all life's business, appears closely connected to organized statuses and the particular expectations or norms surrounding those statuses. Life is institutional. For example, childhood and adulthood are general and universal categories, but particular styles of being children and being adults are always related to specific cultures and their patterning. They are "institutional." Similarly, there persists a very general status, "citizenship," but each society will fit this status to its own fabric of meanings and organizations. Citizenship, like childhood, is a special institution for each culture. Not only the "long view" of citizenship, but also what Margaret Mead calls the "comparative context," is mandatory, whether one studies childhood (as Mead)[2] or citizenship (as Merriam).[3] By nature, the institu-

1. *A Grammar of Motives* (New York: Prentice-Hall, 1945), p. 45. See also Anselm Strauss, *Mirrors and Masks, The Search for Identity* (New York: The Free Press of Glencoe, Illinois, 1959), p. 40.

2. See Margaret Mead and Martha Wolfenstein, eds., *Childhood in Contemporary Cultures* (Chicago: University of Chicago Press, 1955), p. 9.

3. See Charles E. Merriam, *The Making of Citizens, A Comparative Study of Methods of Civic Training* (Chicago: University of Chicago Press, 1931), pp. 7–13; and Gabriel Almond and James Coleman, eds., *Politics of the Developing Areas* (Princeton: Princeton University Press, 1960).

tional approach to citizenship requires comparative study. And while leadership (or the "elite") increasingly attracts political scientists and theorists, serious citizenship studies continue few and mixed in quality. Merriam even suggested that one must compare, not only various cultures in their citizen training, but different generations within single polities—a space-time multidimensional approach. One may dispute Merriam's view (a view of considerable influence) that the political's function encompasses "co-ordination, balancing, and integration of patterns . . . maintaining . . . the equilibrium of integration . . ." but still appreciate his approach to civic education systems as parts of total social situations.[4] Indeed, his insight seems scarcely changed from Aristotle's famous distinction between the "good citizen" and the "good man," the citizen's excellence always relative to the constitution of his particular *polis;* that is, "political" or "public" virtue. Such a man is not a "good man," because of any single absolute excellence, but a "good citizen."[5] Understanding the citizen means knowing not only the man but also his institutional (or "constitutional" in Aristotle's terminology) context, including the specialized institution of citizenship.

To serve the polity faithfully, civic education must renew itself constantly according to the special changing needs of particular political communities. Such education must also preserve a certain continuity so that it does not confuse its students. Always, therefore, citizen training includes an ingredient of traditionalism. But in such an era as the present, when fervent but flimsy nationalism and cults of self-interest universally cheapen the citizen's role, it is well to recall Aristotle's image, directly applicable for a context different from the modern nation-state, but compelling nevertheless, of a special kind of virtue belonging to citizenship—a virtue taught according to rational precepts, commonly called the "public interest." Does the public interest have any empirical substance? This the next section will attempt to ascertain. The "realist" position, represented by Arthur F. Bentley's belief that a social whole has no

4. *Op. cit.*, p. 11.
5. *Politics*, 1276b.

reality, is itself as unverified as the opposing position.[6] Another problem of citizen training involves redefining the text of civic virtue for each generation, to preserve the relevance of governmental and political institutions for the living. Since education is almost universally public in modern states, at least through primary school, defining and redefining common practices and purposes, consistent with the autonomy of individuals and their nonpublic associations, remains a basic human problem in the twentieth century. From California school boards to Russian education commissars, public authorities are universally tempted to employ civic training for "indoctrination" purposes.

As a political actor, the citizen need not contribute much politically. Belonging to a given polity, because he is born into it, the citizen's birthright makes him a full member, destined to be cannon fodder, commissar, elector, according to the lot fortune assigns him. Everywhere the single citizen (or organized group of citizens) acquires scant control over the course of political events, unless he (or they) possess social power. The ordinary man, "ordinary" because he has little or no control (power) over affairs in the world around himself, appears universally victimized by circumstances environmentally determined, a member of institutionalized, political arrangements (unless he is temporarily implicated in an alien society). Individual fortune fuses with communal history, but the latter's destiny generally remains beyond the citizen's personal control. Yet no matter how binding his obligations or blind his commitments, the citizen can always disobey. In other words, he is always fully and irrevocably responsible for his obedience.

Quibbling here about distinctions between "subjects" and "citizens"—presumably subjects merely "obey," citizens also

6. "Usually we shall find," Bentley wrote, "on testing the 'social whole,' that it is merely the group tendency or demand represented by the man who talks of it, erected into the pretense of a universal demand of the society. . . ." *The Process of Government* (1908), edited by Peter H Odegaard (Cambridge, Mass.: The Belknap Press of Harvard University, 1967), p. 220. An eloquent plea for reason and common interest in political life is found in Joseph Tussman, *Obligation and the Body Politic* (New York: Oxford University Press, 1961).

"participate"—seems a distinction of only marginal utility. In monarchies, absolute and constitutional, full members are called "subjects," although they are "citizens" too. No one would imagine that a "citizen" of Franco's Spain participates politically as much as a "subject" of Queen Elizabeth II. The distinction may also be symbolic, inherited from Rousseau and the French Revolution. It was imperative then to draw a suppressed populace into the republican ambience, so "citizen" actually became an honorific title, as it was in Athens. And it signified a similar communal interest of the general will linking all full members together. It was Rousseau who attempted, in his *Social Contract*, "to find a form of association which will defend and protect with the whole common force the person and goods of each associate, and in which each, while uniting himself with all, may still obey himself alone and remain as free as before."[7] This "associate" (*associé*) was the citizen.

Useful as his idea of "associate" was (an idea developed later in this chapter), Rousseau's attempt to solve the paradox of freedom and obedience belonged with other rationalizations for obligation to legally constituted authority, although somewhat more congenial to modern tempers than Hobbes's apologetics for absolutism.[8] Writing one of the few works in the history of political ideas devoted to the citizen, Hobbes used the terms "citizen" and "subject" interchangeably. Citizenship invariably means the special duties and obligations connected with the pleasures and potentials ("rights") of belonging, whatever else may be added: fullest legal membership entails fullest obligation to obey the rules of the polity. Every association, private and public, has the same requirement; otherwise there would exist no concord and hence no co-operation. From the institutional view, instead of placing main accent on some phase of participa-

7. *The Social Contract*, Bk. I, Chap. 6, in *The Social Contract and Discourses*, translated by G. D. H. Cole (London and New York: Everyman's Library, 1913), p. 12.

8. The principal writers on this subject were Plato, Aristotle, Spinoza, Hobbes, Locke, Rousseau, and T. H. Green. See T. H. Green, *Lectures on the Principles of Political Obligation* (1879–1880) (London: Longmans, Green & Co., 1941), Lectures B, C, D, E.

tion as an essential criterion for citizenship (and "participation" is always part of "rights" in general), it is more accurate to use legalistic guidelines when outlining. Following the latter procedure, "full membership," defined by specific societies, is stressed. Also, participation and subjection are not necessarily antinomies within organized settings.

On the contrary, Hobbes's *Leviathan*, one of the most trenchant defenses of absolutism ever written, explored at some length and with considerable ingenuity the many facets of political obligation. He seemed more dedicated to rationalizing subjection than to sanctifying absolute power. For Hobbes, obedience was hardly passive, though he indicated it was "simply" the subject's duty to obey his sovereign. "Subject to the higher powers," citizens participate in government because such subjection helps sustain the state common to all citizens. "Good citizens" are usually thought to be those who obey their community's laws (or are disobedient within its organized, legal framework) and work for its betterment according to these rules; they undertake the "activity of obedience" (see the third section of this chapter).[9]

Where these rules forbid active participation by the mass of citizenry, obedience is no less essential for "good citizenship" within institutional confines. On the other hand, where the individual's autonomy verges on cultural fetishism, as in modern America, obeying the law seems all the more important. Observing American youth, one often gains the impression of misplaced nonconformity; while frequently acceding unconsciously to every fad and fashion, they "rebel" against legally constituted authority or feign indifference to its claims. They forget the dictum of that most famous rebel against fashions and stereotypes, Socrates, that the price exacted from every citizen for the pleasures of full citizenship is loyalty and obedience to his state. Only where those called citizens are, in reality, denied the privileges of full citizenship, and these rights are consistently denied them over time—American Negroes and poor, for example—is

9. *De Cive*, edited by Sterling P. Lamprecht (New York: Appleton-Century-Crofts, 1949), for example, at p. 169.

revolt justified.[10] As every student of political thought knows, however, grouped with the question of obligation come the issues of equality, liberty, justice, disobedience, and revolution. And who is "really" justified to ask questions about obedience is never clear.

This discussion of the institutional aspects of obedience does not presume that "obeying" constitutes the same activity as, say, "giving orders." Governmental leadership is the most conspicuous political action and one different from citizenship; written history generally chronicles decision-making and acting by leaders. But law, as a whole, can be divided analytically into two parts—what H. L. A. Hart calls the "relatively passive aspect" and the "relatively active aspect."[11] The first type requires obedience from all citizens, the second gives power and responsibility to officials only. Compared with leadership, obedience is *relatively* passive, if the yardstick of leadership action is used. More important, however, the activity of obedience involves an activity different from leadership. At the same time, citizenship connotes not simply followership, since both leaders and followers are involved. Citizenship comprises the activity of obedience to the common good, in which, because all share, all are obliged. Obviously, where individualization and diversification have progressed steadily—in England, France, and the United States—

10. "Revolt" is used broadly—here both literally and figuratively. Aspects of Negro resentment against American society have been stated brilliantly by the contemporary essayist and novelist James Baldwin. See in particular his "Letter from a Region of My Mind," *The New Yorker*, XXXVIII (Nov. 17, 1962), 59–144. For the student of citizenship, Baldwin's queries about equality, justice, and consensus in American society are disquieting. On the more general subject of the American poor, in which Negroes play much too large a part, see Michael Harrington: "In almost any slum there is a vast conspiracy against the forces of law and order." *The Other America, Poverty in the United States* (New York: Macmillan Co., 1962), p. 16. Baldwin's essay centered around the Black Muslim movement. Since 1962 not only Black Muslimism but "Black Power" more generally have spread.

11. *The Concept of Law* (Oxford: Clarendon Press, 1961), p. 60. Hart later calls these two aspects of law "primary" (relatively passive) and "secondary" (relatively active) rules. *Ibid.*, pp. 78–79.

citizenship's participative aspects have greater value, at least in official ideologies.[12]

Using common association, full membership, and mutual obligation under law as the elementary criteria for citizenship, it is now possible to generalize from the experience of individual societies. That is, cataloguing the relations of citizens in and to their polities can now be simplified by certain categorical generalizations about factors common to all citizenships. Only after such broader categories are established can institutional theories be devised. Hence, a legal category, citizenship, characterizes all polities, even though some have no written law, no organized law enforcement, and no expression for citizen. According to the anthropologist Lucy Mair, who has made an extensive study of governments in primitive East Africa,

> Every primitive society recognizes in some way that fellow citizens have mutual obligations which do not extend to aliens, and in societies which have the least government these obligations are concerned with the limits of the use of force. If we give a very broad meaning to the word "law" we can express this fact in the proposition that there are social groups which recognize the rule of law among themselves, but do not consider outsiders come within it; and if we give the very broadest meaning to the phrase "the rule of law," we can say it is a situation in which peaceful relations are regarded as normal, and there has to be something to justify a breach of these relations.[13]

Here, mutual obligations, limits to force, and normally peaceful relations characterize the political community, but threats of enforcement and sanctions are usually present too. Citizenship status, viewed from outside a commonwealth, encompasses full legal membership in that polity's communal arrangements, using "law" in its broadest sense as obligatory rules (written

12. Assuming there is "progress" in the first place and that historical and social progress entails greater individualization and diversification. See Emile Durkheim, *The Division of Labor in Society*, translated by G. Simpson (Glencoe, Ill.: The Free Press, 1949), pp. 172–181; Edward Hallett Carr, *What is History?* (New York: Alfred A. Knopf, 1961), p. 190.

13. *Primitive Government* (Harmondsworth, Middlesex: Penguin Books, Ltd., 1962), p. 35.

and/or unwritten) sanctioned by force (organized and/or un-organized).[14] Rules may be accepted without being written and enforced without organized law enforcement, as Miss Mair's examples from East Africa amply demonstrate. Obedience signifies acceptance. Still this comprises "government," she insists, if one views government functionally for what it does, protecting "members of the political community against lawlessness within and enemies without; and . . . [taking] decisions on behalf of the community in matters which concern them all, and in which they have to act together."[15] In some societies, however, rules include two rather formal varieties: "primary rules"—those imposing duties on human beings to do or desist in certain actions; and "secondary rules"—those conferring powers, public and private.[16] Such law presumes legislative and adjudicative organs, plus organized sanctions. It seems evident, however, that government, on its more elementary level (as once practiced among the Nuer, for example), does not contain any clear notion

14. See Hart, *op. cit.*, Chapter V.
15. Mair, *op. cit.*, p. 16. See also Hart, *op. cit.*, p. 84: "Rules are conceived and spoken of as imposing obligations when the general demand for conformity is insistent and the social pressure brought to bear upon those who deviate or threaten to deviate is great . . . When physical sanctions are prominent or usual among the forms of pressure, even though these are neither closely defined nor administered by officials but are left to the community at large, we shall be inclined to classify the rules as a primitive or rudimentary form of law."
16. *Ibid.*, pp. 78–79. Hart claims that by combining these two types of rule, he has found "the key to the science of jurisprudence," which Austin mistakenly thought he had discovered earlier (see p. 79). Hart's claims to discovery include political theory as well as jurisprudence (pp. 95–96). Closer inspection reveals, however, that Hart is not as far from Hobbes and Austin as he would like to think, particularly in Chapter 4, Section 3, entitled (echo or parody of Hobbes?) "The Elements of Law" (pp. 89–96). This section is the keystone of Hart's concept of law. His distinction between "primary" and "secondary" rules here is scarcely an improvement on Hobbes, though the language (of crucial importance in Hart's linguistic analysis approach to his subject) has changed. It is clear that the transition from purely primary law (duties but no enforcement) to secondary law (law enforcement apparatus) is, for Hart, "a step from the pre-legal into the legal world" (p. 91). In other words, enter that familiar *deus ex machina*, the sovereign.

of governing authority: more basic is "the principle that certain actions are offences, and that a person who has suffered an offence is entitled to redress."[17] A "state of nature," lacking common governmental authority, presents a misleading fiction; contemporary societies exist (or did before more recent colonialism and national independence movements intervened) where government operates without recognized authority and life is neither "poor, nasty, brutish and short" (Hobbes), nor rife with "smouldering vendettas" (Hart).[18]

Human beings do not "need" government's apparatus, they simply have it, for better or worse. At least the two questions, why they have it and why they need it, are logically distinct. Among those peoples lacking recognized institutions and sanctions of authority, common rules are enforced because each person (or family) stands ready and willing to retaliate immediately against offenders. Even in the most modern societies with complex governments, this same principle insures obedience to the common rules, as all persons give certain signs (or at least many give signs) that they consider these rules to be common ones. Simple acquiescence furnishes the usual signal.

In most polities, both private individuals and governmental agencies undertake such retaliation. For example, given all the laws adjusting private property relations in Illinois, they operate effectively because both officials and aggrieved parties may retaliate against intruders (including the state itself) by summoning their available force (usually the force of legislation and adjudication, although sometimes personal force as well). How many property owners are ready to react violently, in word if not deed, against invasion of their domain, even in the most civilized states? Is not this a deterrent to aggressors? Obviously, such willingness to use personal force does not constitute a "state of nature."

The requirement that all citizens obey the rules binding their common association is sometimes rationalized as the "need" evil humans have for government: but this requirement is sustained

17. Mair, *op. cit.*, p. 36.
18. *Cf. ibid.*, Chapter I.

in fact because each citizen is prepared to use violence—private and/or public—to maintain these common rules. All the testimony needed for the utility of governmental arrangements and for the political tension and conciliation surrounding the expansion, interpretation, and use of these common rules can be traced to mutual willingness to force obedience on recalcitrants. Motives for obedience vary; consequently government's usefulness cannot be proved logically from them, unless one could catalogue definitively all such motives; nor is law concerned with motivational problems, or at least it is only infrequently.

Important for law (and should be important for political theory) is the nearly unanimous agreement by community members—for various reasons—that there are common standards applicable to all, and that individuals may appeal for redress to these common standards, receiving satisfaction thereby. Such satisfaction, together with fair hearings for grievances, generally constitute "justice." Applying a religious metaphor, law-abidingness has many substances, but only one form.[19] The "loyal" include all those who agree (explicitly or tacitly) that there are common standards. Disagreements will arise over what this commonalty actually entails, but few will ignore completely common or public interests. Qualifying this argument is the expression "*nearly* unanimous agreement." Those who do not agree face punishment until such time as they can defend themselves or change the rules or acquiesce. Recalcitrants confront a certain "terror" (T. H. Green), be this terror organized law enforcement and adjudication, the pressure of public opinion, threats of personal violence by the aggrieved, or any combination of these.

The associational-institutional character of citizenship encourages exclusiveness. There are associates, "citizens," bound together by rules, who perform specialized roles following certain expectations and traditions connected with their given statuses. From this grows a sense of corporativeness and common involvement, an in-group solidarity against the outside world. Inside, "members" count more than "aliens": outside, these

19. See T. H. Green, *op. cit.*, Lec. G, p. 129.

members are distinguished, by their particular association, from those who do not belong. Everywhere he travels, the citizen is both free because of his status and yet bound by particular characteristics which mark him as an American, Briton, or Japanese. He gains attention and respect throughout the international community because he has that peculiar, official mark signifying membership somewhere—citizenship.

Viewing citizenship both internally and externally, it constitutes man's most fundamental and important political characteristic. "Belonging together in common governmental association" has as much ubiquity as "power," or at least the above examples from East Africa seem to indicate this. Conversely, statelessness, or exclusion from political community, signifies the most punishing interdiction. A parallel to this exclusiveness can be found in popular legislative bodies, supposedly accessible to outsiders ("constituents"), but actually closed corporations where sharp distinctions are made between members and non-members, inside and outside the legislature, in terms of information, perquisites and privileges. Hence, when observed by the individual citizen as member of a polity, citizenship forms his life in common with a large number of others, at least a larger number of others than in any other governmental institution; in this life together, particular rules, sanctioned by force, apply to this group and to no other.

In this citizen association there are usually symbols for the public business, such as buildings, flags, and personages. All Shilluk in East Africa compose one nation because they share a common interest in the single center of their political life, the Reth, or "Divine King," whose most important functions center on ritual rather than command.[20] Such a single focus makes it easy to demarcate the "common interest." Not so simple are the lines dividing common or public interest and private interest in the United States, as a nation, or even in any city within that nation. Yet if citizenship retains any meaning, this division must be constantly analyzed and nurtured. Dividing public and private, in order to define the area common to all citizens, has all

20. Mair, *op. cit.*, pp. 69–70.

the more urgency in a society such as America that seems dedicated, both in practice and civic ideology, to obfuscating this distinction. Without a clear sense of the public space (a question to be covered in the next section), there can be very little mutual association and common purpose. If this space has ceased to exist in "real life"—and this subject still needs much investigation—then statesmen and philosophers alike should recreate it. Public virtue, "good citizenship," cannot flourish minus a public ingredient. And those arrangements concerning all citizens in common never involve merely sublimated private interests, as the long tradition from classical economics would have it. Nor should "public" be confused with "social," since the latter includes all those mundane areas of everyday life where government and politics find little attention. "Public life" represents that common life promoted by mutual sharing of a single governmental focus which, going beyond all groups, creates a common allegiance regardless of other social ties.

There is no need to specify where a given community's boundaries are located: these develop territorially, as in modern states and cities, or by combining territory and lineage, as among East African tribes, or by organizational genesis and development, as in the numerous "private governments" typifying modern, pluralistic societies.[21] Everywhere these boundaries are known to and communicated by the citizens involved and thus include, not merely territorial or patrilineal or organizational considerations, but spiritual and symbolic ones as well; in this sense they presume elements of personal imagination carried about, even outside the geographical confines of a particular public area, as cognomens, ideas, issues, dilemmas and dreams.[22] Completing the circle, these ideas build, as no mere

21. See Walton Hamilton, *The Politics of Industry* (New York: Alfred A. Knopf, 1957), *passim;* Grant McConnell, *Private Power and American Democracy* (New York: Alfred A. Knopf, 1966), Part I, Chapter 5; Arnold M. Rose, *Theory and Method in the Social Sciences* (Minneapolis: University of Minnesota Press, 1954), Chapter 3.

22. "The *polis,* properly speaking, is not the city-state in its physical location; it is the organization of the people as it arises out of acting and speaking together, and its true space lies between people living together for this purpose, no matter where they happen to be . . . action and

lines on a map ever could, the community's boundaries. War and peace, life and death, freedom and capture, as well as lesser issues, all stem from that symbolic nexus called communal identity. Even *Realpolitik* depicts an intellectual vision of the public interest, a symbolism which transforms simple cartography into political geography.

Common citizenship produces symbolic patterns of national, provincial, urban, tribal identities and is nurtured by these patterns. Such common allegiance and association are not necessarily "above" other allegiances, though the issue of loyalty raises this question again and again. While numerous interconnections between the commonweal and other areas exist, the "otherness" of the public area causes friction between public and private spheres. The "otherness" of public space, together with the special membership in this space, citizenship, constitute the two fundamental foci of this study. They present complementary, not distinct, problems when dealing with citizen action.

Typically, citizenship associations have a "way of life," or "norms," found in a "political culture" (Almond-Verba) or "arrangements" (Oakeshott) common to a society of citizens and learned by them through civic education. More popularly, these learned citizenship patterns are archetypical for the "heritage" or "history" of a given community. Such a heritage includes more than purely political (in the secularized sense)

---

speech create a space between the participants which can find its proper location almost any time and anywhere." Hannah Arendt, *The Human Condition* (Garden City, N.Y.: Doubleday Anchor Books, 1959) (Originally published by the University of Chicago Press, copyright © 1958), p. 177.

"The important thing about any given urban world is not that it is rooted in space. That is merely what often strikes the eye first, just as it attracted the attention of the nineteenth-century journalists and twentieth-century sociologists. What is important about a social world is that its members are linked by some sort of shared symbolization, some effective channels of communication. . . . The important thing, then, about a social world is its network of communication and the shared symbols which give the world some substance and which allow people to 'belong' to 'it.' " Anselm Strauss, *Images of the American City* (New York: The Free Press of Glencoe, Illinois, 1961) (copyright © 1961 by The Free Press, a corporation), p. 67.

items, accommodating as well other totems relevant to a tribe or polity. Modern Western societies appear highly secularized in their politics, and so, in large measure, do their political heroes, myths, symbols, totems. Of course, the further back into Western history symbols are projected, the more sacred (in the religious sense) they become. Yet even religious figures, such as Joan of Arc, have secular significance as well, especially when viewed through twentieth-century eyes. Western cultures find it simpler to outline the "dignified" and "efficient" parts of a constitution, as Bagehot did for politics in nineteenth-century England or Machiavelli in sixteenth-century Italy.

Politics has become more overtly instrumental; that is, largely missing are obvious transcendent symbolisms, but normative standards still measure civic virtue and responsible citizenship. Where societies have not experienced the modern temper's full impact, secular politics and spiritual symbols more closely interconnect (in countless subtle, as well as obvious, ways). This holds true even for contemporary Western polities relatively untouched by secularized modernity, such as Spain and Ireland, and for those in the West which have intentionally abjured modern symbolism for something more bizarre, figuratively if not in practice, such as Nazi Germany, to say nothing of such newly developing non-Western nations as U Nu's Burma before 1962, where different modes of "modernity" may yet appear.

Citizenship encompasses, therefore, an institutional complex composed of the following structures: initial determinations and subsequent readjustments of member status; legislation and adjudication of rules—normative and instrumental—governing citizenship; adjustment of relations between citizens; civic education, acculturation and symbolism. Fruitful generalizations will come only after these structures have been examined. Such generalizations all retain action content in the sense of focusing on the acting citizen as contrasted to his institutional context, but they concentrate mainly on the citizenship institution as a whole (its genesis, development, transmutations, support by citizens); certain of its complex institutions (description, comparison); individual groups related to institutions of citizenship (for example, the "tension" of citizenship, loyalty, "good citizenship"); ideas about these problems held by political thinkers; or any combination of these.

Institutional approaches to citizenship have dealt with the following subjects. First, there is what might be called spatial-contemporary theory. Here, more or less systematic generalizations are based on contemporary examples from a wide or narrow range of samples. The citizenship studies authored under Merriam's encouragement and summarized in his *The Making of Citizens* (1931) would be examples of this approach; these monographs encompassed a wide contemporary canvass, from American and German societies to the Duk-Duks. With allowances for the effects of colonialism and national independence on tribal government, Lucy Mair's *Primitive Government* (1962), sampling a restricted geographic compass of East African societies, yet containing prolix styles of government, should be included also. Her work is all the more instructive for its narrower scope, because East Africa offers a wide range of polities in a relatively limited area.

This first type of generalizing derives from individual studies. A second spatial-contemporary variety of citizenship study would be one wherein a conceptual scheme, involving institutions such as public opinion and elections, is first devised and then selected or nonselected examples are fit. Current "political" or "civic" culture theories, notably the work of Gabriel Almond and Sidney Verba in *The Civic Culture* (1963), belong to this group, although they also claim to be action theories because of certain behavioral predilections. Such theories form a part of much broader attempts at general theorizing in comparative government.

A second kind of generalizing theory might be called the "temporal approach" with several subtypes. For instance, citizenship might be studied historically, with no prior conceptualization and only limited conclusions. This hardly represents "theory" in any sense, particularly when the conclusions cover one period only. Yet such detailed historical studies as A. N. Sherwin-White's *The Roman Citizenship* (1939), of which there are too few, serve as cautions against hasty generalization. Another variety of the temporal approach is found in H. Mark

Roelof's book, *The Tension of Citizenship, Private Man and Public Duty* (1957), which views citizenship from lofty historical vistas, beginning with ancient Greece and ending in modern America with a rewriting (Roelof's) of the Declaration of Independence. This work also has a conceptual scheme, where history politely serves as handmaiden.

A similar but more modest approach, from a sociological viewpoint and dealing only with recent English history, is T. H. Marshall's *Citizenship and Social Class* (1950). Conceivably, a history of citizenship in the West could be written, and in one unpretentious attempt, T. H. Haarhoff's *The Stranger at the Gates* (1951), a beginning was made. Haarhoff's imagery of the walls of citizenship and the stranger (or outsider) at the gates, written with an eye on his native South Africa's citizenship laws, suggests several important considerations.

Werner Jaeger's monumental *Paideia* (1933–43), a citizenship study of ancient Greece, belongs in the temporal category too. But any proposed definitive work, covering Western civilization as a whole, would be a staggering enterprise. Also, using historical examples has certain dangers here, so closely do citizenship institutions relate to the social fabric of existential societies.

Finally, in the historical, temporal mode, would be a history of ideas or philosophies of citizenship; for example, the contributions of one theorist such as Aristotle. Or several philosophers might provide insights into man the political animal, using T. H. Green's commentaries on Spinoza, Hobbes, Locke, and Rousseau, in opening his *Lectures on the Principles of Obligation* (1879–80), for inspiration. Actually, Green's investigations into the history of political ideas proved less interesting than his own views on citizenship and obligation.

Closely related to the temporal approach, is a third kind of generalizing, a free-wheeling combination of contemporary and historical. Here all institutions and ideas, past and present, reciprocate. One could comment on, investigate, or even polemicize on current citizenship trends in one's own country or elsewhere. Contemporary examples are Joseph Tussman's *Obligation and the Body Politic* (1960), D. W. Brogan's *Citizenship Today* (1961), and Robert Lane's *Political Ideology* (1962).

In conclusion, the particular institutional context of citizenship, with its municipal panoply of law and sanction, defines the status of citizens. It also tells something about their activities within any polity. The statuses and relations between citizens are institutionally and legally outlined in particular communities. Also, differences between classes of citizens and between citizens and noncitizens are made. In most governments, such complex arrangements find expression in general compendia of laws specifying the rights of citizens and aliens and their respective obligations, such legal provisions accounting accurately for what citizens do in most societies (assuming there is written law).[23] Hence, only citizens vote in the states of the United States, because laws provide their singular eligibility. Also, United States citizens, unlike their counterparts in some countries, carry no "identity papers" while traveling within their own country, because laws requiring aliens to register and visitors to carry visas as well as passports remain silent on citizen registration, and no other similar ordinances deal exclusively with citizens.

Notice that such laws say little or nothing about *why* there are (or are not) such laws, although judicial decisions often will, but they summarize what citizens *do*. Law does not describe or prescribe role-playing styles; only the general status of citizens has legal sanction. American citizens vote, hold public office, serve on juries, perform military services; aliens do not, although they might be recruited for duty in the American armed forces during certain emergencies. Above all, because they enjoy citizenship status, Americans are "obliged," whatever their motives, to obey their nation's laws with fullest dedication. For citizens alone the state's most opprobrious epithets of "disloyal" and "traitor" apply. Conversely, American citizens are forbidden to vote in elections, hold public office, or serve in the armed forces of foreign states, except under certain unusual circumstances in the last instance. And whatever else they face punishment for, they cannot be "treasonous" and "disloyal" to any foreign state, except in very special instances (as mercenar-

23. Both legislation and judicial precedent. For a discussion of the distinction between the two, see Hart, *op. cit.*, pp. 121–132.

ies, expeditionaries, or revolutionaries they risk being called "traitors" or "disloyal" to one or another cause).

This list by no means exhausts the "dos" and "don'ts" for American citizens. No static catalogue in any case, even a complete list changes over time, subject to evolving law and developing legal interpretations. Generalizations about citizenship, based on institutions and laws of citizenship and on contemporary commentaries (by legislators, lawyers, judges, philosophers, professors, and others) about such institutions and laws, are perfectly reliable guides to what citizens do now and what they have done in the past. *How* they act and for *what* reasons, especially the activities and decisions of individuals, go beyond strictly formal approaches. And since the state never concerns itself about the hows and whys, so long as law-abidingness continues widespread in the community, it follows that these last questions have scant relevance for strictly legalistic analyses of the citizenship question.

*Political Nature*

Much as institutional and legal analyses are useful for indicating what citizens do, they have an even greater utility for political theory. Such analyses demarcate political space and political time, this space and time making up together "political nature." Political nature includes only situations within the ambience of governmental arrangements, particularly for this study, the institutions of citizenship. According to Sheldon S. Wolin, political institutions, as arrangements of power and authority, "serve to define, so to speak, 'political space' or the locus wherein the tensional forces of society are related, as in a courtroom, a legislature, an administrative hearing, or the convention of a political party."[24] Institutions also divide time into political units of "decision, resolution, or compromise."[25] Institutional foci, providing for the confrontation of individuals and groups in society and necessitating relations between them in such confrontations, furnish the "situations" or "field" of politics. In this

24. *Politics and Vision* (Boston: Little, Brown, 1960), p. 7.
25. *Ibid.*

discussion of the political nature bounded by governmental arrangements,[26] the following expressions, all signifying a given
area of considerations marked off from other areas, will be used
interchangeably: "political nature," "political ground," "political situation," and "political field." While these indicate something "given," they by no means imply an area "fixed" and
"stable" either in space or time.

Without political theorists and philosophers, politics would
still exist, although quite a few persons might see political life
differently. Independent political arrangements limit the scope
of political study. More particularly, citizenship's institutions,
while not fixed for all time, are "givens," and of necessity
theoretical analysis is bounded by them. This means that there
are boundaries to discussions of political action, and these are
provided by the "nature" of political phenomena. An analogy
may be drawn (hesitantly and imperfectly) from two very
different approaches to human action, both bearing on the idea
of field or situation, one by the American sociologist Talcott
Parsons, the other by the French social philosopher Jean-Paul
Sartre.

In Parsons's action theory, "the point of reference of all terms
is the action of an individual actor or a collectivity of actors."[27]
But such action, for sociological theory, is not the physiological
process of the individual organism but "the organization of the
actor's orientations to a situation."[28] Obviously, all social acts,
including political ones, have situations, because there is always
someone else acting too. By definition, "social" means more than
one person, and more than one is the number needed for a social
situation. Needless to say, for social science theory, simple numbers are less important than the relations between two or more

26. For Wolin's discussion of "political nature" see *ibid.*, pp. 6–7.
27. Talcott Parsons and Edward A. Shils (eds.), *Toward a General
Theory of Action* (Cambridge, Mass.: Harvard University Press, 1951),
p. 4.
28. *Ibid.* "This organization of action elements is, for the purposes of
the theory of action, above all a function of the relation of the actor to his
situation and the history of that relation, in this sense of 'experience.'"
Talcott Parsons, *The Social System* (Glencoe, Ill.: The Free Press,
1951) (copyright © 1951 by Talcott Parsons), p. 5.

persons, but the convenient dividing line between psychology and social science is that demarcating the individual from the group—"personality system" and "social system," using Parsons's terminology.[29]

There exists, therefore, a very general relation between political acts and social acts, because politics inheres only in social situations. This does not mean, however, that the "political" may be grouped under the more general "social," except in the most self-evident sense discussed above. Political life involves certain special concerns, specific "situations." Frequently, social scientists are carried away by the self-evidence of their basic proposition that "where more than one is gathered, there will be the social," without distinguishing qualitatively between political relations and other social relations. This error will be discussed shortly, when the political ground is more fully charted.

Approaching the same question of action and situation from the viewpoint of French existentialism, it is found that "the structures of society, created by human endeavor, define for each person an objective situation of departure."[30] Sartre hastens to add, however, while the truth of a man (*la vérité d'un homme*) is his labor and his salary, "he defines it [this truth] to the extent that he constantly surpasses [*dépasse*] it by his practice."[31] But the social situation includes, not only the objective situation of departure (Marx's social or material forces), but "the relations between men" (Marx's social relations) as well.[32] In fact, there

29. Parsons and Shils, *op. cit.*, p. 7.

30. Jean-Paul Sartre, *Question de méthode*, in *Critique de la raison dialectique* (précédé de *Question de méthode*) (Paris: Gallimard, 1960) (copyright © Editions Gallimard), p. 64. My translation is a trifle inexact, because it does not preserve the Marxist flavor of Sartre's writing. This Marxist "flavor" is more explicitly discussed by Wilfred Desan, *The Marxism of Jean-Paul Sartre* (Garden City, N.Y.: Doubleday, 1964).

31. *Ibid.* "Practice" encompasses all aspects of life in the total situation, not only social relations, but also the relations of men with nature. This latter subject enables Sartre to include "passion" in his aspects of life. *Ibid.*, p. 68. Elsewhere, Sartre writes that whatever a man does, from writing to tying his tie, he represents everyone. *Les Temps Modernes*, I (October 1945), 13–14.

32. Sartre, *op. cit.*, p. 68.

are only men and their relations. "Collective objects" are real enough, but their reality is "parasitical" (*parasitaire*).[33] "Parasitical" has a somewhat more prosaic parallel in Parsons's statement that institutions and collectivities are two aspects of more basic status-role relationships, which, in turn, derive from the social interactions of individuals.[34] Sartre's existentialism finds "the singular man in the social field," a field shaped by social interactions.[35] This field has been charted largely by Marx—at least it has for Sartre.[36] The idea of "field" or "ground" in philosophy and social science has been a persistent one, for example, in the work of Koehler, Koffka, Lewin, and Merleau-Ponty, but the matter will be pursued no further here.

"Nature," however, is a perplexing subject, whether this is the nature of the physicist, artist, sociologist, or political theorist. In the first place, nature, as the "given," is not fixed, but in flux, as are new discoveries of nature. Likewise the institutions that limit political nature change constantly. Political theory,

33. *Ibid.*, p. 55.
34. *Social System*, p. 39.
35. Sartre, *op. cit.*, p. 86. "Reduced to the simplest possible terms, then, a social system consists in a plurality of individual actors interacting with each other in a situation which has at least a physical or environmental aspect, actors who are motivated in terms of a tendency to the 'optimization of gratification' and whose relation to their situations, including each other, is defined and mediated in terms of a system of culturally structured and shared symbols." Parsons, *Social System*, pp. 5–6.
36. Sartre claims that his existentialism is an "ideology" in the penumbra of Marx's "philosophy"; that is, his philosophy is derived from the only real school of philosophy (according to Sartre) since Hegel and Kant—Marxism. But he is careful to distinguish his own version of Marxism from Soviet Marxism. For his theory of "philosophy and ideology" and existentialism's relationship to Marxism, see Sartre, *op. cit.*, Chapter I. Most of Sartre's criticism of Soviet Marxism parallels Herbert Marcuse's in the latter's *Soviet Marxism*. In both, there is an anguish over Soviet deviation from Marx's social democratic tenets, a deviation blamed on bureaucratization of Marxist theory in the USSR and subsequent separation of theory and practice. According to Albert Camus, however, the "historical rebellion" at the base of Marx's thought contributed to this cynical separation. See *The Rebel*, translated by Anthony Bower (New York: Vintage Books, 1956), pp. 209–226.

while limited by political phenomena, has proliferated during severe historical crises, when the lines of politics metamorphose or even break beyond repair. Institutions appear most fascinating for theory's creative talents precisely when most disorganized and doubted. Although every thinker (indeed, every person) perpetually occupies that lacuna between past and future, the "present," as contemporary physicists (like Heisenberg), philosophers (like Arendt, Heidegger and Sartre), historians (like Carr), and novelists (like Kafka) remind us, the political philosopher, much as the artist and musician but also as some physical scientists, seems to find most congenial those particular "presents" when directions change and shadows appear everywhere.

Yet the presentiment of flux is nothing novel—most philosophers have wrestled with its specter and its reality. There remains a still more elementary reason why "nature," in all its manifestations, should be problematic. What nature signifies to men changes, not simply because nature changes, but, much more important, because men change intellectually. Put differently, the external realities of physical nature have not changed much during man's civilized era, but man has. First, humankind has evolved physiologically, though scarcely at all since the founding of civilization. But second, and relevant to the present discussion, man's civilizations and societies, and thus his explorations and perceptions of nature (including his own nature), have changed toward greater diversification, individualization, and rationalization.[37]

Politics being "natural," because it represents a given albeit created product of civilization, undergoes a double transfiguration: its nature changes and so do the ways men look at it. But still there endures the political situation or political nature. Even physical science has found, during the last five or so decades, that its "nature," as object of investigation, appears much less autonomous from the observer than classical physics had thought. Man's conception of nature defines "nature" for him. There is no absolute, fixed, and objective natural world com-

37. See footnote 12, this chapter.

pletely apart from the perceiving subject, yet nevertheless a human product. Physical science too evolves under the impact of changing cultures.

This does not mean, as classical logical positivism would have it, that objective truth derives only from sensory experience of the individual observer, and that theories of "fields" and "situations" must constitute more or less gratuitous conclusions drawn from discreet data. There is a higher reality than this—a real nature outside sensory experience awaiting discovery.[38] For this reason Charles Sanders Peirce, embued with scientific philosophy yet a realist rather than a nominalist, could describe the three "modes of being," the being of positive qualitative possibility ("firstness"), the being of actual fact ("secondness"), and the being of law that will govern facts in the future ("thirdness").[39] Hence Peirce, while very non-Hegelian, was attracted to Hegel's chief topic: the importance of continuity in change, "the very idea the mathematicians and physicists had been chiefly engaged in following out for three centuries . . . My philosophy resuscitates Hegel, though in a strange costume."[40]

Recognizing positivism's powerful attraction for physical scientists, Max Planck argued, in opposition, that "(1) There is a real outer world which exists independently of our act of knowing; and (2) The real outer world is not directly knowable."[41] These two theorems "form together the cardinal hinge

38. See Max Planck, "Where Is Science Going?" translated by James Murphy, in *The New Science*, p. 41, published as Volume III of Planck's *Complete Works* (New York: Meridian Books [Greenwich Editions]), 1959. Planck rejected positivism in science. A similar view, from the social science standpoint, is found in George Herbert Mead, *The Philosophy of the Act*, edited by Charles W. Morris, et al. (Chicago: University of Chicago Press, 1938), p. 43. Planck was more wedded to classical physics than others, such as Einstein.

39. *Collected Papers of Charles Sanders Peirce*, edited by Charles Hartshorne and Paul Weiss, 2 volumes (Cambridge, Mass.: Harvard University Press, 1960), Vol. I, paragraphs 20–26, pp. 6–7.

40. *Ibid.*, paragraph 42, p. 18. Hegel had great contempt for scientists though, a fact Peirce notes.

41. *Op. cit.*, p. 41. Planck rejected the doctrine of "as if" in scientific theory.

on which the whole structure of physical science turns."[42] Since the two preceding statements seem mutually contradictory, there must be "an irrational or mystical element which adheres to physical science as to every other branch of human knowledge."[43]

All this discloses a constantly expanding science, discovering new aspects of nature through fruitful collaboration between theory and experience, in conjunction with imagination.[44] Similar to physical science, any other endeavor of thought, such as political theory, has its particular analytic field and canons of discourse known to its students, which govern to a greater or lesser extent the vocabularies and conclusions of that enterprise.[45] Yet a given subject matter and a particular tradition of ideational co-operation do not eliminate imagination (or "vision") and innovation: science's most exciting characteristic is its unfinished business.[46]

42. *Ibid.*

43. *Ibid.* See also *ibid.*, p. 33, where Planck asserts, "The ordinary scientist, who does not believe in the positivist attitude, admits the validity of the aesthetic standpoint and the ethical standpoint; but he recognizes these as belonging to another way of looking at nature." And Werner Heisenberg, when discussing the framework of classical physics: "The fact that this machine as well as the whole of science were themselves only products of the human mind appeared irrelevant and of no consequence for an understanding of nature. Only the extension of scientific methods of thought far beyond their legitimate limits of application led to the much deplored division in the world of ideas between the field of science on the one side and the fields of religion and art on the other." *Philosophic Problems of Nuclear Science*, translated by F. C. Hayes (New York: Pantheon Books, 1952), p. 22. On the "sense of mystery" in human affairs, from a Thomist point of view, see Yves Simon, *Philosophy of Democratic Government* (Chicago: University of Chicago Press [Phoenix Editions], 1961), pp. 91, 277; from a phenomenologist's perspective, Maurice Merleau-Ponty, *The Phenomenology of Perception*, translated by Colin Smith (London: Routledge & Kegan Paul, 1962), pp. xiii, xx.

44. Planck, *op. cit.*, pp. 41–42; Heisenberg, *op. cit.*, Chapter 3.

45. See Wolin, *op. cit.*, pp. 22–23, on the tradition of discourse in political theory.

46. See Planck, *op. cit.*, pp. 41–42. Also, the relation of imagination and innovation to political theory, see Wolin, *op. cit.*, pp. 17–21, 23–27;

Nature, for the political theorist, changes not only with expanded discoveries or enlarged perspectives but in its external reality as well. A protean subject matter complicates and troubles the effort to acquire and compile political truths. Nevertheless, though the "rules" of political theory differ somewhat from those of atomic theory, an external field, changing as man's conceptions expand, persists for both. Hence, the world of contemporary political thought diverges from ancient Greece, and no one need think that political nature today should resemble ancient politics, either in its external substance or in the way observers perceive it. This applies to the study of citizenship too. Yet certain institutional forms have had extraordinary tenure in Western civilization, and this longevity has been equaled by persisting categories in the history of political ideas. Greek political life, centered in the *polis*, no longer exists, nor do the legislative and adjudicative arrangements suiting that kind of polity: but the institution of citizenship and the citizen role, about which Aristotle wrote with reference to the *polis*, have continued. Why? One reason seems obvious: the citizen is "political man," the full member of his state, whatever the latter's form. And "man" always creates political symbols.[47] Theorizing about this part of political nature has as long a continuous tradition as atomic theory, which dates back to Democritus, and about which modern physicists (and modern philosophers like Russell) appear eager to speak.[48]

Yet the political theorist must ask himself, as the modern atomic theorist asks about Democritus' theory of the atom, not only why and how much today's citizenship differs from that of ancient Greece, but also why and how much modern political

---

for science, see Peirce, *op. cit.*, Vol. I, paragraphs 46–48, pp. 20–21. See Arnold Brecht on the unfinished business of empirical political science in *Political Theory* (Princeton: Princeton University Press, 1959), Part Four.

47. Which does not mean that people devote more energy to politics than other affairs. See Chapter Five.

48. Heisenberg is interested in delineating similarities and differences between the atomic theory of Democritus and that of the moderns. But in the process he by no means disdains Democritus, who had not benefited from two thousand years of scientific advance. See *op. cit.*, Chapter 2.

theory perceives politics and the citizen differently from Aristotle. Both continuity and discontinuity persevere in the "field" of citizenship. Adopting the method of microphysics, as he conceives it, to his own social theory, Sartre writes,

The only theory of understanding that can be valuable today is that founded on this truth of microphysics: the experimenter is part of the experimental system. This alone permits the discarding of every idealist illusion, only this points out the real man in midst of the real world. But this realism necessarily implies a reflexive point of departure, which is to say, the *discovering* of a situation is accomplished in and by the practice [*praxis*] which changes it. We do not put the influence of consciousness at the source of action, we see there a necessary moment of action itself: action gives, *in the course of accomplishment*, its own knowledge.[49]

In other words, the theorist both reflects on and lives in his situation; his thought and action coincide at numerous junctures. The field of politics remains at once fixed, being acted in at every given moment, but changing, since action always surpasses the present moment as participants act. Political theorists themselves live within the political field, acting because their reflection is grounded in the "on-goingness" of politics in which they find themselves implicated. Thought "rationalizes," "reflects upon," "delimits," "organizes," "expands" and "contracts" the field of action. As in Sartre's literature, words comprehending political communications provide "toboggans, forgotten, unnoticed, and solitary, which will hurl the reader into the midst of a universe where there are no witnesses. . . ."[50]

In political space lives political man, the citizen, as contrasted to biological man, psychological man, and so forth. And this situation defines his activities. Surely, the political community embraces "individuals," but the statement must be qualified by adding that these are peculiar kinds of individuals, that is, citizens, who carry the attributes of political nature. Life is

49. *Op. cit.*, p. 30, n. 1. See also Heisenberg, *op. cit.*, pp. 70–71, 73. In this same connection see the sociologists, Parsons and Shils, *op. cit.*, p. 167; and the historian, E. H. Carr, *op. cit.*, pp. 7–10.

50. Jean-Paul Sartre, *What is Literature?*, translated by Bernard Frechtman (New York: Philosophical Library, 1949), p. 229.

loosely enough compartmentalized that in real life politics will not stand separately from other human endeavors, at least in any artificial fashion. Man is naturally political in this sense anyway. Nevertheless, political nature provides an abstraction, useful for analyzing citizenship, but an abstraction always suggesting concrete activity.[51]

Also, politics, no matter how labeled, constitutes an action field involving actors who specialize in political matters and who act *as if* politics were isolated for their official and professional endeavors. This applies to the actions of individuals in their official citizen roles (voting, holding public office, being loyal) as well. The theorist need not employ "as if" abstractions, since the political realm already provides a continuous, institutionalized area. He abstracts that which is already political. It was noted earlier how valuable are institutional and legalistic approaches in this respect.

Aside from the obvious territorial limits surrounding formal citizenship, focal tensions and attempts to control the violence associated with such tensions appear to be the most significant phenomena of political nature.[52] Political space comprises that space demarcated physically and mentally from other spaces in life, by focusing or concentrating social tensions from many differing kinds of associations within the boundaries of governmental arrangements. Finding the borders of this political ground presents an explorative, not definitional, set of problems. Obviously this space goes beyond ordinary public institutions and activities commonly associated with "politics"; it is particularly clear that "politics" appears, latently at least, in most social groups.

Again, as with political nature, the idea and experience of government pervades most social situations. Whatever their ori-

51. A similar point is made by David Easton and those influenced by him in their theories of the "political system." The political system approach is not used here, because it appears too mechanical.
52. This view accords with Bertrand de Jouvenel's of "politics" as the "tussle" preceding decisions and of "policy" as the course adopted. *Sovereignty*, translated by J. F. Huntington (Chicago: University of Chicago Press [Phoenix Editions], 1963), p. 16.

gins, such governmental arrangements confront those tensions concomitant with interacting, socialized participants. Because rewards remain scarce in every community, interactive violence is no mere specter manufactured by apologists for the *Machtstaat*. So pervasive are scarcity and violence that governmental institutions also become points for violence. Focusing social tensility into orderly, authoritative procedures, government provides that imperfect, frequently unsuccessful attempt to control violence.[53]

But government's very presence as controller, stimulates competition between individuals and between groups for capture of its vital rewarding and punishing agencies. The actual tension within governmental situations defines political space and the agendas for political time. Needless to say, such space fluctuates constantly. Politics transpires only within governmental arrangements, but not all government is political. Hearings conducted by ostensibly "nonpolitical" administrative agencies may invite tensional focus and perhaps tensional exacerbation, while a piece of legislation with no opposition can be entirely nonpolitical.

Also, a spectrum of political tensions might indicate that intrigues surrounding a Vatican Council meeting in 1962 would be far more political, because of the more far-reaching conflicts and more lucrative rewards offered for controlling the Roman Catholic Church, than much of the business transacted by either house of the United States Congress. Yet political scientists, even today, focus a great deal more attention on agencies such as Congress than phenomena of political nature such as Vatican Councils.

Finally, the arrangements of government extend well past formal institutions, including the areas those institutions affect and the responses made to actions taken by those institutions among the citizenry at large. Tension is the key to politics and government provides tensional focus. If what has been argued

53. By "authoritative" is meant, at the minimum, "recognized by the community." Investment with power to enforce decisions is another matter. For societies with authoritative government, but little or no law enforcement, see Lucy Mair, *op. cit.*, Part One.

here about the wide variety of forms within political nature has validity, then the notion of citizenship itself needs emendation to accommodate modern man's citizenry in multiple political settings within his national community.

The configuration of governments and their politics in a given total society delineates the structure of tensions for that society. A national political community—where official citizenship is assigned—comprises a unique structure of tensions which can be compared with others. Such a general structure involves, at the minimum, agendas or schedules of past, present and future concerns; lists of priorities; and the six factors of association, decision, resolution, reward, punishment, and publicity, all related to the schedules of concerns and lists of priorities for a particular total community.

These schedules or lists are figures of speech, denoting past, present, and future controversies and conciliations and appearing in the on-going actions of the society rather than in party declarations and official pronouncements, though the latter phenomena are symptomatic of underlying compromises and conflicts. For example, the American President's State of the Union message has political importance because it focuses tensions—past, present, and future—for either controversy or conciliation. Similarly, the report of a Soviet Party Congress augurs politically significant things when it exemplifies resolved or unresolved tensions in Soviet society and the Communist world—tensions which have made some impact on governmental decisions. In this respect, political pronouncements are like art (or what some persons like to characterize as art)—they are "representational" or "nonrepresentational" or perhaps both; that is, they possess direct political significance or they do not, or they may contain both significant and nonsignificant elements.

No society, however advanced, has completely subdued that potential product of tensions—violence. In fact, modern societies have actually multiplied and perfected the means of violence between men to such extent that elaborate governmental systems are imperative even in the smallest states. Yet such elaboration seems to encourage even greater violence, for example, by introducing propaganda and terror, thus belying Lenin's implication in *State and Revolution* (1917) that proletarian violence through dictatorship would end all violence (class war) and lead to abolition of the state. Ideational violence cannot be minimized, even in nontotalitarian societies: everywhere political speaking and writing (where written language exists), as weapons of attack, pursuit, liquidation, and defense, have considerable prominence, particularly in societies with advanced communications technologies.

On the other hand, primitive peoples often manage with only minimal regulation, even though violence appears more overt than in the civilized world. This need not be the case, of course, particularly if speaking and acting are both included.[54] Thus all societies possess political arrangements, and where pluralistic group structures complicate matters, politics and governments proliferate. In modern societies extreme cases of specialization and fission foster politics in nonconventional, private settings outside state and public agencies. Emphasizing tension and incipient violence, the present analysis of political nature encompasses a good deal more terrain, potentially at least, than traditional "public" or "formal" governmental institutions allow. Likewise, man owes allegiance to various polities.

Speaking in modern terms, however, citizenship conventionally means membership in the state; that is, full membership in "a compulsory [territorial] association with continuous organization . . . [with] its administrative staff successfully [upholding] a claim to the *monopoly* of the *legitimate* use of physical force in the enforcement of its order."[55] Even here, the political situation finds it difficult to squeeze into formal, public institutions, and citizenship discovers the same problem. Citizenship, though a highly formalized kind of membership tradition-

54. See Arendt, *The Human Condition*, p. 177. Arendt's ideas are adopted in this sentence, the full import of these ideas is not accepted. While acting and speaking, in the sense Arendt uses them, seem unusually profitable means of locating "the political," her view that this kind of politics is declining in Western thought and practice is debatable. See Chapter Four below for a fuller discussion.

55. Max Weber, *The Theory of Social and Economic Organization*, translated by A. M. Henderson and Talcott Parsons and edited by Parsons (Glencoe, Ill.: The Free Press, 1947), p. 154.

ally reserved for the state, is still an ambiguous term even when confined to this realm or its equivalent.

An illustration of this ambiguity actually precedes the rise of the modern secularized state in St. Augustine's conception of citizenship. Conforming to the conventional requirements that citizens are full members of cities and that ancient religions were civic in structure and temper, he stretched classical notions to accommodate the very unclassical "City of God," and then posited a dual citizenship, one to earthly municipalities, the other to the heavenly city. Although this oversimplifies Augustine's intent and method, the point is clear enough: political nature, for him, included something more expansive than traditional political usages allowed. So he adjusted older conventions to newer situations.

Another, more contemporary approach might abjure the tradition, inventing instead new conceptions to describe novel situations. Faced with increasing diversification and individualization, some modern observers disregard old-fashioned "state" and "sovereignty" conceptions, favoring a new sociological vocabulary which seemingly accounts for pluralism, increased division of labor, and so on. Then, in terms of this up-dated viewpoint, traditional politics would seem less central to social life, perhaps even peripheral or inconsequential. Citizenship could now be interpreted, as modern pluralists usually interpret it, as membership in a plurality or series of social groups, a notion not altogether different from Augustine's but expressed in modern symbols.[56]

Since conceptions of situations help determine behavior in those situations, however, the novel view—either expanding the old or inventing a new vocabulary—might lead to actions which help to implement practically the new vision. For example, the

56. Arendt has commented on the modern notion of "society" in *On Revolution* (New York: Faber & Faber, *op. cit.*, 1963), p. 118; *The Human Condition*, pp. 35–45. See also Wolin, Chapter 10. Max Weber, for instance, described the concept of citizenship as three-sided: (1) economic (community of economic interests), (2) political (membership in a state), (3) social class (those strata drawn together by property and culture). *General Economic History*, translated by Frank Knight (Glencoe, Ill.: The Free Press, 1950), Chapter XXVIII.

controversy over whether there is a common interest or only a succession of private interests in politics has never been mere closet disputation. The stand taken on this issue conditions the way one sees the real world, the way one communicates this vision to others, and the way one acts in that imagined world. Hence, a teacher of the "group approach to politics" describes not merely a "real world" for his students but communicates that world to them and conditions their political expectations and actions as well.

In other words, because of political nature's often ambiguous boundaries, perceptions of it are not only scientific but ideological (leading to action). Every political analysis turns prescriptive as well as descriptive, because efforts to delimit political boundaries prescribe where goals begin and where they end. Such conceptions, dealing with an everyday world, rather than with something as subliminal as atomic structure, the spectroscopy of stars, or even the relations of ego and id, influence the views of others orienting themselves as full community members. All political studies, not only political philosophy, have such an ideological component, because they define fields of action as well as fields of contemplation.

For the sake of both precision and outmoded convention, however, political nature will mean here only those conventional institutions of government operating within the territorial boundaries of the "state," even though squeezing citizenship into such limits ignores much in the political field. Citizenship constitutes full membership within these conventional arrangements and encompasses all political activity taking place within their confines. This by no means excludes politics occurring outside such formal institutions, in churches, for example, but only places certain conventional limits on the present discussion. From the lives of individual citizens come the main tensions that characterize politics. Other factors contribute; for example, aliens and foreign states produce conflict. But a polity's response to its problems—even to external problems—comes from the structure of tensions within that political community, which in turn, accords with the kinds of persons and the types of associations enjoying full status in that community.

At the same time, however, the prior existence of political nature, its "given-ness" or "tradition" from the past and its "trends" toward the future, encourages—even requires— projection of citizen disputes into this particular space; tensional focus already exists. While deliberate provision for an on-going (in the sense of "having been," "is now," and "going toward") focal point for social conflict may threaten the political community, it is still requisite if sudden ruptures among citizens are to be avoided. Life needs continuity, even if this continuity includes revolutions and civil wars. Actually, "political community" would disappear entirely without political nature and its continuous attributes, so the very threat to the body politic from partisan strife really comes from the political's natural workings.

Note that politics provides the "deliberate provision of an on-going focus for social conflict" and yet can be called "natural," since life without such a focus could not be sustained for very long and thus such a focus remains mandatory, that is, natural, for political life. Here, at the focal point, the individual acts in his institutional capacity as citizen. From this point flow laws, decrees, activities, loyalties, and defections. Relative to this nexus of tensions, the political field, a citizen frames his private hopes and fears, as well as his solicitude (if any) for his commonwealth. It is this focal point which circumscribes the citizen's role and within which his activity occurs. On the other hand, these private hopes and fears help form the structure of tensions peculiar to a society.

What, under these circumstances, are the limits of political nature? Such a question has no direct answer. Speaking in oversimplified terms, everything is potential politics. "To focus" brings individual cases under *common* headings. Or, to change metaphors, focusing sharpens inchoate, blurred images. So politics functions to focus social tensions into common concerns, blurred disputes into magnified, sharpened problems, dramatizing in bolder tones previously thinner outlines. Or at least such tensions appear in common governmental institutions of society —in the public marketplace or public square—whether or not most of the community has any awareness of their presence.

Of course, during political give-and-take, clouds of rhetoric obfuscate issues, but these issues at least appear in the open, as publicly discussed problems of communal concern. Someone deliberately uses public government's arrangements to confront, but not necessarily to surmount, tensions, even where these tensions seem falsely presented. Confronting social tensility on an official level, not surmounting such tensility, forms the basis of politics. Each societal tension, however, remains only potential politics, unless someone or some group adjusts the common interest to consider new tensions.

Each society makes choices, therefore, as to what questions will achieve public prominence, and such choices then become part of the common concern—a concern shaped by symbolic forces and modes peculiar to that polity. Conversely, an issue may be denied or divested of common significance after enjoying considerable prominence. Hence, the same tensions are not integral to political life in every society (although there are remarkable similarities between societies of the modern world), because each political community defines its interests uniquely and changes them incessantly. Observers must cognize both political space and political time, not only in the macrocosmic terms of each community, but in the lives of individuals and lesser groups within each community.

Once problems enter the public domain, however, new political stresses arise. Novel considerations are introduced, others disappear, attentions and priorities shifting their weights with varying degrees of perceptibility. Politics become more complex through additional introjections, but as certain tensions ease, government's fabric seems simpler again. Perhaps leadership has no desire to "rock the boat," and few new items are placed on the community's agenda; such slogans as "Keep Cool with Coolidge," or "Peace, Prosperity and Ike's Sincerity," exemplify essentially conservative, go-slow episodes in recent American history, even though many social tensions clamored for attention at the time. On the other hand, the dynamism, the new priorities infolded by conundrums such as "New Freedom," "New Deal," "New Frontier," appear obvious. Here leadership even chooses to introduce new tensions, to revive dormant unsolved problems, and to admit certain issues previously suppressed.

No problem is automatically a political one, but once injected into the public domain its tensions become focused in the already crowded schedule of common involvements. The ordinary citizen may have little awareness that such a schedule exists; he may know some of it in detail and has, some hope, at least a rough idea of these common problems and why these are political (tensional) and others are not. More than likely, he simply listens to what persons important in his life tell him. He hears conflicting versions about where politics should end, on what issues it should center, what should be its agenda of priorities—if he listens at all. He knows vaguely that new tensions have arisen and modified schedules of communal considerations seem likely.

But he possesses no clear conception of details, and since most politics lies on the margin of his life (he tells himself, often mistakenly), he has no incentive to learn. Democracies usually stage public disputes over these priorities and the limits of the schedule, at least on major issues, but most citizens take no part. Those who do generally engross themselves in political drama and its rhetoric, focusing their attentions on certain issues through symbolizations provided by their particular faction or party. We assume, on very spotty evidence, that every society, no matter its regime, allows at least private disputation on public priorities.

Whether or not he pays any attention to politics, the citizen is involved in political nature. His status as full member of his commonwealth places him there, like it or not. Because of his status, *the* community presumes it is *his* community. He must follow, obey, serve. Knowledge of communal problems might or might not improve his perspective on these matters, but it never changes his obligations. Laws and decrees, revolutions and restorations, the final results, if any, to political tensions, require obedience. Further, the citizen, as full member, *must* obey, however sophisticated his rationalizations or behavioral his motivations. The only relevant motive for obligation, from the political point of view, remains the citizen's acceptance of his community's tensions as his own—that he participate in common involvements with his fellows, whatever really other causes shape his responses. It is simply assumed that the citizen, not merely "human" but a "political human" vested with the status and perquisites of political membership, feels obligated to his community. He may have no awareness at all of the "others" who are also citizens and have no knowledge of the issues at stake. His "there-ness" or "membership" may be rationalized in Chief Justice Earl Warren's lofty phrase, as "the right to have rights," or simply as a citizen's subjection to a Saudi Arabian prince.

Whatever the rationalizations, citizenship has as much cogency as, though a good deal less immediacy than, family membership. Making matters worse, the individual often has far less choice about his citizenship, because the deprivations attached to expatriation are frequently more severe than simply "leaving home." And political banishment from the "homeland" forecasts heavier penalties for most than does disinheritance by their biological family. The focal ground of politics intersects in each individual citizen, but their problems compose the common focus in the first place. Hence, citizens can be either responsible or victimized. For their own interests—and on this individualistic premise, modern democracy was founded—better they be knowledgeable and hence responsible. Obversely, the community is always maintained and improved best by an enlightened citizenry—independent men rather than dumb sheep. But citizenship as an institutionalized role requires only ("only" is qualified in the next section) obedience and a sense of obligation which insures spontaneous, rather than forced acquiescence in common undertakings.

## Obedience and Obligation

A particular society's focal point of tensions, found in its institutionalized political arrangements, comprises the common good for that society, paradoxically equating tension and good. Politics knows no other life. Why make this common good some mystical entity? As noted before, "focusing" means bringing into sharp relief blurred images, and such focusing furnishes a vital political function. Political arrangements, beset by obfuscation, complicated by self-seeking ambitions, hindered by anomalous institutions, seldom perform optimally. But life without politics is unthinkable. Lacking a common tensional center, an institutionalized "sovereign" as the older tradition would say, social existence, as known everywhere over the centuries, seems highly improbable, or at any rate inconceivable.

The common good, therefore, presents a concrete activity with a vital function and not an illusive specter fascinating to speculative philosophers and no one else; elementary and essential, it can be interchanged with other expressions such as "common concern," "common (or public) interest," "common involvements," "political nature." Common to all, the political focus must be public, because privacy undermines commonalty. And the "common" means, by definition, that shared among others. For large numbers sharing an enterprise, there must exist some mutual body of knowledge and experience known to all and participated in by all.

If there existed no elaborate institutional structure or effective participant mechanisms, the citizen would still participate in the common good or public interest; as citizen, he must at least establish identity with his community. Always problematic, such identity relationships between individual and polity are never absolutely secured, but identification goes on nevertheless, even if only in negative relations. The focal center demands allegiance from citizens as it does from aliens. It always "pays" to know one's way about, for self-interest if no other reason. But the citizen, as full member (unlike the alien), must "feel obliged," even when it no longer suits his interest; he must share in a common good, which amounts to a communal enterprise. He should be "willing" to obey, to serve, to die. His state automatically assumes this and feels justified in forcing him to do its bidding for the common interest's sake. The price for the privileges of full membership (such as they are) is obligation. For citizen, "I ought," is superseded by "I am obliged"; not "I am forced to do such and such," but "I am willing to do such and such."

This obedience flows from will, not force. But willing conduct entails responsibility for that conduct. Needless to say, the feeling of obligation is a model attitude, but every state presumes it in the main, though recalcitrants are anticipated. Brute force cannot sustain that common focus of considerations and tensions—political community. Where only force prevails no community exists, only occupied territory. Yet with time even such territory may develop commonalty.

Citizens join together, therefore, with ties of amity, concord, equity, peace, and will. In other words, as public persons undertaking the focal tensions of common association, their reciprocities involve active allegiance to their community. Mutually loyal in their common involvements, their very mutuality precludes purely passive obedience, introducing the many questions that accompany "identity" and the activity of "identifying." Loyalty's frequent dilemmas appear, because, bound together and looking to a central political life, citizens can never be "merely" or "only" passive. No matter how cowed by fear, individuals may move out of line, thwart association, disengage their loyalties, and risk punishment. They always retain powers of identification and the responsibilities going with these powers, as they constantly seek and transform their own identities.[57]

Threatening their community by living in it, citizens retain at least a latent activity. And their internal symbolizations can never be completely dominated by even the most totalitarian community. Hence, every age witnesses elaborate concessions to public opinion, even in barbaric despotisms. Likewise, careful precautions against defection are devised, because citizens may also temporize. By its attribute as an incomplete bridge between private individual and public action, citizenship cannot, in any culture, stand too much stress for too long.

Of course, the resiliency of citizenship institutions depends upon the particular political community. More than likely, American citizens would endure greater demands from their state than full members of the Haitian dictatorship would from theirs. Put another way, the prospects for revolution appear

57. Anselm Strauss, *Mirrors and Masks*, p. 139.

brighter in Haiti than in the United States. On the other hand, free peoples, accustomed to better treatment from their communities, may have lower tolerances for abuse than those virtually enslaved by tyrannies. According to this view, the American colonists revolted in the eighteenth century because they once enjoyed the "rights of Englishmen" of that era but were then denied liberties few peoples possess even in the twentieth century. In contrast, the suppressed citizenry of contemporary Saudi Arabia cannot have much spontaneous regard for liberty.

When citizens feel obligated to obey and serve their political community, as contrasted to being forced to obey, one says they "owe allegiance" or "feel obligated." Such allegiance is active, not passive. Since not all states are democracies and even those that are have imperfect institutions for positive participation, the activity of allegiance, citizens identifying with and making "a" community "their" community, appears basic to all citizenship, no matter what kind of commonwealth. This allegiance also lies at the base of the question of obligation, or why one feels obliged to obey a government.

At least this can be expected from citizens: presumably they will obey willingly (feel obligated). In this sense they all participate, because willingness indicates an identity with the common interest, when and where demanded, but surely an incompleted identity, since the common interest can never include every private concern. While not identical, however, private and public interest share identity. The key to citizen obligation is participation, but this participation can be interpreted broadly to include *tacit* acceptance through allegiance, as well as *explicit* agreement with community policies.

As full political membership, citizenship knows only the particular community at given points in space and time; it concerns the stable polity recognized by international arrangements or other ways (such as incorporated cities), which labels the members Haitians, Paraguayans, Saudis, Americans, Chicagoans, Parisians, and so on. States that enslave their citizens (and enslavement may take many forms) vitiate good citizenship. And such nations as Nazi Germany and South Africa that deliberately exclude large parts of their total populations from full citizenship as a matter of public policy are execrable. Nevertheless, good citizenship remains relative to concrete political institutions, at least when citizenship is approached from the institutional point of view, a civic style tailored for better or worse by the constitutions of particular states and the ways of life under those constitutions. Institutionally speaking, citizenship is synonymous with loyal membership. Even the United States and Great Britain, two nations priding themselves on their citizenry's freedom, emphasize the primary attributes of loyalty and service. Further, loyalty and service involve an identification between individuals and political nature, providing in the process forms of civic action.

Modern democratic arguments for participation seem to suggest the problematic nature of allegiance. Why should not citizens participate in state decisions which contravene their private interests? Also, granting the proposition that identity underlies good citizenship, how can identity be established between individual and community when most individuals are not allowed a voice in that community's arrangements? Would not active participation by the whole citizenry in the common good, argued Rousseau, insure that each, "while uniting himself with all . . . still obey himself alone, and remain as free as before?" Of course, the question for democrats was never creating more citizens, so that additional persons could be admitted to active decision-making. This would have been the issue in ancient Athens, where the citizen was also full participant in affairs of state.

But another citizenship, described so well by the sixteenth-century *politique*, Jean Bodin, prevailed in the West: citizen role and positive participation have not been synonymous.[58] The central issue for democratic theorists never was the quantity of citizens, but the quality of citizenship. All, or at least most, were already citizens because they were subjects of the realm, and this group or some significant part of it was to control the

58. *Six Books of the Commonwealth*, Book I, Chapters vi–vii.

common good, thus changing citizenship for most from arbitrary sacrifices to privileged decision-making about what those sacrifices should entail.

Since the rise of modern democracy accompanied exaltation of human reason, it could further be argued that men should not be expected "reasonably" to serve the commonweal when they had no political voice (Hobbes, of course, used reason to defend exactly the opposite argument). The best democratic theorists never thought all men basically rational, but their rationalism supported an obligation based on reason, not so much vindicating "reason" as "reasonableness." They believed that men of good will could agree on this latter point, even if some doubt lingered about how much reason or what kind of reason most men possessed.

The common man of early democratic eras hardly qualified as "enlightened" by seventeenth- and eighteenth-century standards (a time when ambitious criteria measured rational enlightenment), but he was reasonable and could be cajoled by rational arguments aimed at his self-interest. Furthermore, the force of such reasoning indicated that one could not expect active obedience or a sense of lively obligation from a purely "subject" community. Ants make poor citizens, yet their social life exhibits admirable organization, and their mechanisms of social control remain peerless. But good socializers hardly make good citizens. Finally, the political community offered a certain limited expansive potential for individuals, but this potency could be exploited only if every individual participated actively in state affairs (Hobbes again argued the contrary). Any other expectations would be unjust and unreasonable. The nineteenth and twentieth centuries widened this earlier democratic argument to include economic and social participation, as well as political.

For the citizen, allegiance means commitment to the state's purpose. In fact, this distinguishes him from slave and alien. As a full-fledged member, he should "care" and "identify." For him alone the following issues, all involving obligation or active obedience, have relevance. The citizen performs loyally or disloyally, dutifully or undutifully, steadfastly or treasonously, patriotically or unpatriotically, knowledgeably or ignorantly. Considered from an institutional standpoint, good citizens score high on loyalty, service, patriotism, participation, and civic knowledge. Even law-abidingness, something required from every person residing in a given jurisdiction, has especially meritorious overtones for citizens. Conversely, opprobrium follows the disloyal, treasonous, unpatriotic, alienated, anomic, and ignorant.

One caveat is necessary, however. Absolutist arguments lay full onus for good citizenship on the individual: the state and its leaders can do no wrong. More realistically, citizenship provides a bridge between individual and state and requires support from both sides. As citizenship begins to waver and disintegrate, unfirm political ground may not sustain loyalty and service among citizenry. Blurred identities develop concomitant with an alienation often traced to those characteristics of political nature which repel citizens and cause disaffection. At the same time, however, the individual always interprets social symbols for himself, so that his society, outside very wide controls, has no guarantee that even the "best of all possible worlds" will satisfy everyone or prevent disillusionment. Recalling an earlier argument, the individual always retains his power of identification. He constantly seeks himself and, in so doing, incessantly transforms his identity. One modern poet, Charles Olson, pictures us all, "Around an appearance, one common model, we grow up many."[59] This individual autonomy will be discussed more fully in later chapters.

As political space furnishes an abstraction for isolating the special field of politics, so allegiance to institutionalized arrangements confines the special action form of citizenship. The unique political focus requires a corresponding actor. This actor is a common or public person, the citizen. He wears the single mask or plays the typical role of citizen, sharing it with others who also possess many different attributes and accomplishments. Citizenship being a formal institution, its role-players, the citizens, occupy stereotyped positions in a ground of common involvements. No society tolerates so much divergence in citizen style

59. From "The Kingfishers" (1949), in *The Distances* (New York: Grove Press, 1960), p. 8.

that the political field, where these citizens participate, no longer provides a common place for all. But each community judges divergencies from the single pattern differently. Whatever the limits, beyond them citizens cease treating the cracks and fissures in the common ground as natural or inevitable and become alienated from the community; they no longer recognize *this* polity as *their* polity.

From the state's point of view, common loyalty to the community constitutes the extreme circle beyond which dissidence finds no toleration. However variegated citizen motives for obedience and obligation, the state usually interests itself only in outward obedience and obligation, although questions about hypocrisy arise in modern revolutionary situations.[60] Communities that want to remain communities—places where sharing and associating take place—must attend to such formalities. Formal citizenship institutions continue very important and grow increasingly complicated, their problems involving not so much individual differences as how, given these differences, a common life still can be maintained. The vital problem of maintaining commonweal in the face of human idiosyncrasies, without destroying these idiosyncrasies, makes citizenship training an awesome responsibility and the highest pedagogical calling known to human societies.

Situated as an actively obedient subject in political nature, the citizen provides a paradigm or "type" amenable to analysis. Such active allegiance to or identification with the common focus involves the following basic questions, considerations which will occupy Chapters Four, Five, and Six of the present study. First, the task of separating public action from private attitude, so as to establish a point (or points) for common or focal tensions, seems elementary. Second, symbols and mechanisms for obligation have wide currency and necessitate classification and comparison. Finally, connections between personality and obligation, or congruencies between private individuals and public order, universally pervade political organizations and have important relevance for citizenship study.

60. Arendt, *On Revolution*, pp. 91 ff.

Other problems immediately suggest themselves but will be ignored to a considerable extent here; for example, too little time will be expended in analyzing the political act itself, or its dimensions of actor, action, situation, and effects. Yet any understanding of the individual in political nature benefits from discussing the three main questions raised above. The citizen becomes in any social enterprise "a participant or party in a conjoint undertaking" (to paraphrase John Dewey slightly), but the citizen's undertaking, distinguished from the Rotarian's (who is citizen as well), involves a political and public focus since he encounters his community's tensions and these tensions impart a peculiar situational reality and the responsibilities incumbent in that reality. No one commands the Rotarian to identify with his community at large, but the citizen must.

Political nature and the citizen role found there converts the private individual into a political man. Citizenship provides what social psychologists call "collective identity," but a particular kind of identity—the imperfect union between individual and political nature, or, in more conventional terms, the relation between citizen and state. In another patois, citizenship delineates the political "alter ego" of each individual. Establishing identity and developing a fairly congenial relationship between ego and this special institutionalized alter ego is the function of obligation. The rubrics of congruence—the traditional issue of obligation plus the actual feeling of being obliged—rationalize such identity relationships.

As a postscript, it may seem bewildering that the terms "community," "state," and "polity" have been used interchangeably here with little care for technical distinctions. All denote the same thing from the citizen's standpoint, namely, citizens sharing a common institutional focus in their society. This common sharing never means, however, that every citizen knows every other citizen (Aristotle's "ideal state") or shares anything tangible in common (Plato's "ideal state"). From the standpoint of a shared focus, the enterprises of community, state, and polity are highly symbolic, the more so as societies grow in organized complexity.

Perhaps Erving Goffman's interesting discussion of the "colleague" role in social interaction might clarify this last point as it relates to modern societies. Goffman's discussion also serves as a fine transition from citizenship as an institutionalized status, with all the ambiguities we have noted in what such a status means to those who occupy it, to citizenship as a problem in action and symbolism, a problem which will concern the remainder of this book. "Colleagues," distinguished from "team-members," present a standard routine to an audience but do not participate together simultaneously as a team would do. Accordingly, while not all on the same stage at the same time, colleagues still share "a community of fate."[61] Whatever their individual languages, they come to speak the same social language.[62] Conversely, there always remains the possibility that a disaffected colleague will turn renegade and sell out to an audience the secrets of a dramaturgical act his erstwhile brethren are still performing.[63] Colleague groups vary in the strength of their corporate ties, ranging from those wherein members rarely share responsibility for misbehavior of their associates to closer corporate groups.[64] While the ideas of colleague and collegial

61. *The Presentation of Self in Everyday Life* (Edinburgh: University of Edinburgh Social Science Research Centre, 1956), p. 102.
62. *Ibid.*
63. *Ibid.*, p. 105. Goffman views the dramaturgical approach to the "social establishment" ("any place surrounded by fixed barriers to perception in which a particular kind of activity regularly takes place"—p. 152) as one of five possible perspectives. The dramaturgical perspective concerns outward display in social interaction. Another of these perspectives is the "political," characterized by Goffman as "the actions which each participant (or class of participants) can demand of other participants, the kinds of deprivations and indulgences which can be meted out in order to enforce these demands, and the kinds of social control which guide this exercise of command and use of sanctions." (p. 153) The political and dramaturgical may be combined for added insight into action and communication. Power must be clothed in effective means of displaying it, and it will have different effects depending on how it is dramatized. Naked power—physical coercion—is often neither objective nor naked, "but rather functions as a display for persuading the audience; it is often a means of communication, not merely a means of action." (p. 155) Machiavelli, of course, was most appreciative of political dramaturgy.
64. *Ibid.*, p. 106.

apply immediately to many professional associations, Goffman also includes "mothers" as a loosely knit corporate group.[65]

Extending the colleague model to politics, the community or state is collegial in all the ways noted above and the notion of colleague provides a useful analogy for citizenship, at least generally speaking.[66] More particularly, however, the political community was initially a residential association, something which cannot be said for other colleague groups. "The constitution of the polis." Aristotle wrote, "involves in itself some sort of association, and its members must initially be associated in a common place of residence. To be fellow citizens is to be sharers in one state, and to have one state is also to have one place of residence."[67] Tangible geographic and institutional spaces always demarcate specific polities, but civic identity is at least as symbolic as it is tangible.

65. *Ibid.*

66. If the citizen is more colleague than team-member, it follows that the rules binding civil society together, that is, its laws (which affect aliens too, but do not bind them in any sense of obligation), are more like "professional ethics" than "rules of the game." Yet the latter kind of rules are most frequently compared with law, at least in the English-speaking world, where high premium is placed on sport as a social and socializing activity. In the sense that law carries with it the obligation to obey and this obligation is instilled in citizen members through civic education, it makes more sense to draw parallels between political rules and professional rules. Also, law frequently regulates the rules of collegial groups, but seldom interferes in the rules of games. Finally, the strategies operating in political nature are more like those in corporate bodies than like those in games; the current fad of applying "game theory" to political situations is misleading, perhaps. In this connection, any political investigation may have fruitful and interesting results in terms of what that investigation sets out to accomplish; whether a given inquiry is relevant to political nature is another matter. Here, as elsewhere in political studies, the scientific approach, simply because it is science, is not necessarily as useful as, say, literature. From a social scientist's viewpoint, see the reservations held about game theory in the study of interorganizational conflict, in James G. March and Herbert A. Simon, *Organizations* (New York: John Wiley, 1958), pp. 131–135.

67. *Politics*, 1260b–1261a.

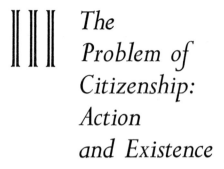

# III The Problem of Citizenship: Action and Existence

THE preceding chapter approached the citizen as an institutional actor playing a role and occupying a status. Viewed as such an actor, the citizen is not a type of person, but an occupant of a particular status.[1] Such an actor wears the citizenship mask, suggesting a personage only in the sense that "mask" and *persona* coincide in meaning. For example, in law the legal person is distinguished from the natural person.

It thus arises that all agency before the law is personal agency, the action not of men but of maskers. The context of legal relations into which the natural individual is born confers upon him the sole responsibility which he may claim by right. He may not extricate himself from the masks of society; it is given to him only to exchange masks within society. To be without a mask, to wear no mask at all, is, in human society, to exist without personality and without title, to

1. See Ralph Turner, "Role-Taking: Process versus Conformity," in *Human Behavior and Social Processes, An Interactionist Approach*, edited by Arnold M. Rose (London: Routledge and Kegan Paul, 1962), Chapter 2, at p. 24.

suffer the condition of having no status, to be slave or outcast beyond that pale of the law, which requires that every legal relation be a relation between persons and will suffer with equanimity any desecration of men, so it be not done to the masks of the law is designed to protect and men are predestined to wear.[2]

The legal "person" and "mask" are synonymous, both connoting a fixed condition of reliable conduct. The citizen role, much like any other social role, furnishes a "socially structured world of experience" and comprises many dimensions, only one of which concerns role-playing.[3] Thus, the last chapter presented a legalistic, stereotyped citizen, in order to depict the citizen actor as a socially ideal type. An ideal form deliberately stresses consistent behavior, even though actual behavior threatens surprises; social order and "folk judgment" demand homogeneous expectations, if not consistent performances. Through idealized roles every person orients himself, idealization itself limited by shared cultural perceptions. So imperative is this quest for consistency that whenever many individuals characteristically act from two or more given roles simultaneously, society will devise a single role into which the two may merge.[4] Thus both Plato and Aristotle defined "the citizen" as he who both ruled and was ruled in turn. Citizenship encompassed two different roles, and its dualistic structure still shapes citizenship's basic composition.[5]

But the political problems of citizenship arise precisely where natural persons confront legal statuses, citizenship being one

2. John F. A. Taylor, "The Masks of Society: An Essay on the Foundations of Law in Civil Community," *Journal of Philosophy*, LIV (August 15, 1957), 513–531, at 516. The article appears, as part of a larger study, in John F. A. Taylor, *The Masks of Society: An Inquiry into the Covenants of Civilization* (New York: Appleton-Century-Crofts, 1966), Chapter 4, p. 80.

3. Turner, *op. cit.*, p. 24.

4. *Ibid.*, p. 26. Turner's example is the "politician role" which really includes an individual acting simultaneously as a party functionary and government official.

5. The latest variation may be found in Gabriel Almond and Sidney Verba, *The Civic Culture, Political Attitudes and Democracy in Five Nations* (Princeton: Princeton University Press, 1963), in the orientation of citizens toward government "inputs" and "outputs," pp. 15–16.

institutional means for connecting nature and law. Comparing the God of the Old Testament to the *ens Summum* of medieval theology, the Roman Catholic philosopher, Don Miguel de Unamuno, observed more generally,

> to define a thing is to idealise it, a process which necessitates the abstraction from it of its incommensurable or irrational element, its vital essence.[6]

Most of this essay aims to locate the "vital essence" of that *political* thing called citizenship, which necessitates careful examination of the "incommensurable or irrational element" in the citizenship role, the individual self. "Role-taking" actually signifies, in Ralph Turner's words, "role-making," with military and bureaucratic roles being somewhat atypical, rigid extremes.[7] Something as imprecise (albeit stereotyped) as the citizen role necessarily provides room for diverging approaches and styles by private or natural persons. Citizenship, whose institutions always appear imprecise in varying degrees because so many persons are involved, invites highly stylized, personalized role-playing. This does not mean that a rigid citizen stereotype is never available; American high school civics textbooks provide handy, simplistic images of the "good citizen."[8]

But the citizen role as actually practiced is so widespread and so involved in airy tissues of rights and duties symbolic enough to defy any precise explication in actual policies that close institutional surveillance over all members seems more an Orwellian nightmare than a daily reality.[9] And unenforced, spontaneous

6. *The Tragic Sense of Life*, translated by J. E. Crawford Flitch (London: Macmillan, 1921), p. 159.
7. Turner, *op. cit.*, p. 22. In this connection see Turner, "The Navy Disbursing Officer as a Bureaucrat," *American Sociological Review*, XII (1947), 342–348.
8. Even a cursory review of leading high school government texts reveals an emphasis on hortative discussions of "good" citizenship.
9. "All who possess the status [citizenship] are equal with respect to the rights and duties with which the status is endowed. There is no universal principle that determines what those rights and duties shall be, but societies in which citizenship is a developing institution create an image of an ideal citizenship against which achievement can be directed." T. H. Marshall, *Citizenship and Social Class, and Other Essays* (Cambridge: Cambridge University Press, 1950), pp. 28–29.

melding together of *l'homme civil* and *l'homme naturel* always seems a vain ideal.[10] Because of citizenship's diffusion, individual personality may have greater scope for exercising its prerogatives within this role, so that the self becomes a very important, if not the most important, condition for citizen action.

Historically, the structure of citizen action has seldom been rationalized in bureaucratic or militaristic fashion, at least as bureaucracy and military are understood today. Sparta proved a noted exception, but close conformity to rigid stereotypes of the good citizen there included, not only severe military discipline, but full-time service to the state; and realistically enough citizens (who were all males) did not scrape for their livings, thereby excluding from the picture private interests with their distracting cares.[11] Subsequent events demonstrated that ideal and practice diverged widely. In another direction, Athens also paid its citizens during certain periods.[12]

The present chapter and the one following propose to examine the citizen as a unique self, rather than role actor, with the social actor occupying an integral but not paramount position within the citizen role. In other words, the dimension of institutional actor will be held fairly constant and the structure of the self varied. We shall assume, for the sake of argument, that selfhood varies in predictability and autonomy relative to social structure, depending upon both the particular individual and his milieu. These chapters will argue that "predictions" about citizen behavior must take into account the great latitude ordinarily given the idiosyncrasies of persons within their citizen role. What Whitehead once termed the tendency of symbolic elements in life "to run wild, like the vegetation in a tropical forest,"[13] will be remembered too, since citizenship's symbolism, no matter how vacant its actual meaning, may adversely affect

10. See Jean Jacques Rousseau, *Emile*, in *Rousseau, the Political Writings*, (1915) edited by C. E. Vaughan, 2 vols. (Oxford: Basil Blackwell, 1962), II, 145–146.

11. J. B. Bury, *History of Greece*, third edition revised by Russell Meigs (London: Macmillan and Co., 1959), pp. 131–133.

12. *Ibid.*, pp. 587–588.

13. Alfred North Whitehead, *Symbolism, Its Meaning and Effect* (New York: Capricorn Books, 1959) (Barbour-Page Lectures, University of Virginia, 1927), p. 61.

personal autonomy. Finally, Chapter Six speculates on the congruency between self-needs and actor-demands in modern citizenship: an unresolved tension exists between self and world which is nevertheless not an antimony. In political thought this tension has traditionally been expressed in terms of private and public (see Chapters Four and Five), but this tension rests on a more ontological foundation which must be explored in order to add depth to political analysis. Political actors are *at once* role players and whole persons.

The remainder of this study explores some exciting theories relevant to certain citizenship problems. The problems may sometimes appear abstract, but it is hoped that these abstractions will relate sufficiently to everyday political experience. Philosophies of symbolism will be prominent, as will psychoanalytic theories, logical positivism, psychologies of meaning, modern literature, linguistic analysis, contemporary and traditional political and legal philosophy, administrative theory, and modern theology. Each approach has some relevance to citizenship as developed in this essay. But the continuing dialogue between social science and existential philosophy—often more latent than openly expressed—will dominate what follows. Neither is monolithic. Social science encompasses pluralistic points of view, even concerning human interactions, this study's primary interest. Likewise, existential philosophy is polyglot, particularly when discussing the authenticity expected of individual subjects.

Comparisons between social science and existentialism have been made elsewhere,[14] but not regarding political action in

14. For example, Van Meter Ames, "Mead and Sartre on Man," *Journal of Philosophy*, LIII (March 15, 1956), 205–219; Paul E. Pfuetze, *Self, Society, Existence* (New York: Harper Torchbooks, 1961); Jean-Paul Sartre, "Questions de méthode (I)," *Les Temps Modernes*, XIII (September 1957), 338–417; Maurice Natanson, *Literature, Philosophy, and the Social Sciences: Essays in Existentialism and Phenomenology* (The Hague: Martinus Nijhoff, 1962), Part III; Natanson (ed.), *Philosophy of the Social Sciences: A Reader* (New York: Random House, 1963), pp. 3–26; Edward Tiryakian, *Sociologism and Existentialism: Two Perspectives on the Individual and Society* (Englewood Cliffs, N.J.: Prentice-Hall, 1962).

general or citizen action in particular. Citizenship's major problem involves the interrelation between individual actor and political nature. How do acting subjects "fit" into the world of objective political things? What are their interrelationships? their mutual and specialized responsibilities? This chapter will adumbrate a conversation between social science and existentialism on these crucial matters, reserving full treatment for later chapters. In so doing, the interconnections between action and existence on the one hand, and the interpenetration of subject and object in human thought and action on the other, will, it is hoped, become apparent. The issues remain difficult ones, all obfuscation is unintentional.

The interconnections between action and existence constitute themes explored by nineteenth- and twentieth-century social philosophers, sociologists, social psychologists, and political scientists, and deserve more notice than they usually receive; studying any political action concept, including citizenship, requires attention to these questions. According to social scientists, thought is existentially determined, or, if "existential" sounds too mysterious (it did not to Mannheim, for one), thought is determined by "experience," that is, by configurations adjusting the self to other persons and things. But what determines "existence" or "experience"? "Action," or what amounts to the same thing for them, experiencing through everyday sense impressions and activities, is the answer modern social science theorists give. Karl Mannheim observed at the very beginning of his *Ideology and Utopia*,

Philosophers have too long concerned themselves with their own thinking. When they wrote of thought, they had in mind primarily their own history, the history of philosophy, or quite special fields of knowledge such as mathematics or physics. This type of thinking is applicable only under quite special circumstances, and what can be learned by analyzing it is not directly transferable to other spheres of life. Even when it is applicable, it refers only to a specific dimension of existence which does not suffice for living human beings who are seeking to comprehend and to mould their world.[15]

15. *Ideology and Utopia*, translated by Louis Wirth and Edward Shils (New York: Harcourt, Brace & World, Inc. [Harvest Books], 1936), p. 1.

John Dewey also criticized what he termed "classic philosophy," for impractically conceiving the "office of knowledge" to demand uncovering "the antecedently real, rather than as is the case with our practical judgments, to gain the kind of understanding which is necessary to deal with problems as they arise."[16] Dewey saw "irony in a situation wherein desire and emotion are relegated to a position inferior in every way to that of knowledge, while at the same time the chief problem of that which is termed the highest and most perfect knowledge is taken to be the existence of evil—that is, of desires errant and frustrated. . . ."[17] Philosophers could make genuine contributions "to the central problem of development of intelligent methods of regulation," if they would connect thought and action, and envisage action as sense experience.[18] Criticizing Greek philosophy because it separated (he alleged) activity from what he considered action, namely making and doing (experience), Dewey thought it knowledge's proper office to regulate the experiential realm.[19] Existence comprised no mystic region, but plain ordinary experience, and only with the latter kind of existence should philosophy occupy itself.

If the present study were confined only to social science theory, discussing "existence" would prove bootless. "Experience" is more stylish in social science. By including existential philosophy, however, the present approach—rightly or wrongly —broadens the human condition from the more naturalistic

16. *Intelligence in the Modern World*, edited by Joseph Ratner (New York: Modern Library, 1939), p. 288 (from *The Quest for Certainty*, by permission of Joseph Ratner).

17. *Ibid.*, p. 300 (from *The Quest for Certainty*).

18. *Ibid.*, p. 277 (from *The Quest for Certainty*).

19. *Ibid.*, p. 289 (from *The Quest for Certainty*). For criticism of the modern tendency to associate action with "making and doing," see Hannah Arendt, *The Human Condition*, Chapter 6. Morton White comments on Dewey's attitude toward "classic philosophy": "In one instant Dewey discredited the entire two thousand years that preceded him in philosophy, meanwhile expressing the temperamental aversion to formal, 'rigid' logic and 'hairsplitting' which has been part of his philosophical personality for almost seventy years." *Social Thought in America* (Boston: Beacon Press, 1957), p. 189.

(and instrumental) "experience," to the more mysterious (if not entirely metaphysical) "existence." And behind the expression "existing" move problems so complicated, paradoxical, and insoluble, that they seem "scandalous" (perhaps even farcical) to the simplifier, the superficial conceptualizer, and the pedant busily getting his "blind-spots-structuralized-into-dogma."[20]

Jumping from "experience" to "existence" is not gratuitous, because the so-called existentialist philosophers, in varying degrees, reject that metaphysics which finalizes the universe in technical systems, but retain metaphysics as the study of what lies "outside" or on the "boundaries" of empirical objectivity.[21] For example, the following lines from one of Lawrence Durrell's novels pose a profound metaphysical problem with important ramifications for contemporary citizenship. Such a question interests existential philosophies too and makes these philosophies relevant to political studies, yet it involves a non-transcendent issue. One might describe the difference as one between a transcendent problem with experiential implications and an experiential problem with implications going beyond the obvious. Here Durrell analyzes one character's predicament.

He was not to know, however, how much worse than a simple death a war could be, with its power to deaden and whip the sensibility into emptiness; he was not to foresee the dreadful post-war world

20. This refers specifically to the history of the psychoanalytic movement but has other applications as well. See *Existence, A New Dimension in Psychiatry and Psychology*, edited by Rollo May, *et al.* (New York: Basic Books, 1958), p. 7.

21. See Martin Heidegger, "What Is Metaphysics?" translated by R. F. C. Hull and Alan Crick, in *Existence and Being*, edited by Stefan Schimanski (Chicago: Gateway, 1949), pp. 344–345; Karl Jaspers, *Way to Wisdom*, translated by Ralph Manheim (New Haven: Yale University Press, 1960), pp. 34–36; Ronald Grimsley, *Existentialist Thought* (Cardiff; University of Wales Press, 1960), pp. 86–89 (on Heidegger) and 153–155 (on Jaspers). Merleau-Ponty refers to these boundaries as a "horizon of meaning" in a wider, pre-objective field of experience, *The Phenomenology of Perception* translated by Colin Smith (London: Routlege & Kegan Paul, 1962), p. 15. For an interesting attempt to fill "experience" with the full meaning of "existence" see Ronald D. Laing, *The Politics of Experience* (New York: Pantheon Books, 1967).

which became a frantic hunt, not for values, but for the elementary feelings upon which any sense of community is founded.[22]

Existence, for these new philosophers (actually "old" philosophers by Heidegger's reckoning, since he finds the basic issues in pre-Socratic philosophy[23]), harbors the same active, everyday connotations, only with much more impressive depth and richness, that experience has for pragmatists and instrumentalists. At the same time, however, while rejecting a metaphysics of technique,[24] existential philosophies also abjure pure technics without any metaphysical dimension whatever. Just as the modern existentialist cannot be Cartesian or Kantian, he cannot be instrumentalist, positivist, or philosophic analyst. As a corollary to this animosity toward technical philosophy runs the existentialist revolt against the bondage of modern technology with its artificial isolation of analysis and synthesis.[25] "Existence" constitutes "being-in-the-world," a nexus of relations with oneself, other persons, other things, "Nothing" (Heidegger), and, for some theologians, God as well. "Experience," as generally used in the social sciences, has more naturalistic, socialized connotations and poses none of the dreadful, true-to-life malignities which challenge common sense and yet populate that existence featured in existential philosophy.

Dewey's animosity toward Freud's psychology typifies naturalism's flattening of human experience into motives and drives, amenable to the methods of a psychology even undergraduates can practice, though Freud may ultimately prove more powerful than Dewey.[26] Indeed, it would not be unfair to say that Dewey's

22. *The Dark Labyrinth* (New York: E. P. Dutton and Co., 1962), p. 62.

23. See Thomas Langan, *The Meaning of Heidegger* (New York: Columbia University Press, 1959), Chapter 8.

24. *Ibid.*, Chapter 9. My discussion of Heidegger throughout this book relies extensively on Langan's excellent study. See also Karsten Harries, "Martin Heidegger: The Search for Meaning," in *Existential Philosophers: Kierkegaard to Merleau-Ponty*, edited by George A. Schrader, Jr. (New York: McGraw-Hill, 1967), Chapter 4.

25. F. H. Heineman, *Existentialism and the Modern Predicament* (New York: Harper Torchbooks, 1958), pp. 26 ff.

26. John Dewey, *Human Nature and Conduct* (1922) (New York: Modern Library, 1930), pp. 86 ff.

5

use of experience represents a deliberate attempt to speak more technically, but that his philosophy still presented enough ambiguities as it aspired to technical applications. Paradoxically, for an avowedly practical man with an explicitly practical philosophy, Dewey was most imprecise exactly where techniques confronted practicalities, namely, connecting means to ends and goals.

Technics are presumably neutral, because they apply to any number of ends and circumstances. But practical applications of such means involve concrete situations with tangible goals—at least in social and political action they do. And goals encompassing the means of their achievement are politically relevant; the rest is simple engineering devoid of practicality. "What is to be done?" and "How is this to be done?" are seldom, if ever, separate problems in political life, even if it proves convenient for political scientists to separate them analytically.

Even in analytical terms such separation leads to irrelevancies and vacuities. For example, one can hardly separate the role of military leader as a calculator of means designed to promote national policy from the role of military leader as an executor of these plans in life. Very crudely and simply put (with hope that later discussion will amplify and clarify), what existential philosophers iterate, and what appears so relevant for political action and political theory in the present age, is that everyday human projects, contrasted to physics in the laboratory, psychology in the maze, political science in the model, are barely technical, and the means for understanding and expressing human existence must therefore suit human beings in their experiential totality,[27] an experience partly technical and objectifiable but also charged with metaphysical energies stirring the human depths of anxiety, being, dread, existence and meaning.[28] But what constitutes this totality?

27. Hannah Arendt, "Understanding and Politics," *Partisan Review*, XX (July–August 1953), 377–392. Of course, physics, psychology and political science, as they become relevant to the everyday world, are *more* than technical also. Better put, the neutral values of science, as science is practiced in the laboratory, become ambiguous when pure knowledge mixes in socio-political action.

28. Heidegger, Merleau-Ponty and others have been deeply influenced by the *Lebenswelt* phenomenology of Edmund Husserl.

Heidegger's inquiry into experience goes beyond scientific "what-is" to questions surrounding the problem of "Nothing," which in turn are presaged by dread (*Angst*) arising from experience itself. Suddenly, by introducing negation, human action assumes new dimensions. Experiencing dread varies from person to person, depending upon their different sensitivities.[29] The simple, rational negation of "logic" indicates that Nothing resides in what-is. But better still are the affective premonitions presaging annihilation (Durrell's "elementary feel-ings"?) —"harshness of opposition and violence of loathing . . . pain of refusal . . . the mercilessness of an interdict . . . the bitterness of renunciation."[30]

Products of daily experience, such events are freighted with pregnant metaphysical meanings ignored by instrumentalists and positivists (or at least the latter schools reject metaphysical implications). "The very idea of 'logic,' " Heidegger writes, "disintegrates in the vortex of a more original questioning." Yet he insists that the "Nothing" beyond "what-is" remains within the bounds of real experience, since it surrounds and encompasses the empirical as the latter's ground; "Nothing" fluctuates on the empirical's periphery, but no philosopher can legitimately summon transcendent absolutes to explain it. Indeed, conjuring absolutes, just as pandering empirical reason, debilitates insight. While metaphysical, therefore, Heidegger's Nothing is "integral to Being of what is."[31] Experience widens and deepens when based on *Dasein*, or all-embracing Being grounded in the world.

Political theory and citizenship theory require this "more original questioning." True, once political studies needed, in Bentley's words, "a glow of humanity" rather than an "injection of metaphysics," but humanity and metaphysics need not be

29. "Dread is there, but sleeping. All Da-sein quivers with its breathing: the pulsation is slightest in beings that are timorous, and is imperceptible in the 'Yea, yea!' and 'Nay, nay!' of busy people; it is readiest in the reserved, and surest of all in the courageous." Heidegger, "What Is Metaphysics?" *op. cit.*, p. 343.

30. *Ibid.*, p. 342.

31. *Ibid.*, pp. 342–346. Also, Merleau-Ponty, *Phenomenology of Perception*, pp. 23–24.

incompatible, if existential ambiguities and responsibilities in-
fusing basic human feelings are emphasized instead of theological gratuities. Again, Planck's ruminations on that mystery
latent in all knowledge quickens thought.

Returning to Dewey and Mannheim, both argued that philosophic thought, as traditionally constructed, could not apply
where living human beings sought to comprehend and explain
their daily worlds. In Durrell's words, why fret over philosophic
values when the community searches frantically "for the elementary feelings upon which any sense of community is
founded"? Isn't there something missing from the so-called
value-fact dichotomy? Where occur the elementary feelings? Do
they constitute "values" or "facts"? Or are they something else?
In what semantic pidgeonhole does this political commentary by
one of Durrell's characters fit?

Sometimes, Baird, I think there is only politics left for you—the last
refuge of the diseased ego. You notice how all the young men are
burning to reform things? It's to escape the terrible nullity and
emptiness and guilt of the last six years. They are now going to
nationalize everything, including joy, sex and sleep. There will be
enough for everyone now because the Government will control it.
Those who can't sleep will be locked up.[32]

How do philosophers and political scientists handle the relationships between politics on the one hand, and "joy, sex and sleep"
on the other? Are these relationships relevant to citizenship?[33]

But Dewey and Mannheim connected experience, on the one
hand, with thought (comprehension) and action on the other.
Compelled by his interest in ideology, Mannheim emphasized
the axis of experience and thought but did not exclude the
correlative dimension of experience and action. He was quick to
observe thought's "rootedness" in action. Such awareness did
not preclude evaluations from the "new type of objectivity in the
social sciences," but did stimulate a "critical awareness and
control of them." Not only thought but everyday experience is

32. Durrell, *op. cit.*, p. 78.
33. See here James C. Davies, *Human Nature in Politics* (New York:
John Wiley, 1963); and some of the early work of Harold D. Lasswell.

grounded in activity. Finally, this activity is "collective activity."[34] The intimate relationships between action, thought, and experience was implied in Mannheim's conception of social science's proper goals.

In order to work in the social sciences one must participate in the social process, but this participation in collective-unconscious striving in no wise signifies that the persons participating in it falsify the facts or see them incorrectly. Indeed, on the contrary, participation in the living context of social life is a presupposition of the understanding of the inner nature of this living context. The type of participation which the thinker enjoys determines how he shall formulate his problems.

. . . . . . . . . . . . . . . . . . .

Man attains objectivity and acquires a self with reference to his conception of his world not by giving up his will to action and holding his evaluations in abeyance but in confronting and examining himself. The criterion of such self-illumination is that not only the object but we ourselves fall squarely within our field of vision. We become visible to ourselves, not just vaguely as a knowing subject as such but in a certain role hitherto hidden from us, in a situation hitherto impenetrable to us, and with motivations of which we have not hitherto been aware. In such moments the inner connection between our role, our motivations, and our type and manner of experiencing the world suddenly dawns upon us. Hence the paradox underlying these experiences, namely the opportunity for relative emancipation from social determination, increase proportionately with insight into this determination.[35]

Dewey advised that men's values needed "concrete security" in the realm of experience (note his accent on "values" rather than on "elementary feelings," but his values are avowedly practical ones). He contended,

34. *Op. cit.*, p. 5. See Dewey, *op. cit.*, pp. 385–400, 962, 970; George Herbert Mead, *Mind, Self and Society*, edited by Charles W. Morris (Chicago: The University of Chicago Press, 1934), p. 7.
35. Mannheim, *Ideology and Utopia*, pp. 46–48. See also Theodore Abel, "The Operation Called Verstehen," in *Readings in the Philosophy of Science*, edited by Herbert Feigl and May Brodbeck (New York: Appleton-Century-Crofts, 1953), pp. 677–687.

The chief consideration in achieving concrete security of values lies in the perfection of *methods* of action. Mere activity, blind striving, gets nothing forward. Regulation of conditions upon which results depend is possible only by doing, yet only by doing which has intelligent direction, which takes cognizance of conditions, observes relations of sequence, and which plans and executes in the light of this knowledge.[36]

The Danish philosopher Søren Kierkegaard, for one, doubted that intelligence and action could be unified with objective security, at least not for living actors. And Hannah Arendt suggests a "threefold frustration" of political action.[37] Needless to say, such dissents have never found a large audience in pragmatically oriented American social science. Dewey assumed it folly to assert that thought and action were disparate. Yet his writings contain some curious ambiguities concerning this question: the unity of thought and action and their relations to experience sometimes appear as an "ought," other times as an assumption of existential modes of valuation (philosophers notwithstanding), and still other times as apparent despair over consummation of that union. Further, Dewey's philosophy holds that thought itself is experiential, paralleling here Mannheim's sociology of knowledge. And "every experience is the result of interaction between a live creature and some aspect of the world in which he lives.[38]

For Mannheim's social science, as Einstein's physics, God does not gamble, provided the scientist wholeheartedly and paradoxically emancipates himself from social determination by dedicating himself to this same determination. Accuracy and freedom derive from knowing the secrets of social relativity. And only initiates attain to such secrets divorced from all mystery. But this suggests a familiar theme in all deterministic theories, relativist as well as absolutist. Attempting to show how free are individuals bound by historical necessity, the Marxist Plekhanov claimed,

36. *Op. cit.*, p. 300 (from *The Quest for Certainty*).
37. *The Human Condition*, p. 197.
38. Dewey, *op. cit.*, pp. 966, 970 (from *Art as Experience*).

if I know in what direction social relations are changing owing to given change in the social-economic process of production, I also know in what direction social mentality is changing; consequently, I am able to influence it. Hence, in a certain sense, I *can make history*, and there is no need for me to wait while "it is being made."[39]

So dedicating himself to this paradox, the scientific observer (Marxist, Mannheimian, etc.), because he knows (and believes) passionately these paradoxical terms, frees himself from social ignorance and acts effectively ("effectively" and "efficiently" meaning here, "freely"). Since collective action ruled human existence and consequently dominated human thought grounded in that existence, the dimensions of existence and thought were supported for early social science by the dimensions of action and experience.

For political theory's interest in the action vocabulary of politics, modern social science's action-experience dimension will always be extremely important. As an action term in the political lexicon, citizenship remains problematic precisely because it prompts questions about action and existence; at once there is political activity, but also relations to wider social life and to human nature's basic questions. Observed as spatial and temporal "objects," man's activities enmesh themselves in the subjective selfhood each possesses—a possession related, in turn, to others in social and political space. But selfhood constitutes an existential, as well as psychological problem, because it refers to being, or to existence in a deeper and wider sense than the mundane experience common to all, yet it encompasses such experience.

Paul Tillich, for one, considers the self as part of being. And this self participates in the world, the self's polar counterpart. "Ontological principles have a polar structure of being, that of self and the world. The first polar elements are individualization

39. George Plekhanov, *The Role of the Individual in History* (New York: International Publishers, 1940), p. 61. For a criticism of historical and social determinism see Isaiah Berlin, *Historical Inevitability* (London: Oxford University Press, 1954), pp. 19–25; and the rejoinder by E. H. Carr, *What Is History?* (New York: Alfred A. Knopf, 1961), pp. 120–124.

and participation."[40] Existential philosophy furnishes its keenest insights into individualization, where the self deviates from common experience, yet is firmly grounded in that experience. Read, for example, Kierkegaard and Heidegger on "dread."

Social science, on the other hand, has traditionally investigated participation. It is this study's central thesis, however, that existentialism and social science, as they focus together on the interrelations between action and existence, give a remarkable composite image of human beings acting in political nature. More specifically, despite very different approaches, their united considerations on action and existence may illuminate, better than either can accomplish separately, the subject of man-the-citizen. According to both views, and the different schools within each, "to participate somehow" describes the one frightening (or exhilarating for some) requirement for every living person.

Normal people accurately assess their social environment's relevancy and cogency for themselves. This by no means implies that "normality" impels conformity; accuracy may signal an alien, antithetical, hostile environment. Several factors drive the neurotic and psychotic to misinterpret their social situations; reasons within their neuro- and psychopathological structures, or their will so to misinterpret, or prevention by social forces from coming to grips with their futures.[41] Ignorant persons are

40. *The Courage to Be* (New Haven: Yale University Press, 1952), p. 86. Merleau-Ponty (in *The Phenomenology of Perception*, p. 63) insists that phenomenology, in contrast to existentialism, stands *between* the polar tension of self and world (subjectivism and objectivism, Sartre's "for-itself" and "in-itself"), while at the same time recognizing the tension as real, in contrast to modern behavioral psychology. Merleau-Ponty's unsuccessful (in my estimation) attempt to resolve the tension warrants a separate treatment as this resolution relates to political theory. As noted earlier, the political tension point called "citizenship" provides an ideal case study for a social science of tensions, and because of their concern with "polar tension" existential philosophers seem most interesting for the study of citizenship.

41. The last point about social forces raises the possibility that the alienated person, as member of either an oppressed or oppressor group, both accurately and inaccurately perceives his social and political situation. Hence, in an essayist like James Baldwin is found an impression of

powerless, and research indicates them to be most prone to mental illness. And despite the apologists for the common man, ignorance of social things negatively correlates with formal education, at least in American society where complexity and literacy are both taken for granted; in other words, the poor possess more mental deficiencies and disorders than any other class.[42]

The polity demands its own ambiguous and perplexing participation: political action proffers "the unpredictability of its outcome, the irreversibility of the process, and the anonymity of its authors. . . ."[43] Such action occasionally demands reckonings from participants of what they have done and why. Responsibility is expected even for active obedience, not to mention those accountings exacted from leaders. No wonder citizenship remains only a part-time, frequently no-time enterprise! Great effort in the citizen role might prove unendurable.

Existential philosophy and certain areas of social theory currently inquire into action and existence. For Talcott Parsons, the common foundation of the social and personality systems (note the similarity to Tillich's "individualization" and "participa-

---

America which may or may not coincide with the white's (Baldwin says it almost never does), but is alleged to be an accurate view of America from the Negro's perspective. This may be inaccurate, however, even from the Negro point of view, since a social force, racism, intervenes in perception. But the white ruling-class view may be no more monolithic, since the same social force intervenes. Both racial groups are alienated from social reality, and this alienation (which itself may be reality) not only distorts their respective views, as a whole, but also prevents any unified group picture. Such is the essence of Marx's theory of alienation based on social class and class conflict: class conflict is a contagious disease infecting oppressors and oppressed alike with the social and personal blight of alienation. Not only are there warring classes, but class "solidarity," as in military units, is as close to unity as people can come under these circumstances, true community being impossible. This should be contrasted to Durrell's comment that community is absent where the "elementary feelings" (joy, sex, sleep) are wanting (footnote 22 above). See Paul Tillich, "Existential Philosophy," *Journal of the History of Ideas*, V (January 1944), 44–70, at 65.

42. Michael Harrington, *The Other America, Poverty in the United States* (New York: Macmillan, 1962), pp. 122–127.

43. Arendt, *op. cit.*, p. 197.

tion") is not the individual, but *action* as the basic stuff of both systems.[44] Social theory must avoid crude, old liberal dichotomies pitting individual against society. Similarly, even though Sartre's existentialism hails "l'homme singulier," he is no solitary from the underground, but a rather special kind of individual engaged in historical combat.

> This is the single [*singulier*] man in the social field [*champ*], in his class within the milieu of collective objects and of other single men, this is the alienated, reified, mystified individual, the division of labor and exploitation having made him such, but struggling against alienation by the means of improper tools and, in spite of everything, patiently winning from the field.[45]

True, other forms of existential philosophy seem less socially minded, as Sartre notes.[46] But their very concentration on the nonobjectifiable, thinking subject, outside normal social intercourse (for example, the problem of dread) makes them significant for social theorists (including political theorists), as these problems add depth and breadth to social analysis. This study will employ most branches of existential philosophy as occasions warrant.

Parsons's conception of the social and personality systems and their basic action units is not unusual in its fundamental design. Aristotle first linked action and existence (selfhood) for a classic citizenship model. Although he pointed out that the good man and the good citizen were not the same, even though the two might coincide under ideal circumstances, he adamantly argued that the adjective "good" had very definite ethical and metaphysical meanings no matter where applied. Citizenship did

44. *The Social System* (Glencoe, Ill.: The Free Press, 1951), p. 18.

45. *Question de méthode*, in *Critique de la raison dialectique* (précédé de *Question de méthode*) (Paris: Gallimard, 1960) (copyright © Editions Gallimard), p. 86.

46. For Sartre's sketchy criticism of Jaspers and Kierkegaard, see *ibid.*, pp. 21–22. Sartre warily leaves open the difficult case of Heidegger, *ibid.*, p. 21, n. 1. See also Albert Camus' criticism of "le suicide philosophique" (among others, Jaspers and Kierkegaard) in *Le mythe de Sisyphe* (Paris: Gallimard, 1942), pp. 46–72.

not sustain different standards of conduct from other stations in life, but only a particular position within virtue's total plan.[47]

Aristotle's linkage of sociopolitical action with selfhood pervades modern social thought. During the nineteenth century, Durkheim considered a "social fact" as "every way of acting, fixed or not, capable of exercising on the individual an external constraint; or, again, every way of acting which is general throughout a given society, while at the same time existing in its own right independent of its individual manifestations."[48]

Freud's psychoanalysis dealt with action problems embracing the individual's inner "struggles" and "repressions." Although Freud discovered (quite independently) repression, "the foundation-stone on which the whole structure of psychoanalysis rests,"[49] Otto Rank showed him how similar was this discovery to Schopenhauer's idea of insanity as "the struggle against acceptance of a painful part of reality."[50] Parsons has synthesized Durkheim and Freud,[51] although his first mentors in action theory did not include Freud.[52] Modern theorists of the self,

47. *Politics*, 1295a–1295b.

48. *The Rules of Sociological Method*, translated by S. A. Solovay and J. H. Mueller, edited by G. E. G. Catlin (Glencoe, Ill.: The Free Press, 1950) (copyright © 1938 by the University of Chicago), p. 13. Social facts are those in a category consisting of "ways of acting, thinking, and feeling, external to the individual, and endowed with a power of coercion, by reason of which they control him. These ways of thinking could not be confused with biological phenomena, since they consist of representations and actions; nor with psychological phenomena, which exist only in the individual consciousness and through it." (*Ibid.*, p. 3) Freud's psychology does not fit Durkheim's picture of "psychology," but Durkheim formulated his ideas in *Les règles de la méthode sociologique* (1895) before the Freudian revolution.

49. Sigmund Freud, "On the History of the Psycho-analytic Movement," (1924) in *Collected Papers*, translated by Joan Riviere, *et al.*, five volumes (London: Hogarth Press and International Psycho-Analytical Library, 1956), I, 287–359, at 297.

50. *Ibid.*

51. See "The Superego and the Theory of Social Systems," *Psychiatry*, XV (February 1952), 15–25.

52. Principally, they were Durkheim, Pareto, and Weber. Talcott Parsons, *The Structure of Social Action* (Glencoe, Ill.: The Free Press, 1949).

combining psychological and sociological evidence ("social psychologists"), frequently emphasize the action base of human existence. George Herbert Mead, a seminal thinker in social psychology and sociology, observed,

The self has a character which is different from that of the physiological organism proper. The self is something which has a development; it is not initially there, at birth, but arises in the process of social experience and activity, that is, develops in a given individual as a result of his relations to that process as a whole and to other individuals within that process.[53]

A neo-Freudian psychoanalyst, Karen Horney, pictured the human self in action terms: one's relation to oneself and to others provides the context within which the self grows.[54] Politics and government, a branch of human experience, comprised, according to Arthur F. Bentley, "first, last and always activity, action, 'something doing,' the shunting by some men of other men's conduct along changed lines, the gathering of forces to overcome resistance to such alterations. . . ."[55]

Connecting social science action theories to philosophies and social theories of existence at first seems a precarious, superficial venture. Have not sociologists outgrown metaphysics and antiquated systems of ideas? What possible connections appear between empirical theories of human experience and problems of existence and being? As a matter of fact, while social science action theory disclaims metaphysical inquiries, it reintroduces their substance, though not their form, in its investigations. When discussing membership in political society, Aristotle experienced no misgivings about drawing analogies between ethical and political matters and then binding these to metaphysical arguments concerning the mean, distributive justice, parts of the soul, and the hierarchies of Being and *telos*. Indeed, he provided

53. George Herbert Mead, *Mind, Self and Society*, edited by Charles W. Morris (Chicago: The University of Chicago Press, 1934) (copyright © 1934 by the University of Chicago), p. 135.
54. *Neurosis and Human Growth* (New York: Norton, 1950), p. 368.
55. *Op. cit.*, p. 176. The configuration of this activity is "the group struggle."

such later political theorists as Aquinas with a classic citizenship
model of action and existence fused together yet concentrating
on the isonomy of political life. He was the first to show that
citizenship's "problem" included linking a particular kind of
action, political action, to general human nature in both the
widest sense of metaphysics and in the practical field of ethics.
He was at once moralist, philosopher, political theorist, and
sociologist. By the nineteenth century, however, social theorists,
pursuing an empirical human understanding, considered Aristotle's somewhat felicitous union of action, existence, ethics, and
metaphysics gratuitous.[56]

Nevertheless, the central problem of human existence stub-
bornly endures despite our blindness: man combines within himself a magnificent technical apparatus and a highly individualized being. He is nonobjective in a prolix world of observable
objects which include himself—subjective and objective inter-
penetrate everywhere. Even the most empirical social theory, if
it deals with men as they are, must struggle with this issue, no
matter how expressed. All other pictures are inaccurate. To
meet such an imperative on a nonmetaphysical level (by referring to naturalistic experience rather than ontological existence)
and in nonethical terms (by excluding valuation from social
inquiry), nineteenth-century sociology devised new methods and
terms. While resisting metaphysical and religious solutions for
the ancient problems of man the social animal and the relation
between action and existence, at the same time undertaking (to
reverse Kierkegaard) a "nonteleological suspension of ethics"
(Kierkegaard's was a "teleological suspension of ethics"[57]),
these social scientists, particularly Durkheim, could not reject
the venerable idea that wholes differ from their parts and that
parts have organic relations to wholes. For now sociology possessed a key concept, "society," manifestly experiential and
unblemished by transcendent theologies.

56. Nineteenth-century social science was emulating the earlier rejec-
tion of Aristotelian science by the new natural science of the seventeenth
century.

57. Søren Kierkegaard, *Fear and Trembling*, translated by Robert
Payne (London: Oxford University Press, 1939), p. 69.

But was it pure nontranscendence? Not quite. Society, rather than the hierarchies of grace and legal order drafted by Aquinas, presumed all opposites and paradoxes; but now society appeared as pure immanence. So reasoned Durkheim. He rejected objections that positivistic sociology's "empirical fetishism" displayed systematic indifference to ideals and their relationship to reality. On the contrary, Durkheim argued, values are socially given products of individual reason and are thus well within sociology's embrace.[58] They originate in society and have collective origins, though they spring from individual consciousness. What society represents is synthesized individuality, "a psychic life of a new genre. . . ."[59] No wonder sociologists competently explain relationships between ideals and reality!

Durkheim considered sociology equipped, not only for measuring social problems, but also prepared for answering qualitative questions about ideals, reality, and human self. If only the entire social universe could be transferred to an empirical and scientific plane from a visionary and mystical one, then social science would deal, in its own fashion, with the timeless problems of existence, as well as with sense data. So Durkheim concluded, with what was really his premise (or at least his wishful thinking), that "society"—sociology's subject matter—presented the universal terminal point. Was not social science, therefore, equal (indeed, called) to encompass ideals within its own studies? Society,

fulfills all the necessary conditions for taking into account these opposing characteristics. It also comes from nature, while dominating it. Not only all the forces of the universe come to end in it, but,

58. "Judgments de valeur et jugements de réalité," *Revue de Métaphysique et de Morale*, XIX (1911), 437–463, at 452. The title of this review is suggestive of the connection in Durkheim's own mind between empirical sociology and questions of metaphysics and morals. The position stated by Durkheim is also Weber's (though terminology differs considerably). See Max Weber, *The Methodology of the Social Sciences*, translated and edited by E. A. Shils and H. A. Finch (Glencoe, Ill.: The Free Press, 1949), pp. 53–54.

59. Durkheim, "Jugements de valeur et jugements de réalité," *op. cit.*, 447.

even more, they are synthesized in a manner giving birth to a product which surpasses in richness, in complexity and in power of action, everything serving to form it. In a word, it is nature, but nature reaching to the highest point of its development and concentrating all its energies in going beyond itself in some manner.[60]

In this one felicitous passage, a remarkable blending of action and existence for man-in-society (there was no other "man" for Durkheim but the social creature) occur. It was not written by schoolman or existentialist, but by a founder of modern social theory, in a journal dedicated to metaphysical and moral inquiry.

No doubt Durkheim, like his mentor Auguste Comte, aimed at eradicating mystery from social studies; there had been enough pseudoscientific social magic. Now forward with real science! But Planck's dictum that a residue of mystery always remains in every science held true even for Durkheim's efforts to demystify society.[61] Sentiments born of a group possessed an "energy" impossible in any single individual.[62] But collective life was not only more "intense" than individual life, it was qualitatively different (the whole-parts situation) as well. Picturing a self undertaking collective action with its confreres, Durkheim suggested some remarkably Rousseauian, if not Aristotelian, consequences: "carried away (*entraîné*) by the collec-

60. *Ibid.*, 452–453.
61. Durkheim was not the first. Hume's social realism remains the *locus classicus* for all subsequent attempts to demystify society. Hume also illustrates the conservative potentialities of a demystification which superficially appears liberalizing.
62. Nineteenth-century social thought was fond of force analogies drawn from classical physics. These metaphors best served to emphasize the power of history and society over individuals. There was a connection made between history and force. Proudhon wrote of the "seriation" of historical stages. Comte noted the "cumulative" nature of history. And Marx spoke of "productive forces." In all cases, the individual was "pressured" by these forces. This line of reasoning was in keeping with the "social physics" of Quetelet and the "sociology" of Comte. Comte's disciple, Durkheim, asserted with reference to social compulsion and control, "pressure accepted and submitted to with good grace is still pressure." *The Rules of Sociological Method*, p. 104.

tivity, the individual disinterests himself from himself, forgets himself, gives himself entirely (*tout entier*) to the common ends."[63] Precisely during the greatest collective effervescence did individual creativity soar.[64] Hence, to see society as other than the universal vector degrades (*diminue*) it. In the social body "lives a spirit (*une âme*) which is the ensemble of collective ideals,"[65] but these ideals were not abstract ones, as metaphysicians might imagine. Empirically pure, Durkheim held that collective ideals were "natural forces," "motors." Yet on second thought, dissatisfied with the connotation of "motors," he magnified the value of the collective ideal: still an "impersonal" and "natural" force, it nevertheless was no simple "thing" (though motor connotes a thing). "It is his [the individual's] style (*façon*); it has his reality."[66]

Finally, to collective thought, representing "the impersonality of human reason," Durkheim added a certain mystique of metamorphosis, accomplishing functions hitherto performed in metaphysics and still retaining social mystery; he ordered the noumenal world into a "ground of being," but an immanent not transcendent one:

collective thought metamorphoses all that it touches. It mixes rules, confounds contraries, upsets what one would regard as the natural hierarchy of beings, levels differences, differentiates similars, in a

63. Durkheim, "Jugements de valeur et jugements de réalité," *op. cit.*, 447. See also Durkheim, *Montesquieu et Rousseau, Précurseurs de la sociologie* (Paris: Librairie Marcel Riviere, 1953).

64. "Jugements de valeur et jugements de réalité," *op. cit.*, 448. The debate between individual-over-events and events-over-individual still malingers. The battle lines are best seen by contrasting Jacob Burckhardt, *The Civilization of the Renaissance in Italy* (London: Phaidon Press, 1955), pp. 81–103, representing the first view, to E. H. Carr, *op. cit.*, Chapter 2, defending the second (though not excluding the first—he argues for interpenetration of subject and object).

65. Durkheim, "Jugements de valeur et jugements de réalité," *op. cit.*, 449.

66. *Ibid.* Contemporary role theory speaks of the individual actor's "style" in playing his social roles. See Siegfried F. Nadel's distinction between "role" and "status" in *The Theory of Social Structure* (London: Cohen and West, 1957), p. 29.

word it substitutes for a world revealed to us by sense an entirely different world which is nothing else than the shadow projected by the ideals which it constructs.[67]

Durkheim obviously equated impersonality with objectivity and science, and anthropomorphism with subjectivity and metaphysics. His equations misled him into believing that the will to think nonmetaphysically about society, particularly when expressed in demystified language, was sufficient to establish novel, nonmetaphysical propositions. But mere technical language neither erases metaphysical substance in arguments, nor uncovers anything new by so arguing. Nevertheless, Durkheim cut a pattern familiar today in social studies: a depersonalized vocabulary may be employed (usually an unconscious effort, which is all the more tragic) to disguise commonplace, yet perplexing social and political issues. Two magical effects are introduced. First, disguising creates an illusion that what is commonplace really is not and must therefore be a science. And second, now that parsimonious science has spoken, the ambiguous commonplace becomes a simplified noncontradictory datum. Without doubt, however, technical disguising of common social wisdom and pressing political urgencies does not constitute profound science, if it is science at all.

Turning to existential philosophy's interest in action and existence, there seems more concern with the subjective mystery of human activities and the responsibility of *individual* actors in these activities. Such concern is never mere mysticism, although mystical elements appear in Heidegger and Kierkegaard. Surely mysticism and mystification *per se* are rejected by Sartre, a good Marxist. But mystery involves that open choice or "abyss" beyond the present moment, toward which each individual gropes in his own fashion. Each discovers his own "givens" by acting; only this way does he know the "given" for him. Present

67. "Jugements de valeur et jugements de réalité," *op. cit.*, 451. This would place Durkheim generically in the tradition Eric Voegelin describes as gnosticism's fallacious "immanentization of the eschaton." See *The New Science of Politics* (Chicago: University of Chicago Press, 1952), Chapter 4. In this tradition, order becomes an elemental or "given" problem only, with no thought to the existential as well.

alternatives are surpassed in order to discover future possibilities in social and political action, for Sartre at least.

Because of such open choice, there is also a responsibility which has prompted one commentator to label existential philosophy "dreadful freedom."[68] Sartre's existentialism argues—and discussion of this point comes more fully later—that social researchers should ascertain the human "project" undertaken by individuals, this "project" indicating "a passage from objective to objective by interiorization (*interiorisation*) of the project as subjective surpassing of objectivity toward objectivity."[69]

Ignoring for the moment Sartre's jargon, the social scientist must undertake a very complicated kind of analysis according to this view. Sartre's gallicized Hegelianism obscures his basic dissatisfaction with abstract objectivity: social analysis must encompass both objectivity and nonobjectivity (subjectivity), if it really wants to understand the human situation adequately. Human beings engage themselves in projects "interiorizing" the objective world and projecting the resultant self back into the objective world. This engagement of "subjectivity surpassing . . . objectivity toward objectivity" continues throughout life and demands proper explanation. Only such an approach keeps action "alive" during ensuing abstractions about actors and their situations. Subject and object remain alive in constant growth and tension.

In one respect, existential philosophy and modern social theory share a common heritage: both, to some extent, reflect Marx's insistence (and others like him), that existence must be approached empirically, a posteriori. But Marx, unlike most modern social scientists, commanded a complete historical perspective from which he viewed empirical facts. Tracing his social theory to Marx and his historicism (historicism in the nonpejorative sense) to Hegel, Sartre belabors American sociology for an inadequate theoretical foundation, and a fundamentally bourgeois idealist conception of history which deals with social mechanics in the past tense, rather than with society in

68. See Marjorie Grene, *Dreadful Freedom* (Chicago: University of Chicago Press, 1948).
69. Sartre, *Question de méthode*, p. 66.

living, future perspective.[70] In other words, these Americans have lost dynamic vision, a not uncommon phenomenon elsewhere as well.[71]

The "person" encountered in existential philosophy is the immediate subject acting to find his individualized limits. Hence the future's cloudy horizons and the present's desperate, passionate striving for peculiar self-realization are emphasized. According to Kierkegaard, "thought" (speculation as contrasted to comprehension) and "being" constitute separate problems that no amount of dialectical juggling can make one.

The individual who raises the question and himself exists, keeps the two moments of thought and being apart, so that reflection presents him with two alternatives. For an objective reflection the truth must point away from the subject. For a subjective reflection the truth becomes a matter of appropriation, of inwardness, of subjectivity, and thought must probe more and more deeply into the subject and his subjectivity.[72]

Consequently, action in relationship to self-realization (whether this action refers to society, as in Marx and Sartre, to God, as in Kierkegaard, or to dread, as in Heidegger) seems "madness," when measured by speculative philosophy (objective reflection).[73] Sidney Hook's supercilious comment, that existential philosophy is foolishness about irregular verbs, proves that Kierkegaard was not paranoic.[74] For existentialism, the philosopher

70. *Ibid.*

71. See David Riesman, "Some Observations on Community Plans and Utopia," in *Selected Essays from Individualism Reconsidered* (Garden City, N.Y.: Doubleday Anchor Books, 1954), pp. 67–104.

72. Søren Kierkegaard, *Concluding Unscientific Postscript*, translated by David Swenson, completed and edited by Walter Lowrie (Princeton: Princeton University Press and the American-Scandinavian Foundation, 1941), p. 17, also p. 176.

73. *Ibid.*, pp. 173–176. Marx is included here, because in many respects he belongs to the history of existential philosophy. See Tillich, "Existential Philosophy," *loc. cit.*, where Marx is included; and Sartre, *Question de méthode*, where his own existentialism is made an "ideology" of Marxism.

74. "Dialectic in Society and History," in Feigl and Brodbeck (eds.), *op. cit.*, p. 705.

himself must become engaged as an "existing subject" to be an existential thinker. "The existing subject . . . is engaged in existing, which is indeed the case with every human being," Kierkegaard declared.[75] For him, "Socratic ignorance" signified that eternal truth is related paradoxically to the existing individual and that such an individual has no objective transcendence over his immediate situation—this includes the philosopher.[76]

Of course, subsequent developments in the history of ideas, notably contributions by Feuerbach, Marx, Nietzsche, Freud, and Husserl, have changed the face of existential thought considerably since Kierkegaard's time. Then it was only passionate revolt against Hegelianism and formal religion. Now existentialism includes anthropology, philosophy, political philosophy, psychology, and sociology, or so its various French and German proponents insist. Sartre, in fact, has enveloped the Hegelian left within his social theory, so that "history" and "reason," so essential for society but negligible in Kierkegaard's basically asocial, apolitical, religious orientation, figure prominently.[77] And behind all Sartre's writings and activities moves Marx's influence.

Existential philosophy has one unbroken, unified tradition, however, even in Sartre's deviations. The existing individual, nonobjectively and passionately striving through an indefinite, indeterminate future toward ofttimes imperceptible goals realizable only in nontranscendent action (including the groping activity of thought-as-comprehension), occupies the central focus. This opens the long, tortuous, unfinished path to authenticity. Goals achieved remain the individual's alone, and only he bears full responsibility; yet he may not desire these final results at all. Such products stamp on him a unique individuality. This by no means implies a laissez faire doctrine, since each society pro-

75. *Concluding Unscientific Postscript*, p. 176. "The philosophers have only *interpreted* the world in different ways; the point is to *change* it," wrote Marx in his famous *Theses on Feuerbach* (1845).

76. *Concluding Unscientific Postscript*, pp. 169, 176, 180.

77. See here the influential Alexandre Kojève, *Introduction à la lecture de Hegel* (Leçons sur la Phénoménologie de l'Esprit), 3rd ed. (Paris: Gallimard, 1947).

vides limits for personal expansion and these limits vary from person to person. But the *products* of social situations are individuals, and the latter are defined not simply by sociological determinants, but by how they act (or do not act) within these determinations.

Thus important Negroes in American society testify that fame and fortune, for them as Negroes, constitutes a curse as well as blessing, because they became more acutely aware of the Negro ghetto than they might otherwise. In Sartre's jargon, an "interiorization" takes place of an objectivity (race discrimination) by a subjectivity (the individual Negro). This individual interiorization, together with its style, developmental history, and transformations, provides an accurate, external social and political index. Indeed, individual interiorization forms the basic social unit. Viewed internally (from the standpoint of the actor himself), this particular image is "mine"; if such self-definition is unsuitable for me, I must change it somehow, by revolt if necessary. No existential view of man can be external only: every such philosophy demands individual action of some sort.

But action always remains ambiguous. For Kierkegaard, not even the Knight of Faith (in *Fear and Trembling*) could step outside himself long enough to take a clear, objective look at his own image and its direction. Kierkegaard criticized all attempts by speculative "modern philosophy" (Hegelianism) to purchase this privilege for man by cheap intellectual tricks.

Modern philosophy has tried anything and everything in the effort to help the individual transcend himself objectively, which is a wholly impossible feat; existence exercises its restraining influence, and if philosophers nowadays had not become mere scribblers in the service of a fantastic thinking and preoccupation, they would long ago have perceived that suicide was the only tolerable practical interpretation of its striving. But the scribbling modern philosophy holds passion in contempt; and yet passion is the culmination of existence for an existing individual—and we are all of us existing individuals.[78]

He did not argue that "truth" might not be probed objectively. Kierkegaard did question the likelihood that truth—"an objective uncertainty held fast in an appropriation-process of the

78. Kierkegaard, *Concluding Unscientific Postscript*, p. 176.

most passionate inwardness"—could be an object at all. Indeed, objective reflection and speculation seemed curiously indifferent to subjective truth (the truth of existence). "Quite rightly, since as Hamlet says, existence and nonexistence have only subjective significance." Admittedly, objectivity might secure itself from the madness haunting subjectivity. Yet does not objectivity face its own kind of madness, the absence of passionate inwardness and personal responsibility? "The objective truth as such, is by no means adequate to determine that whoever utters it is sane. . . ."[79] While not precluded, objectivity is clouded by the premonition that knowledge of man will always rest on incompleteness and mystery, because men are nonobjective: in Sartre's world, they are always "projects," restlessly moving from subjectivity to objectivity, interiorizing the latter and pushing on once more.[80]

A branch of social theory, the symbolic interactionist much influenced by George Herbert Mead, cautions today against forgetting the living actor and his subjective interpreting process in contemporary sociology's haste to objectify itself in "structure," "function," "equilibrium," "stimulus-response," and so forth. Herbert Blumer warns,

These various lines of sociological perspective and interest, which are so strongly entrenched today, leap over the acting units of society and bypass the interpretative process by which such acting units build up their actions.[81]

79. *Ibid.*, pp. 182, 173, 174. On a possible inverse relation between objectivity and sanity see also Merleau-Ponty, *The Phenomenology of Perception*, p. 23.
80. Dostoyevsky observed that man is pre-eminently a creative animal "predestined to strive consciously for an object and to engage in engineering—that is, incessantly and eternally to make new roads, *wherever they may lead. . . .* he is instinctively afraid of attaining his object and completing the edifice he is constructing." *Notes from Underground* (1864) in *Existentialism from Dostoevsky to Sartre*, edited by Walter Kaufmann (New York: Meridian Books, 1956), pp. 76, 77. To lay the blame for human engineering at the feet of modern technology, as Jacques Ellul and others have done, is to ignore Dostoyevsky's wisdom.
81. "Society as Symbolic Interaction," in *Human Behavior and Social Processes*, edited by Arnold M. Rose, Chapter 9, at pp. 188–189.

Speaking of developmental theories, Anselm Strauss, also an interactionist, declares that neither of the two prevailing schools, attainment over time (Gesell scale, for example), or variations on a basic theme (Freudianism) capture "the open-ended, tentative, exploratory, hypothetical, problematical, devious, changeable, and only partly unified character of human courses of action." He proposes instead a third model, one furnishing a series of related identity transformations during life.[82] Dedicated to empirical research and to the socially organized nature of human interaction, Blumer and Strauss nevertheless argue for action's open-endedness, a view not far removed, in spirit at least, from existential philosophy and psychiatry.[83]

Now appears the time for political theory, as Arendt insists, to face squarely the open-endedness and *responsibilities* of that action which "initiates" rather than "responds," abjuring misleading analogies to "system" and references to human "patterns" (Bentley) and human "things" (Parsons). Existential philosophy's salutary effect on all social theory would come from its emphasis on action's incompleteness and on that despair and mystery shrouding the future of each subjectively striving individual. Citizens, as they act politically, likewise implicate themselves in the existential calamities and responsibilities dictated by action.

Notice that the really salient issue is not determinacy versus indeterminacy—one in which contemporary political studies flounder and may finally succumb to stagnation. Nor does the question of individual against society have much meaning. Rather, the real issue involves the "typical" contrasted to the "atypical" (open-endedness, incompleteness, the future joined with the past through present moments). Relying either on the dead, absolutist hand of the past, or on the superficial, relativity

82. "Transformations of Identity," *ibid.*, pp. 65, 66; also Anselm Strauss, *Mirrors and Masks, The Search for Identity* (New York: The Free Press of Glencoe, Illinois, 1959), Chapter 4. See also Erik H. Erikson, "The Problem of Ego Identity," in *Identity and Anxiety, Survival of the Person in Mass Society*, edited by Maurice R. Stein, *et al.* (New York: The Free Press of Glencoe, Illinois, 1960), pp. 37–85.

83. See in this connection Rollo May, *et al.*, editors, *op. cit.*, particularly the relations between Ludwig Binswanger and Freud, pp. 4–7.

of the present, modern political theories hardly consider the problem of the future related to political action or the ambiguous present moment connected to past and future. When they do, it is most often a question of "predictability" or "depth-interviewing."

The single exception, Hannah Arendt in her important but neglected book, *The Human Condition*, and in her book of essays, *Between Past and Future*,[84] dares an unfashionable argument for political action's unpredictability. And yet political behavioralists take inordinate pride in predicting future states, believing this a "science." Their opponents argue this cannot be done for human beings and amounts to "determinism" and "historicism." Neither position—behavioralist or obstructionist—seems convincing, unless each seriously recognizes the future as a special action dimension related to past and present, and then describes this future as a particular mode in space and time.

Predictable (symmetrical, typical) and unpredictable (asymmetrical, atypical) areas permeate human life. A valuable political theory describes and explains the unpredictable, not simply as statistical asymmetry, but in all its various attributes, as found in literature, the arts, philosophy, and even the social sciences. The prediction, for example, that 51 percent of Americans will vote for candidate Smith, if confirmed by the subsequent voting event, only illustrates the technical proficiency of predictors. The really important question, however, remains, "What *if* candidate Smith wins?" Predictions on the latter point require a prescience denied human beings at present.

Nevertheless, the last point is the relevant query, and not that of which of two candidates might win an election. And these are qualitatively different problems. There is a difference, therefore, between predicting a future *event* (that is, the winning of an election) and predicting a future *state* (the course of all events subsequent to victory by one or another candidate). Some might argue that "of course" many unforeseen factors, including for-

84. *Between Past and Future, Six Exercises in Political Thought* (New York: The Viking Press, 1961).

tune itself, will enter into any future state as just adumbrated. Constructing political theory on the basis of this "of course" necessarily leads to imaginative, even intuitive, dealings with premonition as well as prediction, not simply shrewd guesses, but philosophic states of mind which will recognize the darkness which lies at every unexperienced turn in the road ahead and will furthermore incorporate this darkness into systematic inquiry.

The following study of three citizenship dimensions—public action, private symbolization, and political order—utilizes existential philosophies and social science theories, as well as certain other contemporary philosophies which could make important contributions to citizenship theory. No syntheses are attempted, except for the subject at hand. An imperfect world, made up of analysts always limited by their own subjective strivings and by what fruit these may bear and what dead branches may accumulate, has no room for designs both grand and valid. Motives, with their peculiar grammars and rhetorics (following Kenneth Burke), always intervene. Also, given the present proliferated and diversified information about man, there appears scarcely any hope (if one really desires it and I do not) that the study of mankind can ever be consolidated. But social science and existentialism interact in the sense that human behavior connects to existence, and existence means "being-in-the-world" where subject and object always meet.

For some this presents a frightening prospect; for others (including most social scientists) it seems no cause for alarm, since man without society can hardly be man at all. However, the crucial problem for an existentialist such as Sartre, if his play *No Exit* has any social significance, is a question not often asked in the social sciences; namely, the "hell" of other people. No one in Sartre's play *chooses* his particular setting, yet each interiorizes this setting, making choices about how they will confront this given situation. Hence the play fashions a gratuitous trap for each. A desperate struggle ensues, waged by human beings who seriously face the responsibilities of living together with their alienated social interactions and reinforced by both their loathing for these mandatory interactions and their disparate personal anxieties. Such an experience has traumatic effects for both players and audience, yet this kind of "experience" is not ordinarily glimpsed in systematic social science treatises. Perhaps Sartre's characters prove too cerebral: most persons seem not so afflicted by relationships as the three strangers in *No Exit*. More than likely the cerebrations of Sartre's characters are more common to ordinary life than many suppose. As the playwright Arthur Miller notes, our Anglo-Saxon prejudices make us demand a "realistic" drama of emotions without facing the equally important problems of knowing. But the latter problems persist anyway.[85]

A long line of "strangers" and "outsiders" do present themselves in modern literature, psychology, and social science. The sociologist Georg Simmel has observed that the stranger is a *social* problem. Citizenship can be a trap with no exit, a maze few people choose to enter of their own volition and one in which many may feel "trapped" and "estranged" because they cannot bring themselves to commit their conscious energies to what they perceive as a political community irrelevant to human dimensions. Still, as citizens, most have responsibilities and duties to perform which require a conscious commitment. "If at times we seemed to prefer justice to our country," Albert Camus wrote his fictitious German friend, "this is because we simply wanted to love our country in justice, as we wanted to love her in truth and in hope."[86]

Action problems concern not only manifest collective activities, such as voting, but the person developing in relation to himself as well. Hence, any action problem—even of the political variety—encompasses both self and others related to the self. Assuming here that all relations remain imperfect (in the sense of being asymmetrical), hence in disjunction as well as conjunction, and that actions within these relationships will likewise be

85. Miller is commenting on "the decidedly mixed reaction" to his play *The Crucible* when it first appeared. See *Arthur Miller's Collected Plays* (New York: The Viking Press, 1957), pp. 44–45.

86. "Letters to a German Friend" (1943–44), in Albert Camus, *Resistance, Rebellion, and Death*, translated by Justin O'Brien (New York: Modern Library, 1960), pp. 3–25, at p. 10.

"conjoined" and "disjoined," we may best describe this situation as "asymptotic" (see the last chapter below), a term expressing each private life's uniqueness when considered as total existence, and becoming manifest when the private person acts in public space—as citizen.

As an expression of human action in society, citizenship shares a problem common to all social roles, namely, the manner in which relationships between self and society encompass public actions. Since there are obvious disjunctures between individual citizens and public enterprises, it follows that the citizen shares responsibility for his community's action when he complies (even passively) with such actions because these disjunctures between private and public present an element of *choice* for citizens as they cross the bridge from personal life to public action.

The single citizen's identification with his state—symbolic, tangible, or both—expresses an act of will, a choosing of political identity, and as such, devolves responsibility upon the actor. Hence, we say that citizenship constitutes the *activity* of obedience, because it carries with it premonitions of personal responsibility. One cannot retain an identification with something and then disclaim personal responsibility for that identification. Even an unconscious identity affects the personality of the self making such an identity, particularly that political identity which involves persons in great collective efforts leading to massive virtues and crimes.

# IV Action

## The Public Realm

JOHN DEWEY's operational distinction between "public" and "private" provides, in adequate instrumental terms, a brief, convenient beginning for discussing the public realm. According to him, human acts have consequences, some "private," some "public." "The line between private and public is to be drawn on the basis of the extent and scope of the consequences of acts which are so important as to need control, whether by inhibition or by promotion."[1] Further, etymologically speaking, "private" may be juxtaposed to "official."

The public consists of all those who are affected by the indirect consequences of transactions to such an extent that it is deemed necessary to have those consequences systematically cared for.[2]

1. *The Public and Its Problems*, (Chicago: Gateway Books, 1946), p. 15.
2. *Ibid.*, pp. 15–16.

Hannah Arendt, on the other hand, approaching the problem more from an existential view (as the very title of her book, *The Human Condition*, indicates), refines still further the distinction between "private" and "public," giving it noninstrumental depth. Here, public embraces two separate but interrelated phenomena: "everything that appears in public can be seen and heard by everybody and has the widest possible publicity";[3] and "the world itself, in so far as it is common to all of us and distinguished from our privately owned place in it."[4] Accordingly, the public realm surpasses, or goes beyond, private lives and appropriates a vision not seen from any private perspective.

Whether this public be the "others" of existentialism or the "order" of idealism is not very important for present purposes (though it would be elementary for a nonidealist such as Sartre).[5] In either case, the public has wider ramifications, encompassing more "others" than do private relationships, and establishing simultaneously common or shared relationships. Riverting to considerations raised in the second chapter, the public realm provides the area of common interest or common involvement. For Arendt, the public realm sustains immortality itself by guaranteeing the survival of successive generations.[6] Differ-

3. *The Human Condition* (Garden City, N.Y.: Doubleday Anchor Books, 1959) (Originally published by the University of Chicago Press, copyright © 1958), p. 45. Chapter 2 is entitled, "The Public and Private Realm."

4. *Ibid.*, p. 45.

5. The difference amounts to one of "others" acting (and reacting too), contrasted to an "order" going beyond all existential actors and possessing an autonomy of its own. Compare Arendt, pp. 167 ff. ("the frailty of human affairs") with Bernard Bosanquet, *The Philosophical Theory of the State*, fourth edition (1923) (London: Macmillan Co., 1958), p. 119 ("order"). Durkheim definitely adopted the latter position (or perhaps "adapted" is better), even though he disclaimed any idealist philosophy. Both views express the concept of a "public realm," but the similarity ends there. "Others" and "order" have different ramifications for individual actors in the two systems. See the criticism of Durkheim by Georges Gurvitch: "La théorie de la conscience collective de Durkheim vient ici directement rejoindre la religion du 'Grand Être de l'Humanité' d'Auguste Comte et la théorie de l'Esprit absolu se realisant dans l'Esprit objectif de Hegel." *Essais de sociologie* (Paris: Librairie du Recueil Sirey, 1938), p. 165.

6. *The Human Condition*, pp. 50, 176–177.

entiating this paradoxical immortality of the mortal public realm from the fleeting chimera of private affairs constitutes a major task for political theory. Somewhat exasperated in an England beset by radical personal visions of Puritans from left and right, Hobbes declared, "This is the generation of that great LEVIA-THAN, or rather to speak more reverently, of that *mortal god*, to which we owe under the *immortal God*, our peace and defence."[7] In this public area freedom is secured through action.[8]

For Dewey, the distinction between public and private involves a different dichotomy from that between society and the individual.[9] Confusion among these two dichotomies—public and private, individual and society—may stem from confounding action and behavior, a frequent occurrence in modern social science theory (though Dewey did not mention this possibility, of course). "Action" suggests something different from "response," the latter being elementary to those stimulus-response patterns that make up "behavior."[10] Predictability is essential to these patterns. No experimental psychologist—to cite only one approach to behavior—would consider behavior innately unpredictable, the problem being not how to ascertain the predictable features of behavior, since all behavior is patterned, but how any given behavior can be predicted—a technical rather than ontological question.

Action, on the other hand, connotes initiative, and the surprises such individual initiative portends, as contrasted to response and predictability. Blending action and behavior in social

7. *Leviathan*, Part II, Chapter 17, edited by Michael Oakeshott (Oxford: Basil Blackwell, 1955), p. 112.

8. Arendt, *The Human Condition*, pp. 209–210; Bosanquet, *op. cit.*, Chapter 6; Hobbes, *Leviathan*, Part II, Chapter 21 (pp. 138–139). John Dewey's *Freedom and Culture* advances this thesis too.

9. Dewey, *The Public and Its Problems*, pp. 13–15.

10. The "neatness" of the stimulus-response pattern in political behavior theory is found in Robert Lane's "paradigm for the study of electoral behavior." Lane feeds *institutional* stimuli into the "organism" (individual) and retrieves *action* responses ("voting," "electioneering," "contracting," "reading and listening," "contributing," "discussing," "joining"). The confusion of "action" and "behavior" is manifest. See Robert E. Lane, *Political Life* (Glencoe, Ill.: The Free Press, 1959), p. 6. See Blumer's criticism of the stimulus-response approach to social life, *loc. cit.*

science occurs in the work of Talcott Parsons, where he equates the two terms: "The theory of action is a conceptual scheme for the analysis of the *behavior* of living organisms."[11] of course, contriving a problem never guarantees that problem's solution in advance. For Parsons, such behavior is "oriented to the attainment of ends in situations, by means of the normatively regulated expenditure of energy." To be called action, behavior "must be analyzed in terms of the anticipated states of affairs toward which it is directed, the situation in which it occurs, the normative regulation (e.g., the intelligence) of the behavior, and the expenditure of energy of 'motivation' involved. Behavior which is reducible to these terms, then, is action."[12]

Apart from the analytical difficulties in a theory purporting to define action, but subsuming instead only a certain kind of behavior, the Parsons formulation attempts to circumvent what Arendt calls "the threefold frustration of action," stemming from its identification with "initiative" rather than "response." According to her, action frustrates, because of "the unpredictability of its outcome, the irreversibility of the process, and the anonymity of its authors." Exasperation with action is "as old as history."[13] Parsons's accent on the predictable, reversible, and biographical makes his at least a different kind of action theory from Arendt's, concerning technical behavior involving pattern and predictability. Adding the unpredictable, the initiatory, Arendt claims action is not patterned.

In light of modern existential analysis, social science action theory inadequately depicts human action. Jean-Paul Sartre has criticized the mechanistic aspect of American status-role studies and the theories of Abram Kardiner[14] and others, because in these, cultural conduct and fundamental attitudes

11. Talcott Parsons and Edward A. Shils (eds.), *Toward a General Theory of Action* (Cambridge, Mass.: Harvard University Press, 1951), p. 53. See also Parsons, *The Structure of Social Action*, (Glencoe, Illinois: The Free Press, 1949), pp. 43–51, 732–733. My emphasis.

12. Parsons and Shils, *op. cit.*, p. 53.

13. *The Human Condition*, p. 197.

14. See Abram Kardiner, *The Individual and Society: the Psychodynamics of Primitive Social Organization* (New York: Columbia University Press, 1939).

are never understood in true, living perspective, which is temporal, but on the contrary as passive determinations which govern men in the manner that a cause governs its effects. Everything changes if one considers that society presents itself for each as one of *future perspective* and that this future penetrates to the heart of each real motivation and its conducts.[15]

For Sartre, "*Nos rôles sont toujours futurs. . . .*"[16] Heidegger concludes that the fundamental extasis of the *Dasein* is the future, "because Dasein viewed existentially is authentically *creative.*"[17] "Initiative," "future perspective," and "creative" all denote unpredictable (and perhaps nonbehavioral) action.

Each individual citizen undertakes political relations with his fellows—in their public capacities as citizens and possibly as officials—and within these various relationships, expressed in political action, obligations are universally binding, although these obligations change periodically (in the case of informal relations, they may change from minute to minute). Static relationships never finally contain what Arendt terms "the boundlessness of action."[18] Instead the power (*potentia*) resulting from acting and relating together binds political actors. Indeed, "the only indispensable material factor in the generation of power is the living together of people."[19] This "living together"

15. Sartre, *Question de méthode*, (Paris: Gallimard, 1960) (copyright © Editions Gallimard), p. 66.
16. *Ibid.*, p. 72. "Complexes, style de vie et révélation du passé-dépassant comme avenir a créer font une seule et même réalité: c'est le projet comme vie orientée, comme affirmation de l'homme par l'action et c'est en même temps cetté brume d'irrationalité non localisable, qui se reflète du futur dans nos souvenirs d'enfance et de notre enfance dans nos choix raisonnable d'hommes mûrs."
17. See Thomas Langan, *The Meaning of Heidegger* (New York: Columbia University Press, 1959), p. 42; Martin Heidegger, *Sein und Zeit*, eighth unrevised edition (Tübingen: Niemeyer Verlag, 1957), pp. 325, 337. See also Rollo May, *et al.* (eds.) *A New Dimension in Psychology and Psychiatry* (New York: Basic Books, 1958), pp. 41–65–76.
18. Arendt, *The Human Condition*, p. 170.
19. *Ibid.*, pp. 179–180.

is not primarily physical (geographic) at all, but is rather a "space" created by action and speech.[20]

In the public realm each person encounters a special "web of interrelationships"[21] constituting that public; there they act and react during their lives. This pattern of interrelationships changes constantly, and the historian *qua* philosopher (and philosopher *qua* historian), who wishes to capture once and for all this spectacle of flux, seems "destined" to fail.[22] In other words, historical, on-going public action cannot be conceptualized or systematized as a dimension, but only sketched as one. Speaking impressionistically, demarcating private and public appears a futile enterprise. Nevertheless, private and public fields of action can be distinguished, employing such criteria as Dewey's private and official, and Arendt's private and action. Where a public field or ground for action already exists, citizens do too. Using either Dewey's or Arendt's gauge, a similar picture emerges: others constituting a public are affected indirectly (that is, they are relatively anonymous for any one actor[23]) by a

20. *Ibid.*, p. 177; also Arendt on the state of Israel in *Eichmann in Jerusalem*, p. 241.

21. *The Human Condition*, p. 163.

22. The debate over philosophies of history will continue as long as men make history and then look back to behold their handiwork. The best contemporary discussion (or perhaps "argument" is better chosen) has been that between Sir Isaiah Berlin and Edward Hallett Carr in Great Britain.

23. Aristotelian *philia politikē*, a friendship without intimacy and without closeness, insures that the political community can exist despite the essentially anonymous spirit of public action. For Aristotle, fellow citizens were "political friends," if the latter expression is taken as only a crude approximation of his meaning. This love, which is really "respect" for others, corresponds to the more intimate Christian "love" and its "forgiving" nature, although the Greek motive for such love was purely human, while the Christian was grounded in the sacrifice of the Christ for the forgiveness of sins. See Arendt, *The Human Condition*, p. 218; Søren Kierkegaard, *Works of Love*, translated by Lillian M. Swenson (Princeton: Princeton University Press, 1946), especially p. 57; Paul Tillich, *Love, Power and Justice* (New York: Oxford University Press, 1954). The kinship of *anonymous* actors, especially in the politics, seems to be a specifically Western phenomenon. Without *philia politikē*, at least as a citizenship ideal, political life (and political philosophy), as known in the West, could not exist. This also suggests the possibility that political life

private person's action. Dewey also distinguishes between action in private and in public capacities,[24] a valuable division, given modern psychological inquiry and its emphasis on the self's inner relationships.[25] Arendt, on the other hand, insists that all action is public.[26]

In two crucial respects Arendt's theory of "public" and "action" needs emendation, first, by updating the area of public activity, and second, by then extending action's attributes to certain parts of private life. Though her own study relegates work and labor to the realms of "making" and "doing," rather than "acting," the facts protest against excluding work and labor arrangements from the public area on purely etymological and historical grounds.[27] As the American patent lawyer, Walton Hamilton, has observed, there exists no sharp antithesis between public and private anywhere in the American economy:

outside the West may differ significantly from the Western tradition on this point; likewise, the interrelationships between citizens in non-Western communities may have different configurations. Arendt argues this political life has disappeared in the West itself.

24. *The Public and Its Problems*, p. 15.

25. See Karen Horney, *Neurosis and Human Growth* (New York: Norton, 1950), note 39, Chapter 2.

26. *The Human Condition*, p. 160.

27. It is acknowledged here that there may be some differences between the demands of theory construction and a simple description of empirical facts. Such a view is advanced *in extremo* by Eric Voegelin in *The New Science of Politics* (1952), appearing in the work of Arendt and Heidegger as well. This attitude might be termed "suspension of the empirical." On the other hand, the moment empirical facts are interpreted by nonempirical theory constructs and by inspiration, trouble begins. Certain evidence in the experiential world is bound to balk at being squeezed into a conceptual framework which does not provide enough room in the first place. At the same time, one should bear in mind Planck's warning about physical nature: its facts are not directly knowable, and yet they exist, as a body of reality, outside physical science. Such is also the case for political studies. Regarding certain caveats of empirical theory, see Willard Van Orman Quine, "Two Dogmas of Empiricism," in his *From a Logical Point of View*, second edition, revised (New York: Harper Torchbooks, 1963), pp. 20–46; Stephen Toulmin, *Foresight and Understanding*, Chapters 5–6; Maurice Merleau-Ponty, *The Phenomenology of Perception*, translated by Colin Smith (London: Routlege & Kegan Paul, 1962), Chapters 1–4.

all industries to some degree operate as instruments of the general welfare.[28]

Whatever the semantic niceties of "public" and "private," this never absolves trade union leadership from public responsibility or business practices from attention to general welfare needs. In the modern world, even the most private problems are open to legal regulation, for instance, marriage and divorce, yet the most public problems, such as international cartel arrangements, almost entirely escape formal government controls. Indeed, such business groupings form their own governmental systems.[29] One could claim, as Hobbes did, that the Leviathan's reach potentially extends everywhere, but practically speaking, private and public realms shift according to the exigencies of these areas and their temporal settings.

Certain areas of public life are relatively well-insulated from the frustrations of political action. Max Weber saw quite early in this century that "bureaucracy" and "politics," while both public, were not both political.[30] He erred—a mistake made by many in American public administration as well—because he assumed that bureaucratic activity was "less" political (if not entirely nonpolitical) than that area generally called "politics." True, bureaucratic situations usually include less personal risk-taking (what Weber thought was politics) than do nonbureaucratic areas of government. But "political decision-making," contrasted to "personal risk-taking," prevails in bureaucracies,

28. *Op. cit.*, p. 23.

29. "In machine and machine tools, in heavy and light chemicals, in the field of metal products, in the vast area of electronics, the stream of commerce is shaped, not by the action of market forces or by mandates of the political state, but by the decrees of business executives acting in concert." *Ibid.*, p. 119.

30. Max Weber, "Politics as a Vocation," in *From Max Weber*, edited by Hans Gerth and C. Wright Mills (New York: Oxford University Press, 1946), pp. 77–128. See also Guido De Ruggiero's analysis of Weber's views on the relationships between politics and bureaucracy, in *The History of European Liberalism* (Boston: Beacon Press, 1959), pp. 272–274. Reinhard Bendix discusses this problem of "bureaucratization of political leadership" in his book, *Max Weber, an Intellectual Portrait* (Garden City, N.Y.: Doubleday, 1960), pp. 432–449.

if by "political" one means, among other things, focal tension and controlled violence (see Chapter Two).

Politics—the political field—provides a bridge between private and public, where certain societal tensions are confronted. Because confrontation does not automatically lead to solutions, or even guarantee resolution, political action hides much risk. Bureaucratic decisions may not threaten the actors making them with the same urgency that excites the quandaries of politicians, but any situation containing tension and possible violence *has risk for the community.* The crucial "political" question, therefore, in any governmental environment, has nothing to do with the personal fortunes of those making decisions. We measure politics by its relation to *communal* tensility and the impact decisions have for a *community.* Accordingly, rate-fixing by civil servants has more "political" impact than speechifying by legislators on the same subject, if the former focuses tensions and risks, while the latter does not.

Often members of a legislature, to avoid such entanglements themselves, will shift risks and tensions to bureaucratic agencies. In other words, public issues may not always represent political problems; they do so only when they confront and involve tensility. And personal destinies in politics need not be politically relevant: ultimately, politics concerns communal, not personal, risk-taking. Since citizens reside between private and public, in political nature, citizenship encompasses both public action and private attitude. Citizenship, like other political roles but even more so, symbolizes that bond or tie between public and private, in which public and private confront each other in social tensility and a third factor, the "political," enters and surpasses them both.

Operationally speaking, what have changed since the etymological founding of "public" and "political" in the Greek city are the activities and consequently the dimensions of public space. Along with others in the eighteenth and nineteenth centuries, Durkheim noted that the progressive division of labor characterizing modern society stemmed from a "progressive condensation of societies." Populations concentrated in urban centers, cities developed along today's dimensions, and modes of communication and transportation increased in number and improved performance.[31] Durkheim neglected the expanding physical exteriors of societies, accompanied by perfection of their secular symbolisms; that is, he ignored the rise of nation-states, territorially and ideologically, accompanying and interrelating with the "progressive" condensation of societies. But he did see that condensation multiplies intrasocietal relations and tensions ("social volume" and "density").[32] The division of labor in society varies in direct ratio to volume and density, and progresses in a continuous manner during the course of social development because of this greater density and volume.[33] On the foundations of diversification was raised what Durkheim termed "organic solidarity," embracing an interdependence between social actors and regulated by "restitutive sanctions" (the return of things as they were). Such sanctions encompass civil law, commercial law, procedural law, administrative and constitutional law (all contrasted to criminal law).[34]

The ancient *polis* possessed "restitutive sanctions," but such official, legal provisions never attained the formal complexity they have today (being careful, however, not to ignore elaborate *customs* of restitution in primitive societies). These types of law, first developed extensively in the Roman Empire, concern both public and private life, but always flow from public fiat. Such sanctions epitomize increased reciprocity between public and private, an interdependence accentuated by the growing diversity and expansion of social space, promoting thereby public authority's greater relevance for private life and conversely providing more personal escape from government scrutiny.

A peculiar double effect has resulted: while the territorial size of modern states far exceeds that of the ancient *polis*, the old intimacy between public and private found in the *polis* increas-

31. *The Division of Labor in Society*, translated by G. Simpson (Glencoe, Ill.: The Free Press, 1949), pp. 257–259.

32. The idea of "density" is also employed by Herman Finer, *The Theory and Practice of Modern Government*, revised edition (New York: Henry Holt, 1949), pp. 8–9.

33. *The Division of Labor in Society*, pp. 260–262.

34. *Ibid.*, p. 69.

ingly appears in modern nations; yet these same vaster physical dimensions allow citizens more anonymity than ever existed in Periclean Athens. The contemporary impact on citizenship of these two developments has been more state intrusion into private affairs, but less relevance of most governmental actions for all citizens. Hence, political space has expanded and concurrently grown denser, as more private and public institutions invade the once simpler interior of the political community.

But simultaneously, political decisions and political symbols have grown increasingly diffuse, more distant, less personally relevant. Today expanded factors must be taken into account when speaking of the "public." Terminological differences, when discussed brilliantly by analysts such as Arendt, are provocative. But etymology's purity should not blind theorists to the grossness of public problems in contemporary society, nor to the possibility that restitutive sanctions represent the community's partly unconscious attempt to compensate for its growth by retaining a certain intimacy between private and public.[35]

There persist, therefore, two orders of action, if by action is meant that activity which initiates projects and manifests itself through performances. First, political figures act in public capacities, as judges, legislators, citizens, and so on. Second, other persons perform nonpublic roles, but in situations where their private worlds face disclosure to an indirect circle of other persons. Husbands and wives altercate in relative privacy, but sometimes altercations lead to divorce proceedings involving public officials. This gives an example, incidently, where a social

35. In *The Human Condition* Arendt argues that "society" has triumphed over the older public-private distinction and has subordinated both under conformist standards of human interchangeability measured in the division of labor and mass society, and then ultimately expressed in a behavioralist vocabulary. The "emendation" made here to her views of "public" and "action" might well be seen as yet another attempt to substitute "society" and its mundane activities for common, creative political action. This is not intended. On the other hand, surely the idea of "society" involves *reciprocity* or *interaction* as well as conformity, and reciprocity is closer to the political tensions between private and public than is conformity. Durkheim's idea of "organic solidarity" is a case in point; it connotes *both* subordination of the parts to the system and a system that can only function when its parts reciprocate.

tension, confronted in political nature, is "resolved" by not solving it; divorce indicates an irreconciliable conflict.

Accordingly, there exist two levels of action—manifest and latent. Joining public and private, political action threatens the private with disclosure. Arendt herself anticipates such imminent publicity. For her, action and speech have a "revelatory quality." Through action the agent of the act runs the *risk* of disclosing himself.

Although nobody knows whom he reveals when he discloses himself in deed or words, he must be willing to risk the disclosure. . . . Because of its inherent tendency to disclose the agent together with the act, action needs for its full appearance the shining brightness we once called glory, and which is possible only in the public realm.[36]

Applying this to imminent publicity or the imminency of public action, it can be postulated that the actor, when he acts, exposes himself to others and, therefore, risks disclosure of himself. In social interactions, individuals present "fronts" in varying degrees of sincerity and cynicism.[37] Or, actors may wish to be seen by others, but may not be.[38] That not seen (or heard) is private.

36. Arendt, *The Human Condition*, p. 160.

37. That is, the "dramaturgy" of presenting the self in everyday life. See Erving Goffman, *The Presentation of Self in Everyday Life* (Edinburgh: University of Edinburgh Social Science Research Centre, 1956), pp. 10 ff.; Ralph Turner, "Role-Taking: Process versus Conformity," in Rose, *Human Behavior and Social Processes*, Chapter 2; Anselm Strauss, *Mirrors and Masks*, Chapter 3. These "fronts" represent part of what Erik H. Erikson called the "evolving configuration" of identity formation. See Erikson, "The Problem of Ego Identity," in *Identity and Anxiety*, *Survival of the Person in Mass Society*, edited by Maurice R. Stein, *et al.*, p. 49; also Anselm Strauss, *Mirrors and Masks*, *The Search for Identity* (New York: The Free Press of Glencoe, Illinois, 1959), Chapter 4.

38. History is filled with such ironies. Eduardo R. Chibás, a Cuban anti-Communist and foe of former Cuban dictator Batista, attempted to enlist public support against the corruptions of the Batista regime by committing suicide before his radio microphone in 1951. Ironically, he ran over his regularly scheduled time by two minutes and was cut off the air just before he fired the fatal shot. He did not realize this, however, so he committed suicide thinking he was still on the air. See Theodore Draper, "The Runaway Revolution," *Reporter*, XXII (May 12, 1960), 14–15.

Everyone commits legal infractions, such as running red lights, overparking, and speeding, but they are not apprehended or arrested, unless seen by public officials or involved in a traffic accident. One learns early in life that the boundary between private and public shifts continuously. Privacy may be transgressed each time one initiates a new deed that spreads to others by being seen and being significant for them. Every action means potential publicity. Adults and children alike take measures to guard against surprise exposure. Everyone remembers how a slight miscalculation or a careless moment meant detection by someone. Political nature impinges early on personal privacy, usually beginning in early childhood and continuing throughout life. A very young child already knows a rudimentary citizenship, namely, that he belongs to a particular state and that this community has special significance for him.[39]

In the wider, more deadly serious adult world, the same protean forms characterize private and public realms, and political nature has much greater urgency. Totalitarian states (and modern advertising to some extent) now practice "thought control," whereby even private attitudes, before manifesting themselves as acts and public opinions, are considered public business. Even the most private actions, as actions, may be seen by official others and have public consequences. Inaction can be a form of action.

Public disclosure opens privacy, not only to immediate family and close acquaintances, but to more anonymous public and political authorities. Citizen activities have particularly wide ramifications. The citizen performs the most general political role precisely because at least here every full member faces publicity and communal obligations. Citizenship's imperatives appear more difficult to fulfill, in certain respects, than the specifications outlining other political roles, because a citizen's directions are not clearly delineated, and a citizen's duty to commit himself publicly on political matters, not of immediate concern, is considered more-or-less equally incumbent on every-

39. This begins in the preschool years. See David Easton and Robert D. Hess, "The Child's Political World," *Midwest Journal of Political Science*, VI (August 1962), 229–246.

one in a particular community. By choice, one becomes a judge or legislator, but nearly everyone is "born" a citizen and finds expatriation difficult and inconvenient, if not dangerous. A presidential candidate may be "drafted" for his party's nomination and a citizen may be "drafted" for his country's military service, but "draft" means quite different things in the two cases. No one chooses one's parents or birthplace and yet these conditions usually determine one's citizenship.

Citizenship thus proves a continuous, lengthy rationalization for a communal relationship more than likely mandatory. Such rationalizing, as stated earlier, characterizes the activity of obedience and employs the rubrics of obligation. One is a member of the body politic in a way different from that in which one is a member of a legislature; in the first case, one is "ruled" only, at least this is basic to all citizenship; the second case offers the added inducement of being an active "ruler." True, one characteristic of democratic systems is popular control of leaders by the led.[40] In Locke's words, "The people shall judge." But even decision-making affecting the whole body politic usually requires only a limited group of individuals, no matter what the particular regime, since the majority, even where they retain periodic "controls," as in democracies, still do not have any vocational interest in continuous, official decision-making.[41] Tensions seem inevitable when the developing self encounters a given, stereotyped political status like citizenship.

The public-action dimension raises three central issues which will occupy the remainder of this chapter. First, who are those "others" for whom the citizen becomes a public person? Second, what kinds of relationships with these others may be termed public relationships? And third, what constitutes the self-reveal-

40. What Robert A. Dahl calls "polyarchy" and "polyarchal democracy." See Charles E. Lindblom and Robert A. Dahl, *Politics, Economics, and Welfare* (New York: Harper and Bros., 1953), Chapters 10–11; and Dahl, *A Preface to Democratic Theory* (Chicago: University of Chicago Press, 1956), Chapter 3.

41. Dahl, *A Preface to Democratic Theory*, pp. 124 f.; *Who Governs? Democracy and Power in an American City* (New Haven: Yale University Press, 1962), p. 138.

ing quality of publicity and the kinds of revelation possible in public action? Raising these three questions, and the subsidiary problems subsumed under them, one may at least compare *some* contributions modern social science and existentialism have made to action theory generally and the citizenship dimension of public action particularly.

Both approaches to human interaction concern themselves extensively with the complicated problems of others, relationships, revealing of self through public action, and the kinds of revelation possible when the self acts and interacts with others. The fact that existential points of view and modern social science analyses come to rather different conclusions about these topics, does not lessen either's contribution to understanding political action and the citizen's public activities. Both views (and neither is monolithic—see Chapter Three) emphasize a tension between the individual's private life and his public actions.[42] Later I shall examine this tension as a third citizenship dimension, the political order of asymptotic congruence (see Chapter Six), thus completing the public (action) and private (symbolism) dimensions.

The divergence between these two approaches to human behavior does not concern tension per se, but how, given this tension, one relates "that individual" (Kierkegaard's expression) to social structure and the demands that structure makes of both private attitude and public activity. Assuming an initial tension between man and community, social science rationalizes this relationship one way, existential social philosophy another. Early in the histories of social science and existentialism, Durkheim's socialized individual was authenticated as he "inherited" social impulse,[43] while Kierkegaard's asocial actor proved

42. Victor Willi, "Soziologie und Existentialismus," *Kyklos*, VII (1954), 125–164, at 163.

43. Durkheim, *The Elementary Forms of Religious Life*, translated by J. W. Swain (Glencoe, Ill.: The Free Press, 1954), p. 16; *The Division of Labor in Society*, pp. 15, 399, 403; *The Rules of Sociological Method*, p. 123; *Suicide*, translated by G. Simpson (Glencoe, Ill.: The Free Press, 1951), pp. 386–392; *Professional Ethics and Civic Morals*, translated by C. Brookfield (Glencoe, Ill.: The Free Press, 1958), pp. 24–25.

10

114 ACTION, SYMBOLISM, AND ORDER

his authenticity only as he "disinherited" himself.[44] Inheritance
and disinheritance (what Jaspers, with too much facility, calls
the "subject-object" dichotomy[45]) have persisted as separate,
major themes and represent a crucial substantive distinction
between modern social theory and existentialism, no matter
where these two avenues of social thought draw close together.
Using this dichotomy as a departure point, two central issues of
public action may be analyzed—"others" and "relationships."

*Others*

Acting publicly, the individual exposes himself to publicity.
What he thinks of himself in his own private imagination depends, to a greater or lesser extent, on how "others" perceive
him.[46] These others—whether they are directly or only indirectly
related to a given actor—influence that actor's self-image. The
social philosopher George Herbert Mead once stated this succinctly.

No hard-and-fast line can be drawn between our own selves and the
selves of others, since our own selves exist and enter as such into our

44. Søren Kierkegaard, *The Attack upon "Christendom,"* translated
by Walter Lowrie (Princeton: Princeton University Press, 1944).
45. Karl Jaspers, *Reason and Anti-Reason in Our Time*, translated by
S. Godman (New Haven: Yale University Press, n.d.), pp. 34–35.
46. See George Herbert Mead, *Mind, Self and Society*, edited by
Charles W. Morris (Chicago: The University of Chicago Press, 1934)
(copyright © 1934 by the University of Chicago), pp. 154–156.
Pursuing a very Rousseauian analysis of the "self," Mead stated: "The
organized community or social group which gives to the individual his
unity of self may be called 'the generalized other.' The attitude of the
generalized other is the attitude of the whole community." *Ibid.*, p. 154.
See Rousseau, *The Social Contract*, Book II, Chapter IV. It is doubtful,
however, that Rousseau ever inflated his own General Will to the propor-
tions of Mead's generalized other. It may be true, as Bosanquet observed,
that Rousseau implied such a transcendent will in Chapter One through
Three of Book Two, and Chapter One, Book Four of the *Social Contract*.
Yet perhaps it was Bosanquet's own Idealism, inspired by Hegel, which
led him to find such a super community in Rousseau (see *Philosophical
Theory of the State*, pp. 99–115). Mead was influenced by Royce's
Idealism—see *Mind, Self and Society*, C. W. Morris introduction, p. xiii.

experience only in so far as the selves of others exist and enter as such into our experience also.[47]

The "real self," using Karen Horney's expression (though not her meaning[48]), is the "social self," including the public or official self inhabiting political nature. Charles H. Cooley, an early sociologist, clearly pictured this phenomenon.

In a very large and interesting class of cases the social reference takes the form of a somewhat definite imagination of how one's self—that is any idea he appropriates—appears in a particular mind, and the kind of self-feeling one has is determined by the attitude toward this attributed to that other mind. A social self of this sort might be called the reflected or looking-glass self:
> Each to each a looking-glass
> Reflects the other that doth pass.

As we see our face, figure, and dress in the glass, and are interested in them because they are ours, and pleased or otherwise with them according as they do or do not answer to what we should like them to be; so in imagination we perceive in another's mind some thought of our appearance, manners, aims, deeds, character, friends, and so on, and are variously affected by it.[49]

Durkheim rejected any "break in continuity between the individual and society" (as he alleged took place in Hobbes and Rousseau).[50] He concluded that constraint typified all social life, but this "fact" is,

due simply to the fact that the individual finds himself in the presence of a force which is superior to him and before which he bows; but this force is an entirely natural one. . . . By making man

47. *Ibid.*, p. 164.

48. Her conception of the "real self" is more Nietzschean or Kierkegaardian than the social science idea of the real self. Horney defines the real self as "that central inner force, common to all human beings and yet unique in each, which is the deep source of growth." See her *Neurosis and Human Growth*, p. 17.

49. *Human Nature and the Social Order*, in *The Two Major Works of Charles H. Cooley* (Glencoe, Illinois: The Free Press, 1956) (copyright © 1922 by Charles Scribner's Sons), p. 183.

50. *The Rules of Sociological Method*, translated by S. A. Solovay and J. H. Mueller, edited by G. E. G. Catlin (Glencoe, Ill.: The Free Press, 1950) (copyright © 1938 by the University of Chicago), pp. 121 f.

understand by how much the social being is richer, more complex, and more permanent than the individual being, reflection can only reveal to him the intelligible reasons for the subordination demand of him and for the sentiments of attachment and respect which habit has fixed in his heart.[51]

And Talcott Parsons, a contemporary interpreter of Durkheim, completes the picture of the social self interacting with others and publicizing itself thereby.

It follows from the derivation of normative orientation and the role of values in action as stated above, that all values involve what may be called a social reference. In so far as they are cultural rather than purely personal they are in fact shared. Even if idiosyncratic to the individual they are still by virtue of the circumstances of their genesis, defined in relation to a shared cultural tradition; these idiosyncrasies consist in specifiable departures from the shared tradition and are defined in this way.[52]

Such pictures of individual self related to others around it, shared by most social science theorists, follow the premise that human nature is social. Mead held that even man's biological functions were socially conditioned.[53] Robert E. Park, in an observation noted earlier, stated that "man is not born human."[54] The philosopher William E. Hocking discussed the same theme of *social* human nature.

51. *Ibid.*, p. 123.
52. *Social System*, (Glencoe, Ill.: The Free Press, 1950) (copyright © 1951 by Talcott Parsons), p. 12. The conservative implications of this seem obvious, once one moves from the analytical to the empirical level (the distinction is not always clear in Parsons's theory, though the theory is commonly thought to be analytical). See Michael Oakeshott, *Political Education* (Cambridge: Cambridge University Press, 1951), *passim*.
53. *Mind, Self and Society*, p. 133.
54. In Robert E. Park and Ernest W. Burgess, *Introduction to the Science of Sociology* (Chicago: University of Chicago Press, 1924), p. 79. See also Durkheim: "indeed, man is man only because he lives in society. Take away from man all that has a social origin and nothing is left but an animal on par with other animals." *Professional Ethics and Civic Morals*, p. 60. Even in society, man may be "on par" with other animals, at least from the standpoint of one ethologist (who seems to be contradicting the social science tradition and has taken up opposition to modern behavioral psychology), Konrad Lorenz, in his *On Aggression*, translated by Marjorie Kerr Wilson (New York: Harcourt, Brace & World, 1966).

Human beings as we find them are artificial products. . . . Nature has made us: social action and our own effort must continually remake us. Any attempt to reject art for "nature" can only result in an artificial naturalness which is far less genuine and less pleasing than the natural work of art. As to structure, human nature is undoubtedly the most plastic part of the living world, the most adaptable, the most educable. Of all animals, it is man in whom heredity counts for least, and conscious building forces for most. . . . His major instincts and passions first appear on the scene, not as controlling forces, but as elements of *play*, in a prolonged life of play.[55]

Nature creates each man, but "human nature," really "second nature," grows out of societal activity, including political action, a product of interacting with others and becoming subject to social morality. Such subjection fixes the price every society exacts. According to Fichte, man assumes a second nature when conventional morality (*Sitte, Sittlichkeit*) rules him (man actually has no choice).[56] Mead noted, "the social process, through the communication which it makes possible among the individuals implicated in it, is responsible for the appearance of a whole set of new objects in nature, which exists in relation to it. . . ."[57] L. B. Winston, a psychologist, drew contrasts between the "natural person" and the "social and conventional self," in an article entitled, "Myself and I."[58] Albert Keller described the "inheritance of acquired nature."[59]

A particular view of the social self and human nature appears widely shared by early and contemporary psychologists and social scientists. The individual actor not only welcomes publicity and societal scrutiny but would possess no self-identity (authenticity) were it not for social interaction.[60] In this respect,

55. *Human Nature and Its Remaking*, new and revised edition (New Haven: Yale University Press, 1923), pp. 7, 14.
56. Fichte, as quoted by Viscount Haldane in Park and Burgess, *op. cit.*, pp. 106–107. See also Ferdinand Tönnies, *Die Sitte* (Rütten und Loening, 1909), pp. 7–14, who was indebted to Hegel.
57. *Mind, Self and Society*, p. 79.
58. *American Journal of Psychology*, XIX (1908), 562–563; and in Park and Burgess, *op. cit.*, pp. 120–122.
59. *Societal Evolution* (New York: Macmillan Co., 1915), pp. 212–215.
60. Mead, *Mind, Self and Society*, Part III, "The Self."

Parsons has gone so far as to fashion a theory of ego in which Freud, ostensibly skeptical about conventional morality and social repression, becomes Durkheim's ally. Parsons avers that Freud's superego concept provides the "bridge" between the theory of personality (Parsons's) and the social system (Parsons's).[61] Hence, while Parsons carefully differentiates "personality" from "social" system,[62] he nevertheless declares,

Neither what the human object *is*, in the most significant respects, nor what it *means* emotionally, can be understood as given independently of the nature of the interactive process itself and the significance of moral norms themselves vary largely relates to this fact.[63]

Through behavior in society and its public environs, the "individual man," in Robert Park's words, "is the bearer of a double inheritance. As a member of a race he transmits by interbreeding a biological inheritance. As a member of society or a social group, on the other hand, he transmits by communication a social inheritance."[64] Modern social science accentuates the "second nature" each individual inherits when born into interactive situations. Durkheim's last book, *Les formes élémentaires de la vie religieuse*, written in 1912, discoursed extensively on each person's "two beings," the one an "individual being," organic and limited, the other a "social being which represents the highest reality in the intellectual and moral order than we can know by observation—I mean society. . . . In so far as he belongs to society, the individual transcends himself,

61. "The superego provides exactly such a bridge because it is not explicable on any other basis than that of acquisition from other human beings, and through the process of social interaction." "The Superego and the Theory of Social Systems," *Psychiatry*, XV (February 1952), 15–25, at 23.
62. *Social System*, pp. 17–18.
63. "The Superego and the Theory of Social Systems," *op. cit.*, 18.
64. "Education and Its Relation to the Conflict and Fusion of Cultures," *Publications of the American Sociological Society*, XIII (1918), 58–63. Note the importance of communications. Would a communications breakdown (e.g., the rise of warring ideologies) herald disintegration of the social group? See Norbert Wiener, *Cybernetics* (Cambridge: The Massachusetts Institute of Technology Press, 1948), Chapter 8.

both when he thinks and when he acts."[65] Further, this social
world provides comfortable surroundings.

there is not, so to speak, a moment in our lives when some current of
energy does not come to us from without. The man who has done his
duty finds, in the manifestations of every sort expressing the sympa-
thy, esteem or affection which his fellows have for him, a feeling of
comfort, of which he does not ordinarily take account, but which
sustains him, none the less. The sentiments which society has for
him raise the sentiments which he has for himself.[66]

In social science terms, self-authenticity requires that the
individual conform to his "two beings," biological and social.
As noted previously, Mead even went so far as to make the
biologic social. This authenticity might avoid ethical problems
per se, though the existential point of view does not.[67] In social
studies, simple exigencies of "health" require that one man
interact fruitfully with others. Cooley—and it could have been
any one of many sociologists from Comte to Parsons and Merton—stated the health problem as follows,

if one sees a man whose attitude toward others is always assertive,
never receptive, he may be confident that man will never go far,
because he will never learn much. In character, as in every phase of
life, health requires a just union of stability with plasticity.[68]

To be authentic or healthful, the individual self must recognize
that it is creature of a social environment, for better or worse.[69]
If the environment does not promote individual betterment, then
change it.[70]

Obversely, social disorganization can encourage mental disor-

65. *The Elementary Forms of Religious Life*, translated by J. W.
Swain (Glencoe, Ill.: The Free Press, 1954) (copyright © 1915 by
Macmillan), pp. 16–17.
66. *Ibid.*, p. 211.
67. See Marjorie Grene, "Authenticity: An Existential Virtue," *Ethics*, LXII (July 1952), 266–274.
68. *Op. cit.*, p. 207.
69. Durkheim, *Suicide*, pp. 373–374.
70. *Ibid.;* Durkheim, *Professional Ethics and Civic Morals*, Chapter
3, 9; Cooley, *op. cit.*, pp. 256–260.

ganization and even suicide.[71] Just who decides when the environment needs changing and what changes it should undergo no one clearly states. But sociology's founding fathers were neither so coldly "objective," nor so remiss. The world of "others," after all, forms a system observable in its entirety by those with the proper instruments (concepts). In treating society's ills this group has no compulsion to share the patient's plight, any more than a physician must contract his client's disease.[72] For such sociological luminaries as Comte, Marx, Durkheim, and Mannheim, future social practitioners would quite naturally adopt their particular remedies for the socially ill. Hence, various "schools" prevail in the social sciences. Durkheim would have his sociologists act as "counselors" (*conseilleurs*) and "educators" in ways very reminiscent of Comte's "savants."[73] And Mannheim bid his new elite reconstruct and regroup a European society maimed during the holocaust of World War II.[74]

All these arguments have one common ground: man has two natures, one biological, the other social, and the social constitutes his truly "human nature." Chronologically speaking, the latter comes "second," but in every other way it ranks first. This argument has a very conservative tone. Edmund Burke argued a

71. See Robert E. Park, *Social Disorganization*. Durkheim, *Suicide*, *passim;* Everett V. Stonequist, *The Marginal Man, a Study in Personality and Culture Conflict* (New York: Charles Scribner's Sons, 1917), p. 202.

72. Durkheim, *The Rules of Sociological Method*, p. 49. On the "objectivity" of their own forms of the new social science, see also (in chronological order), Auguste Comte, *System of Positive Polity*, four volumes, translated by J. H. Bridges *et al.* (London: Longmans, Green, 1875–1877) IV, 544; and John Stuart Mill's criticism of Comte, *Autobiography* (London: Oxford University Press, 1924), pp. 179–180; Karl Marx/Friedrich Engels, *Historische-kritische Gesamtausgabe. Werke, Schriften, Briefe* (Frankfurt a.M. 1927—Moscow, 1935), VI, 525, and discussed in Hans Barth, *Wahrheit und Ideologie* (Zurich: Manesse Verlag, 1945), pp. 112–113; Max Weber, *The Methodology of the Social Sciences*, pp. 1–112; Mannheim, *Ideology and Utopia*, pp. 161, 162.

73. See Durkheim's very interesting "L'élite intellectuelle et la démocratie," *Revue Bleue*, 5th series, I (June 4, 1904), 705–706.

74. *Man and Society in an Age of Reconstruction* (London: K. Paul, Trench, Trubner, 1944) *passim*.

similar thesis, vis-à-vis politics, in his *Reflections on the Revolution in France* (1790), as he enlisted support from the ancients to buttress his case against the myriad a priori social doctrines spawned during the French Revolution.

The legislators who framed the ancient republics knew that their business was too arduous to be accomplished with no better apparatus than the metaphysics of an undergraduate, and the mathematics and arithmetic of an exciseman.[75]

These ancient legislators "had to do with men, and they were obliged to study human nature."[76] For Burke, men became human only when nurtured by civil society; therefore the study of human nature and the study of citizenship were one in the same. Obviously, being a citizen came after being born (the chicken after the egg), so that citizenship (or "human nature" for Burke) represented a second nature distinguishing men from the "homogeneous mass" of mere biological entities.[77] Burke saw in citizenship what later social scientists saw in society, a human life fulfilled through structured differences,

according to their birth, their education, their professions, the periods of their lives, their relations in towns or in the country, their several ways of acquiring and of fixing property, and according to the quality of the property itself, all which rendered them as it were so many different species of animals.[78]

Social and political life, with special orders and privileges, provide man's richest inheritance. Because this second nature is true human nature, no man could be happy and healthy, that is, genuinely human, unless he adjusted to his own crenelated, gradated community. No wonder the rebel seems "sick," "psychopathic," "abnormal," "anomic," "alienated," "marginal"!

A different, less comfortable world of "others" exists in exis-

75. *Reflections on the Revolution in France* (Chicago: Gateway Editions, 1955), p. 260. See also, Michael Oakeshott, *Political Education*.
76. *Ibid.*
77. *Ibid.*, p. 262.
78. *Ibid.*, p. 261.

tentialism's universe. Has not Sartre written, with dramatic overstatement, that "Hell is other people"? There are different schools of thought within this philosophic approach, rather roughly divided into German and French, nineteenth and twentieth centuries. But a common bond ties together at least the main representatives of existential philosophy, namely the German philosophers in the tradition from Schelling to Heidegger and Tillich: existence must be approached empirically, that is, a posteriori. Here there is no quarrel with social science theory. The difference between them centers mainly on what constitutes existence. According to existential philosophy, one "encounters" the person immediately through his actions and utterances; one confronts initially the immediate personal experience of the existing experiencer who must always be, first and foremost, the observer himself as subject.[79]

But this immediate experience has ethical meaning as well as ontological significance because subject and object cannot be separated. Not the thinking subject (Descartes) alone, but the existing subject (Heidegger) appears ethically and ontologically central. The categories—subject and object, ethics and ontology—become inseparable. In other words, as Tillich observes, this philosophy accentuates the *sum* in *cogito ergo sum;* not on "I think" but on "I am." Existential thinkers possess interest or passion, risking objective uncertainty when they give precedence to "being" or "existence" rather than "thinking."[80] Yet objective uncertainty may be the path to truth.

*An objective uncertainty held fast in an appropriation-process of the most passionate inwardness is the truth,* the highest truth attainable for an *existing individual. . . .* The truth is precisely the venture

79. See Paul Tillich, "Existential Philosophy," *Journal of the History of Ideas,* V (January 1944), 44–70, at 51–52. This is one of the best expositions in English of existential philosophy. Tillich is careful to note that "existential" philosophy is a specifically German creation, but its import is a more general philosophical one. Again, note the importance and influence of Husserl's *Lebenswelt* approach to everyday life here. Merleau-Ponty's contributions, drawn from the same existential background, are important too.

80. *Ibid.,* 52.

which chooses an objective uncertainty with the passion of the infinite.[81]

For Kierkegaard and Nietzsche, social structure and authentic behavior within its confines have distinctly secondary, repressive roles. Instead, the striving individual occupies the central position. Although some might question the sanity of Nietzsche's proposals (are there no limits? did he not go insane?), the way he conceived the truly authentic person nevertheless poses a dramatic alternative to self-authenticity as described by modern social science. As Tillich explains, Nietzsche's "will to power" signified neither power nor will. Rather,

It designates the self-affirmation of life as life, including self-preservation and growth. Therefore the will does not strive for something it does not have, for some object outside itself, but wills itself in the double sense of preserving and transcending itself. This is its power, and also its power over itself. Will to power is the self-affirmation of the will as ultimate reality.[82]

Striving, restlessness, anxiety, impatience with "the public" ("others") and its imperative demands, that is, contempt for any social ethic and life based on what "others" think, constitute central tenets of every existential philosophy. At the same time, however, such impatience with others does not necessarily conflict with civic responsibilities but rather reinforces the individual's personal responsibility in civic situations, not allowing him to escape from personal freedom (whatever its necessary and concrete limits) into the comforts and irresponsibilities of domination. Kierkegaard admired the "Knight of Faith" who resigned every social approbation and yet gained the whole finite world "by virtue of the absurd." "Whoever can do this is great,

81. Kierkegaard, *Concluding Unscientific Postscript*, p. 182. Tillich notes how Kierkegaard, in the *Postscript*, connected Socrates and Christian faith analogically, thus demonstrating the possibility of an existential philosophy, as well as a faith. Tillich, *loc. cit.*, 54.
82. Tillich, *The Courage to Be* (New Haven: Yale University Press, 1952), pp. 26–27.

and he alone is great."[83] In contrast, Kierkegaard's estimate of "others" and that "public" he equated with the amorphous mass,[84] was denigrating.

As far back as I can remember I was in agreement with myself about one thing, that for me there was no comfort or help to be looked for in others. Sated with the many other things bestowed upon me, filled as a man with longing after death, as a spirit desirous of the longest possible life, my thought was, as the expression of a melancholy love for men, to be helpful to them, to find comfort for them, above all clearness of thinking, and that especially about Christianity. The thought goes very far back in my recollection that in every generation there are two or three who are sacrificed for the others and are led by frightful sufferings to discover what redounds to the good of others. So it was that in my melancholy I understood myself as singled out for such a fate.[85]

Nietzsche made a distinction between the "obedient" and the "submissive" self. Wishing to escape the pain of hurting and being hurt, the latter bows to those "blood suckers" who manipulate social controls. But the obedient self commands itself and "risketh itself thereby." Obedience is to self, submissiveness to the collectivized others.[86] And Arendt deplores the illusory escape from action with unpredictable consequences for the individual actor into rule with abdication of personal responsibility.[87]

As far as public action and citizenship are concerned, existentialism reverses everything. "What kind of community can sus-

83. *Fear and Trembling*, translated by Robert Payne (London: Oxford University Press, 1939), p. 69.

84. *The Present Age*, translated by Alexander Dru and Walter Lowrie (London: Oxford University Press, 1939), *passim*.

85. *The Point of View, etc.*, translated by Walter Lowrie (London: Oxford University Press, 1939), p. 79; also Kierkegaard, *The Attack upon "Christendom,"* section entitled "The Christianity of the Spiritual Man/The Christianity of Men."

86. *Thus Spake Zarathustra*, Part II, Chapter 34; Tillich, *The Courage to Be*, p. 29.

87. *The Human Condition*, pp. 197 f. While by no means supporting Nietzsche's position, Arendt will not condone Eichmann's bureaucratic excuses either.

tain the imperative demands of individual authenticity?" replaces "What imperative demands does the community place on the individual?" "Authenticity" becomes the crux of the matter. How can commonweal exist among such peculiar heroic figures as Knights of Faith (Kierkegaard), Zarathustras (Nietzsche), Roquetins (Sartre), and Mersaults (Camus), without bridling, or at least cheapening (existential heroes can be popularized too), their heroism? Basically, the community must fit actors who act for action's sake, because every existential philosophy agrees that *to act is to be free*, including here thought permeated by concern for action.

Arendt's *The Human Condition* remains the most noteworthy attempt to do just this. She insists that the Greek polis, which once provided a common and special public space promoting initiatory action, encouraged human freedom (but not an impossible human sovereignty). Action and speech in that space revealed uniqueness.[88] Action inherently discloses or reveals the agent of the act and, therefore, needs publicity in order to perform this specific function so it will not disappear into museum-like works of art. For good reason "history" usually means political history—an effort to record great deeds not great works.

Because of its inherent tendency to disclose the agent together with the act, action needs for its full appearance the shining brightness we once called glory, and which is possible only in the public realm.[89]

Public action functions to increase personal glory, with political nature providing the widest forum for such self-glorification. "This revelatory quality of speech and action comes to the fore where people are *with* others and neither for nor against them—that is, in sheer human togetherness."[90]

Arendt prizes the greatness of individual personality and what insures such greatness when she writes of public action. Indeed, without political life, nothing would remain but "mo-

88. *Ibid.*, p. 156.
89. *Ibid.*, p. 160.
90. *Ibid.*

tives and aims" which, like psychological qualities, are always
"typical," never "unique." Arendt's social community *must* be
pre-Platonic Athens, not only for etymological reasons (there
the words "political," "citizen," and "public" were first given
significance), but because, in Jacob Burckhardt's words,

we see here more clearly than anywhere else the interaction between
the individual and the community. Since a strong local prejudice
arose that men must be able to do anything in Athens, and that there
the best society and the greatest, or indeed the only stimulus was to
be found, the city actually produced a disproportionate number of
remarkable men and permitted them to rise. Athens always sought
her highest in individuals. Men's supreme ambition was to distinguish themselves there, and the struggle for that goal was terrible.[91]

"Athens always sought her highest in individuals." From Arendt's point of view, Athens (and Burckhardt would have added
Renaissance Florence since his was a nonpolitical approach)
provided the proper setting for great individual actors.

Unlike human behavior—which the Greeks, like all civilized people,
judged according to "moral standards," taking into account motives
and intentions on the one hand and aims and consequences on the
other—action can be judged only by the criterion of greatness
because it is in its nature to break through the commonly accepted
and reach into the extraordinary, where whatever is true in common
and everyday life no longer applies because everything that exists is
unique and *sui generis.* Thucydides, or Pericles, knew full well that
he had broken with normal standards for everyday behavior when he
found the glory of Athens in having left behind "everywhere everlasting remembrance (*mnemeia aidia*) of their good and their evil
deeds." The act of politics teaches men how to bring forth what is
great and radiant—*ta megala kai lampra*, in the words of Democritus, as long as the *polis* is there to inspire men to dare the extraordinary, all things are safe; if it perishes, everything is lost. Motives
and aims, no matter how pure or how grandiose, are never unique;
like psychological qualities, they are typical, characteristic of different types of persons. Greatness therefore, or the specific meaning

91. *Force and Freedom*, edited by J. H. Nichols (New York: Meridian
Books, 1955), p. 194.

of each deed, can lie only in the performance itself and neither in its motivation nor its achievement.[92]

Political action initiates deeds, promotes greatness, encourages the extraordinary, all nonbehavioral phenomena. Indeterminacy and peril haunt the political. Political actors must therefore pay the price for this indeterminacy as they face consequences and responsibilities for their actions. And so must their communities; for example, war's attractiveness is invariably sullied by defeat's specter. Freedom does not, therefore, mean sovereignty: instead, it connotes dangerous choices by no means guaranteeing success.[93] The ideal community for existential social thought must be either Athens, where great leaders were ostracized because they were " 'guilty' of consequences they never intended or even foresaw,"[94] or "La République du Silence" during the French Resistance movement, where enormous, identical responsibilities confronted every actor (*une démocratie véritable*) and a community developed solely on the basis of these mutual responsibilities.[95]

Further, Sartre's "Republic of Silence" possessed no great leaders and no authoritative sanctions against its members; it sustained a more radical ethic, "se choisissant lui-même dans sa liberté, il choisissait la liberté de tous."[96] No ordinary political society, not even Athens, ever depended solely on such "moral virtue" for its cohesion (though some of Miss Mair's examples from primitive East Africa approximate the French Resistance community). And even for the Republic of Silence the hated German supplied a crucial, albeit negative, unity symbol. Yet does not such individual responsibility, or "mutualism" (Prou-

92. *The Human Condition*, pp. 184–185.
93. *Ibid.*, pp. 209–211.
94. *Ibid.*, p. 209.
95. Jean-Paul Sartre, "La République du Silence," *Les Lettres Français* (Paris-Resistance) (September 9, 1944) p. 1. See Arendt's comments on René Char's sadness at France's liberation from the Nazi Germans. "If I survive, I know that I shall have to break with the aroma of these essential years, silently reject (not repress) my treasure." Quoted in *On Revolution*, p. 284.
96. "La République du Silence," *loc. cit.*

dhon), actually form the basis for every society with common interests and public business? Or at least this communal, moral force of mutual sharing complements authoritative social and political institutions. Commonalty's jurisdiction expands and contracts according to time and place, but it must always be present, for a sufficient number of people in every society, or social breakdown seems ineluctable. As Marx observed, even the *unique* individual is a *social* animal.[97]

## Relationships

Human relationships, including those between citizens in political nature, may be classified as three types,[98] each characterized by the priority of either socialized or unique forces at their base. The first relationship is functional. It operates to insure that social and political systems operate normally. Without this relation, patterned regularly and more-or-less predictably, no foundation for social action and social order could exist. This variety may also be called "interest."[99] The relationship of purpose provides the second type. While a good deal of interconnection persists between function and purpose, the latter is more strictly conscious, intentional, principled, and may or may not express

97. From "Economic and Philosophical Manuscripts" (1844) in *Karl Marx, Selected Writings in Sociology and Social Philosophy*, edited by T. B. Bottomore and Maxmilien Rubel (London: Watts and Co., 1956), p. 77. Again, it might be argued that Marx's view represents a victory of "society" over politics and individual uniqueness. But one can also argue that Marx's idea of society gave a richness to individuality and politics denied both conceptions by liberal thought.

98. The basic categories of function, purpose and vocation are found in Dorothy Emmet, *Function, Purpose and Powers* (London: Macmillan, 1958), a very good book to be discussed at length later in this chapter. But the applications of these categories to citizen relationships and the interpretation of these categories for citizenship are mine.

99. For example, while the American philosopher, Ralph Barton Perry, phrases his theory of "interest" in the purposive framework of "expectation," he clearly distinguishes between the often over ambitious intellect and a truly interested act where there is correspondence between expectation and governing propensity. *General Theory of Value* (New York: Longmans, Green, 1926), p. 183.

the interests of the parties involved. Also, certain purposes may prove "dysfunctional."[100] The third relationship is creative or vocational. Here predictability no longer appears a factor. The actor (typically an individual, in the political field) acts because he must; a creative, vital force impels him toward a future where ambiguous consequences await. This type relates to the other two, but surpasses both social utility and conscious purpose.

These three relationships are more completely discussed during the remainder of this chapter. But first a caution. Certain key figures in the history of ideas appear as illustrations in what follows, none of them belonging exclusively under one or another heading. As a case in point, Arthur F. Bentley's followers may cavil when they find him in a "functional" rather than "purposive" position. Leaving aside their liberal desire to be identified with purpose rather than with function (function *sounds* faintly conservative), there is probably some just complaint. Bentley's "interest group," "process" approach surely appears very purposive. After all, interest has long association with purposive activity, particularly under the guidance of liberal theorists wedded to the concept. On the other hand, about the meanings of interest and purpose relative to society few studies have been initiated. As I hope to demonstrate, Bentley's conception of interest, at least as developed in *The Process of Government* (1908) (which remains his most influential political work), presumes interest the subconscious spring for all political activity and not merely an expression for conscious striving after limited political goals. In short, for my purposes, Bentley's group theory leads to functional conclusions. The same considerations apply to other theorists used in this discussion.

*Functional Relationships.* The individual political actor does not simply relate to an amorphous mass of "others." Relationships order themselves in definite systems or structures, readily identified and studied. Within these systems and sub-systems,

100. "Dysfunctions" are "those observed consequences which lessen the adaptation or adjustment of the system." Robert K. Merton, *Social Theory and Social Structure*, revised and enlarged edition (Glencoe, Illinois: The Free Press, 1957), p. 51.

groups and individuals perform functions produced by the inter-relationships between men and the group structures to which they belong (or in which they "participate"). Any ordinary political phenomena—courts, legislatures and political parties—comprehend people acting and interacting in ordered patterns. Hence, functionalism provides a *lingua franca* for modern social science, particularly sociology. Functionalist and/or interactionist theories are too legion to canvass here.[101] For present purposes, Arthur F. Bentley, an early architect of group theory in political studies, will do. Because his theory concerns politics, rather than other functional social systems, he typifies contemporary political science's view of relationships, structure, and function.

Reacting against the "barren formalism" endemic to political science in his day, Bentley strove to induce a "glow of humanity," instead of "an injection of metaphysics," into political understanding.[102] Success crowned his attempts. The "raw material of government" comprised,

First, last, and always activity, action, "something doing," the shunting by some men of other men's conduct along changed lines, the gathering of forces to overcome resistance to such alterations, or the dispersal of one grouping. . . . etc.

101. I recognize marked differences between those social theorists who emphasize function, those who stress structure, those who postulate a combination of the two, and those who concentrate on interaction in a more social-psychological vein. *All* these theories share, however, a common emphasis on the relationships of individuals in certain recognizable patterns (by whatever names these patterns are called), which, in turn, form social entities capable of being abstracted and analyzed. Does any sociologist, for instance, deny that individuals form the basis of group life? Hardly. But the general assumption, following Durkheim (and perhaps Rousseau), is that the group constitutes a different order of life and investigation than the individuals who comprise that group. In other words, the individuals do not provide sociological units of analysis; the group and its role-players do. Another generally accepted tenet, however, is that anthropology, psychology and sociology dovetail to some extent (depending on which social scientist is doing the dovetailing).

102. *The Process of Government*, (1908), edited by Peter H Odegaard (Cambridge, Mass.: The Belknap Press of Harvard University, 1967), p. 162.

This incomplete quotation illustrates Bentley's hypersensitivity to political action. Individuals always act, they can do nothing else. Indeed, human beings reveal themselves only as they relate to and participate in such activity. Ideas and feelings orient individuals in this social activity but do not determine action. Quite the contrary. "There is no idea which is not a reflection of social activity. There is no feeling which the individual can fix upon except in a social form." With his customary flourish, Bentley wrote that the joint activities of men, including governmental activities, "are the cloth, so to speak, *out of which men in individual patterns are cut.*" Again, we refer to Park's dictum, "Man is not born human." From the whole cloth, group action, individual "patterns" are cut.

As noted in Chapter Three, ignoring metaphysics has not meant, for social science, abandonment of the whole-parts idea applied to society. Social science has officially eschewed that transcendental aura surrounding the organic whole. Actually, German idealism still exercises considerable influence in social studies, the "whole cloth" and "patterns" approach being more than vaguely reminiscent of Hegel's transmutations from individual through civil society to the State. Hence, group life appears functional to political life and obversely, political life represents a "function" of group activity. Flowing from group activity and giving particular communities distinctive personalities, purposes are secondary, derivative, and functional.

Bentley's "group theory of politics" stemmed from the preceding supposition that society always forms as a mass of men in groupings cutting across each other. Groups are "vastly more real than a man's reflection of them in his 'ideas.' " Hence, "every classification of the elements of a population must involve an analysis of the population into groups."

The great task in the study of any form of social life is the analysis of these groups. It is much more than classification, as that term is ordinarily used. When these groups are adequately stated, everything is stated. When I say everything I mean everything.

Besides his dogmatism, Bentley's language needs clarification. What does he mean by society as a "mass of men"? Are men simply integers until grouped? Also, exactly how much more "real" are groups than ideas? How much is "vastly more"? Can reality be scaled into more and less? Also, Bentley's equations between reality and concreteness, and between realism and hardheadedness provide troubles because even this realism hides behind an ideational, symbolic system, and a not very precise one at that.

For Bentley, a particular group defines itself in experience by its activities and its relationships to other groups. These activities knit together in a system of competing and intersecting interests with strongly economic goals.[103] Hence, interests operating in a given political field dictate the configuration of group activity in that field. In fact, ordinary political groups are functions of interest.[104] For political analysis, therefore, the most fundamental problem concerns what interests lie behind or underneath apparent group struggle. Accordingly, conscious purposes articulated as ideals represent, at most, "derivations," to use Vilfredo Pareto's expression, such derivations being symptomatic but not causal.

To illustrate this absolute precedence of interests over ideals, Bentley summarily declared that even if every man, woman, and child were a "dyed-in-the-wool idealistic socialist," "the progress of events for the next few years and generations to come would be very little different from what it will be as it is."[105] Again, despite all the ambiguities in "next few years and generations," "very little different," and so forth, his central point never fades: political relationships pattern themselves into a "process" of groups (ranging from legislatures to cat fanciers) based on fundamental, underlying interests (or "lower-lying groups" as Bentley put it[106]), and without these relationships

103. Previous citations, *ibid.*, pp. 176–218. "My interest in politics is not primary, but derived from my interest in economic life; and that I hope from this point of approach ultimately to gain a better understanding of the economic life than I have succeeded in gaining hitherto." *Ibid.*, p. 210.
104. *Ibid.*, p. 211.
105. *Ibid.*, pp. 114–115.
106. *Ibid.*, p. 446.

(an inconceivable thing) political life could not persist.[107] The process of government divides superficially into "discussion" and "organization" groups, but in every case,

they yield to the lower-lying groups with surprising rapidity when the actual change in the balance of pressures takes place. And this explains why it is that no reconstruction of society in terms of the life-history of ideas, or of the life-history of governmental forms, can have more than a crude preliminary descriptive value.[108]

Fundamentally, politics remains a function of interest, and political relationships, being interest-oriented, are functional.

*Purposive Relationships.* Not all relationships are functional, however. Concentrating on the sociological, group approach to politics, to the neglect of more individualized and conscious factors, the unwary observer falls into a neat analytic trap, whereby he imprisons himself in his own categories. If one asserts that politics is based on groups, then one may view all human relationships within the political realm as functional. While Bentley's approach does not exclude intentional or purposive activity, it does subordinate intentions and purposes to derivative statuses under "interest," which explains all and subsumes everything.

Controlling interests determine political actions. Arendt holds a confusion between "action" and "behavior," characterizing behavioral social science, responsible for overemphasis on the necessary and neglect of the unpredictable in contemporary political studies.[109] This criticism, while having some etymological and historical justification, seems too harsh. Arendt stresses public action's "boundlessness" and "inherent unpredictability," but the indeterminate "frustration" caused by action need not arise only because the ancient Greeks said it did. Nor need one contend, somewhat inaccurately (and polemically),

107. See Norman Jacobson, "Causality and Time in Political Process: A Speculation," *American Political Science Review*, LVIII (March 1964), 15–22.

108. *The Process of Government*, p. 446.

109. *The Human Condition*, pp. 40–42. This applies to modern life generally.

that the "behavioral sciences aim to reduce man as a whole, in all his activities, to the level of a conditioned animal,"[110] though zealous behavioralists sometimes make such preposterous claims.

One can simply argue (a "reminder" rather than an "argument" seems better still) that functionalism does not tell the whole story. Political relationships can be studied as functional order and have both descriptive and heuristic value when viewed this way. Nevertheless, function can neither describe nor explain the rather untidy area of purposive action, nor can either function or purpose suffice to explain creativity's teleology. In her book, *Function, Purpose and Powers*, Dorothy Emmet considers the interesting possibility that political analysis needs several languages to describe politics and political action.

If we look at social actions through the bifocal lenses of two kinds of teleological conceptions, the organic teleology of function and the distinctively human teleology of purpose, each in turn may help us to see a different range of problems. What may be seen with the help of the one may be complementary in important ways to what may be seen with the other. But this is not all. Sometimes we need a telescopic lens with the help of which to try and see another range of question, which may seem distant and so obscure compared with those generally looked at with the help of the concepts of function and purpose. Our telescope is still only a primitive and imprecise instrument. It is a third kind of teleological notion related to the inner powers of individuals, which for want of a better term I shall call creativeness, and which, when shown in certain kinds of role, I shall call "vocation."[111]

After reviewing the achievements of functional and structural-functional theory in the analysis of social structure, Emmet supplies another "range of question" for human action, *purpose*. The belief in purpose, she says, represents an intuition that people act intentionally. This enables observers to see action from the actor's standpoint, rather than from the spectator's. In purposive relationships the crucial question is, "What is it we are trying to accomplish?" Functionally, one would ask, "What

110. *Ibid.*, p. 41.
111. Emmet, *op. cit.*, p. 137.

does this particular action effect, when considered in relation to other activities within some system taken as a whole?" While distinct, the two questions are not mutually exclusive. Any political actor can answer the first, but the second requires a trained observer who understands the total system. Quite often the two queries complement each other, the first representing, for any actor, *conscious* intention, the second including *subconscious* or *underlying* motivation. Besides providing a fertile ground for functional, interest relationships, politics naturally embraces many purposive activities as well. According to Emmet:

> In politics people try as participants to give direction to some aspect of social life by getting together to formulate and implement policies, and also to try to prevent other people from doing the same with policies with which they disagree. Politics (in this first order sense of a particular social activity: not in the second order sense of political theory) is something which one cannot do by oneself. It is like a game with partners and opponents.

When we study politics "we shall need sometimes at any rate to put questions in purposive terms and to ask what people are trying to do when they act politically, or what they have set up some particular institution for." A common purpose may even endure, not in the sense of a common mind or collective will, but "people would not be likely to engage in politics unless they believed that in coming together they could plan and collaborate in trying to get something done, or to prevent other people from doing something else." It seems doubtful, however, that a general activity with a single purpose called "Politics" exists *sui generis*. Old shibboleths like "the common good"

> stem from the conviction that without certain common moral attitudes, such as public spirit, and willingness to co-operate to uphold the law, many of the particular purposes promoted through the State are likely to be fruitless. And this is no small thing; as can be seen in times and places where public spirit has been lacking.

Nevertheless, suggestions that a democratic state needs one all-embracing "common purpose" with which to counter totalitarian states should be approached warily. Emmet concludes her discussion of purpose:

If we lose sight of this aspect of purposive action altogether, we are likely to end with too simple an organic, or even mechanistic, a model of society. The model may be deceptive in various ways. It may suggest that a "social system" works automatically in a more economical way than in fact it does.

Unexpected crises will continue and men's efforts during these times may frequently prove abortive. But at least the language of purpose and intention "give people the credit for trying." Emmet could have added, as any study of citizenship must, that an adequate vocabulary of political intention assesses "responsibility" as well as "credit." Intention presumes making choices and choice embraces responsibility.

*Relationships of Creativeness.* Granted that politics has purposive aspects, how does "creativeness" enter political nature? For Emmet, the vocational or creative dimension concerns the problem of morality rather than function or intention. "Social morality" exhibits two main characteristics: reciprocity and a limited group. Durkheim investigating disciplinary society, that is, social morality, seldom mentioned the exceptional individual, hardly surprising, given his approach.[112] Obviously, he was emphasizing only one type of morality (though he sometimes exaggerated its importance).

Henri Bergson made a singular attempt, on the other hand, to distinguish between morality and religion founded on social pressure, or "closed" morality, and that based upon something "beyond" a limited community, namely "open" morality or love of humanity. Accordingly, there persist "two moralities," or rather two faces to a single morality:

a substantial half of our morality includes duties whose obligatory character is to be explained fundamentally by the pressure of society on the individual . . . the rest of morality expresses a certain emotional state, that actually we yield not to a pressure but to an attraction.[113]

112. Previous citations, *ibid.*, pp. 106–141.
113. Henri Bergson, *The Two Sources of Morality and Religion*, translated by R. A. Audra and C. Brereton (Garden City, N.Y.: Doubleday Anchor Books, 1956) (copyright © by Holt, Rinehart and Winston), p. 49.

Bergson's formulation reminds us that functional approaches to morality have limitations. Actually, both moralities complement each other. "The duality itself merges into a unity, for 'social pressure' and 'impetus of love' are but two complementary manifestations of life, normally intent on preserving generally the social form which was characteristic of the human species from the beginning, but, exceptionally, capable of transfiguring it, thanks to individuals who each represent, as the appearance of a new species would have represented, an effort of creative evolution."[114]

So another dimension of public action paralleling function and purpose appears: some individuals and groups surpass existing social structures by their creative powers and by so doing, add something to, or perhaps change these structures.[115] In political nature individuals and groups have, from time to time, operated creatively. Note Mead's conception of the "I" and "me" as phases of the self. Grappling with the same issue discussed above, he urged social science theory to take creativity seriously. His own theory of creativity, though different in its conclusions from the one presented here, nevertheless treated as valid our initial proposition that there persists some disjuncture between individual and social structure. The "me" represents "that group of attitudes which stands for others in the community. . . ."[116] Facing the "me" is the "I." "The 'I' is the response of the individual to the attitude of the community as this appears to his own experience. His response to that organized attitude changes it."[117] Through this "self-indication" humans construct their conscious action.[118] Such responses are anticipated in Mead's proposition that,

The individual not only has rights, but he has duties; he is not only a citizen, a member of the community, but he is one who reacts to this

114. *Ibid.*, pp. 96–97.
115. "Transcend" and "transcendence," as used here, do not necessarily imply an exclusively normative theory of politics.
116. *Mind, Self and Society*, p. 194.
117. *Ibid.*, p. 196.
118. Blumer, *op. cit.*, p. 183.

community and in his reaction to it, as we have seen in the conversation of gestures, changes it.[119]

Whereas the "me" signifies a "conventional, habitual individual," the "I,"

is constantly reacting to such an organized community in the way of expressing himself, not necessarily asserting himself in the offensive sense but expressing himself, being himself in such a co-operative process as belongs to any community. The attitudes involved are gathered from the group, but the individual in whom they are organized has the opportunity of giving them an expression which perhaps has never taken place before.[120]

Mead's view of creativity and novelty, therefore, relates to the social group. As group members, individuals act similarly, yet they react specifically to social experience in different ways.

In a society there must be a set of common organized habits of response found in all, but the way in which individuals act under specific circumstances gives rise to all of the individual differences which characterize the different persons. The fact that they have to act in a certain common fashion does not deprive them of originality. The common language is there, but a different use of it is made in every new contact between persons; the element of novelty in the reconstruction takes place through the reaction of the individuals to the group to which they belong . . . Now, it is that reaction of the individual to the organized "me," that is in a certain sense simply a member of the community which represents the "I" in the experience of the self.[121]

Apparently, Mead did not appreciate how divergent uses of language have intrapersonal, as well as interpersonal significances. That symbolization taking place within an individual's mind (Mead developed this idea himself, but his notion of "mind" precluded solipsism[122]) may easily destroy the unity of

119. *Mind, Self and Society*, p. 196.
120. *Ibid.*, pp. 197–198.
121. *Ibid.*, pp. 198–199.
122. "It is that sort of situation which seems to be involved in what we term mind, as such: this social process, in which one individual affects other individuals, is carried over into the experience of the individuals that are so affected. The individual takes this attitude not simply as a matter of repetition, but as part of the elaborate social reaction which is going on." *Mind, Self and Society*, p. 109.

the "common language" situation Mead deemed essential for any co-operative venture.[123] Social systems comprehending profound heterogeneities obviously have internal communication problems. Even in relatively homogeneous societies there seldom exists a single common-language setting where each person, depending on his interactive situation, constructs his own variations. Mead implied such a common-language situation when he claimed, "the relative values of the 'me' and 'I' depend very much on the situation."[124] And he added,

both aspects of the "I" and "me" are essential to the self in its full expression. One must take the attitude of the others in a group in order to belong to a community; he has to employ that outer social world taken within himself in order to carry on thought. It is through his relationship to others in that community, because of the rational social processes that obtain in that community, that he has being as a citizen. On the other hand, the individual is constantly reacting to the social attitudes, and changing in this co-operative process the very community to which he belongs.[125]

Political society, encompassing exceedingly complex symbolic processes, hardly provides a simple linguistic consensus where individuals "agree to disagree." Intense political conflict may destroy any commonalty: political power can convert a common language into a monolith, anything but a "cooperative proc-

123. Communication was vital to co-operative activities, as Mead envisioned them. He held that communication was more universal, in one respect, than religious and economic attitudes, because it proved the medium serving them both. But in another sense communication was less universal: "There has to be some such field as religion or economics in which there is something to communicate, in which there is a co-operative process, in which what is communicated can be socially utilized. One must assume that sort of co-operative situation in order to reach what is called the 'universe of discourse.' Such a universe of discourse is the medium for all these different social processes, and in that sense it is more universal than they; but it is not a process that, so to speak, runs by itself." In other words, communication presupposes a social process, a social situation. Likewise, political communication presupposes political nature. *Ibid.*, pp. 259–260.
124. *Ibid.*, p. 199.
125. *Ibid.*, pp. 199–200.

ess."[126] As experienced in Nazi Germany, individual and group creativity surpassed the warm-hearted, intellectually fertile community from which it emerged, and transfigured that community, in spite of a common language, into something hideous. And even if totalitarianism seems too extreme an example of fractured commonalty, the student of ideology could nevertheless retort to Mead, "Whose 'common language' are you talking about?"[127] The rise of nihilism in general and National Socialism in particular demonstrate that individuals and groups do not stop with changing, in a co-operative, interactive process, "the very community to which they belong." They might destroy this community and establish, with widespread support, an extreme *Ersatzgemeinschaft* (as Erich Fromm calls it) defying all communication. Or they need have no community whatsoever; they may simply destroy themselves and their fellow citizens irresponsibly.

Bergson saw that the individual's "impetus of love" (he should have added "impetus of hate" as well, but his pre–World War II world was still too comfortable and too naive) could transfigure his social group. This conception of individual action expressed more faithfully than Mead's the dynamic (and often daemonic) power of creative human will. Whereas Mead's community "contained" the individual, recognizing that there were different "styles" of role behavior, Bergson's individual demanded much more from his society:

126. For at least one student of totalitarianism, the penultimate in functional rationality exists in the Soviet Union. Reorganization schemes in the U.S.S.R. seem to be consonant with "the principle of functional rationality which maintains that the components of the social system shall be so constituted and so organized as to contribute maximally to the effective functioning of the system." Raymond Bauer, *The New Man in Soviet Psychology* (Cambridge, Mass.: Harvard University Press, 1952), p. 177.

127. For Marx, the only universal found in any society hitherto (*aller bisherigen Gesellschaft*) was the totality of historical class conflict. This war was manifest not only in concrete economic and political decisions, but in the spiritual world as well—religion and art, man's philosophies of history and self-knowledge, and the scientific knowledge of law, state and economics. See Karl Marx/Friedrich Engels, *Historische-kritische Gesamtausgabe*, VI, 525. Discussed in Hans Barth, *op. cit.*, pp. 112–113.

We are fond of saying that society exists, and that hence it inevitably exerts a constraint on its members, and that this constraint is obligation. But in the first place, for society to exist at all the individual must bring into it a whole group of inborn tendencies; society therefore is not self-explanatory, so we must search below the social accretions, get down to Life, of which human societies, as indeed the human species altogether, are but manifestations. But this is not going far enough; we must delve deeper still if we want to understand, not only how society "constrains" individuals, but again how the individual can set up as a judge and wrest from it a moral transformation.[128]

The basic distinction between Mead and Bergson is this: Mead believed that all human life, including the biological, was "social"; Bergson held that all "Life," including human life, was biological in a vitalistic sense. Mead emphasized, therefore, the elements of co-operation and conflict within organized human (that is, social) life. Bergson recognized human and social life as manifestations of "Life" in general; that is, he perceived both social continuity and aspiration beyond the normal community's limits. Under Bergson's formulation, biological "instinct" or "nature" complemented the "intelligence" of social man, an important contribution to the thinking of an Industrial Revolution intent on "subduing" nature. The pride of intelligence, however, will not admit "its subordination to biological necessities" and suppresses nature and life. For Bergson (and others from Matthew Arnold to Nietzsche), "farewell nature! farewell life."[129] But fortunately,

this independence is limited in fact: it ceases at the exact moment when intelligence would defeat its own object by injuring some vital interest. Intelligence is then inevitably kept under observation by

128. Bergson, *op. cit.*, p. 100. See also Reinhold Niebuhr, *The Children of Light and the Children of Darkness* (New York: Charles Scribner's, 1944 and 1960), pp. 49–50. But Niebuhr distinguishes between "freedom in history" and "absolute freedom in history," the latter denied human beings. The distinction he is drawing is also made by Arendt's "freedom" and "sovereignty"—*The Human Condition*, pp. 210–211.
129. Bergson, *op. cit.*, p. 161.

instinct, or rather by life, the common origin of instinct and intelligence.[130]

Both Freud and Jung agreed that subconscious instinct—*daemon*—moved men to act in creative, albeit (for them) predictable, ways. But neither shared Bergson's optimism that "intelligence is then inevitably kept under observation by instinct, or rather by life. . . ." Freud and Jung asserted that civilization perilously suppresses the individual's unconscious and subconscious desires and needs to such an extent that men forget, detrimentally, the existence of these primal, underlying forces.[131] Moreover, Freud never waxed euphoric when he pictured, as one of "the problems of man's fate," the need to find some "expedient accommodation—one, that is, that will bring happiness—between this claim of the individual and the cultural claims of the group."[132] For Freud, the individual never fully resigned himself to community. Instead, a proper analogy for the relationships between the individual and others would be a planetary system: the individual orbits society and thus relates to his community's life, just as any planet remains in place by its relation to the central in its particular system. Yet each planet, while orbiting, rotates on its own axis, turning its multiple faces toward the center: or, to apply this analogy, the individual revolves about his own axis, related, nevertheless, to his community through a certain gravitational impulse. And this Freudian orbit was intractably elliptical:

Just as a planet revolves around a central body as well as rotating on its own axis, so the human individual takes part in the course of

130. *Ibid.*, pp. 161–162.

131. See Freud, *Civilization and Its Discontents* (1930), in *The Standard Edition of the Complete Psychological Works of Sigmund Freud*, translated from the German and edited by James Strachey, 23 volumes. Copyright © 1961 by James Strachey. Reprinted with permission from the publishers, W. W. Norton & Company, New York, and the Hogarth Press, Ltd., London, the Institute of Psycho-Analysis, and Mrs. Alix Strachey; Vol. XXI. C. G. Jung, "The Phenomenology of the Spirit in Fairy Tales," in *Psyche and Symbol*, edited by Violet S. de Laszlo (Garden City, N.Y.: Doubleday Anchor Books, 1958), pp. 110–112.

132. *Civilization and Its Discontents*, *loc. cit.*, XXI, 96.

development of mankind at the same time as he pursues his own path in life.[133]

Finally, Freud saw that individual response to interaction with others assumes a separate life and logic, sometimes antagonistic to its original social origin. In the fullest sense, reaction to others becomes action in spite of or against others. Writing in 1930, Freud voiced this prophetic pessimism:

> The element of truth . . . is that men are not gentle creatures who want to be loved, and who at the most can defend themselves if they are attacked; they are, on the contrary, creatures among whose instinctual endowments is to be reckoned a powerful share of aggressiveness . . . their neighbour is for them not only a potential helper or sexual object, but also someone who tempts them to satisfy their aggressiveness on him, to exploit his capacity for work without compensation, to use him sexually without his consent, to seize his possessions, to humiliate him, to cause him pain, to torture and to kill him.[134]

In conclusion, two related factors concerning political relationships seem elementary: first, human relationships are not exhausted in what Durkheim called "the elementary forms" of life, that is, in strictly functional relationships; second, politics comprises several orders of relationships (of which political activity comprises one segment, and citizenship an important part of that segment) that do not always exhibit settled and systematic forms. On the functional level "systems" and co-operative "processes" have a crucial place in political analysis. Even social conflict has utility value from this point of view.[135]

133. *Ibid.*, XXI, 141.
134. *Ibid.*, XXI, 111.
135. See Lewis Coser, *The Functions of Social Conflict* (Glencoe, Ill.: The Free Press, 1956). Coser builds his theory on that of Georg Simmel. See Simmel's *Conflict*, translated by Kurt H. Wolff, Glencoe, Ill.: The Free Press, 1955). For Coser "conflict is a form of socialization." He continues: "This means essentially that, to paraphrase the opening pages of Simmel's essay, no group can be entirely harmonious, for it would then be devoid of process and structure. [Aristotle leveled somewhat the same criticism against Plato.] Groups require disharmony as well as harmony, dissociation as well as association; and conflicts within them are by no

But several kinds of questions concerning human relations cluster outside the ambit of functional analysis and its language and require separate methods and different vocabularies. Since political relationships involve "purpose" and "vocation" (creativity, power), as well as "function," it seems necessary to construct several different types of language—which would co-exist more or less peacefully—in order to analyze phenomena properly.

---

means altogether disruptive factors. Group formation is the result of both types of processes. . . . Conflict as well as co-operation has social function." *The Functions of Social Conflict*, p. 31.

# V Symbolism and Attitude

## Private Attitude

IF public action can be characterized by disclosing oneself to indirect others, private attitude provides an inner sanctum for each person. In private attitudes one can hide in privacy. Contrasted to the shifting boundaries of public action, attitude seems very definitely bounded, for it circumscribes the one area of life where individuals possess considerable control, or at least think they do. Related to oneself,[1] one finds a retreat from the "hell" of others, with security rather than adventure the dominant value.

Boundaries appear quite precise in the private world, with the single self ringed by physical and mental characteristics identifying it as a distinct individual. Symbolically, each possesses a

1. Paul Tillich, *Love, Power and Justice* (New York: Oxford University Press, 1954), p. 25. And of course, psychoanalytical theory highlights the relations within the personality.

name as well. More widely, there are certain artifacts and groups closely associated with the self in the family and home. Into such primary relationships public scrutiny from the world of indirect others has only limited access. Indeed, if there are "others" in one's intimate privacy, they are in direct relationship to oneself.[2]

A leading characteristic of such an intimate circle of private involvements is the fact that nonintegrateable elements, possibly disturbing to equilibrium and harmony, are not tolerated on the level of consciousness.[3] "Strangers" can be excluded, if they threaten the security of this circle, and since security remains the dominant value in privacy, strangers often meet suspicion if not hostility. Expressions such as "A man's home is his castle" signify protection and steadfastness in a world of flux. Seemingly one can retreat through the castle gate, pull-up the drawbridge, and elude one's enemies.

Actually, one can delineate the major outlines of privacy with no more precision than those of public action. The above description provides a crude model at best, since it deals only with the level of consciousness. Conscious privacy has always been conditioned by cultural norms (different cultures, for example, treat strangers differently) and today is increasingly assailed by intruders from mass society, such as fads in entertainment. But more important, consciousness itself, probed in the investigations conducted by Freud, Jung and others, seems the most superficial dimension of private life. We learn from psychoanalytic studies that individuals do not possess considerable control over themselves, that privacy hardly affords a retreat from the hell of other people, that security is an illusion, that alienation actually flourishes in the most intimate associations between spouses, between siblings, and between parents and children, to say nothing of alienation within any given personality, so that nonintegrateable

2. John Dewey, *The Public and Its Problems*, (Chicago: Gateway Books, 1946), p. 15.

3. The neurotic personality's "integrating power" is impaired, but only in the sense that there is a lack of spontaneous integration. See Karen Horney, *Neurosis and Human Growth*, (New York: Norton, 1950), p. 171.

elements, while psychologically uncongenial, are nevertheless accommodated in perverted ways as the private self passionately pursues its quest for unification.

In other words, one cannot "retreat through the castle gate, pull up the drawbridge, and elude one's enemies," when there exist many gates, no drawbridges, and ambiguous enemies. Our privacy model must balance two major factors, therefore, and constantly look over its shoulder at a third. Both conscious and unconscious modes of symbolization—and symbolization comprises the major theme of this chapter—must be counted when analyzing privacy and relating this privacy to the public spaces of everyday life, but what Freud called "civilization" and what we shall term "society" or "mass society," that is, inexorable pressures from collective forces beyond personal control, constantly preclude privacy on either conscious or unconscious levels. Furthermore, this chapter suggests that tangible distinctions between public and private, readily apparent to the naked eye, are difficult to make, but distinctions remain possible if one shifts the search from tangible to symbolic differentia (see the following section of this chapter).

Personal, private motivation has two sources: the will to power (*potentia*) manifesting itself in public action,[4] and fear of the risks involved in such a quest, typified by shrinkage of individual interests to orientation and security.[5] Risking disclosure, the actor desires attention from and intercourse with a wider audience than his privacy ordinarily allows. Many persons (if not all people) need larger publics. Obviously, artists and politicians thrive on publicity, but so do the "offenders." Why do painters have "exhibitions," writers "publics," and musi-

4. See Arendt, Nietzsche, Tillich in the preceding chapter.
5. "The driving force in human minds is fear, which begets an imperious demand for security in the world's confusion: a demand for a world-picture that fills all experience and gives each individual a definite *orientation* amid the terrifying forces of nature and society." Susanne K. Langer, *Philosophy in a New Key* (New York: Mentor Books, 1958), p. 138. Reprinted by permission of the publishers from Susanne K. Langer, *Philosophy in a New Key* (Cambridge, Mass.: Harvard University Press, Copyright, 1942, 1951, 1957, by the President and Fellows of Harvard College).

cians "recitals"? But even the untalented can demonstrate publicly a certain prowess (if not expertise) by passing and cutting at high speeds on the highway.

The wider audience provided by other people affords a public that judges an actor, and the fact that this audience so often consists of anonymous members makes its judgments all the more salient, since the actor (for example, the speeding motorist) may presume whatever judgment he wants, for he will probably never face any of these others directly. If creativity in the widest sense means doing something personally satisfactory which one takes to be one's own original effort, then the anonymous audience performs a vital function for creative processes: it expresses an appreciation ambiguous enough that actors can interpret to suit themselves.

What social scientists frequently call "mass society" —involving great numbers, wide dispersal of groups, heterogeneous members, anonymity, disorganization, no common institutions and customs, unattached individuals[6]—lends itself particularly well to amorphous public situations where literally "all is permitted." Too much ink has been spilled over the tyranny of the mob in mass society, and not enough effort has dealt with the irresponsibility allowed individual actors by the mob's inability to express itself authoritatively and specifically.[7]

But privacy affords something other than the risks of creativity in the public world, with the attendant dangers of being seen and criticized by others who are relatively anonymous. The private area of life offers orientation away from the "madding crowd," even if this kind of security proves illusory.[8] At least

6. See Louis Wirth, "Consensus and Mass Communication" (1948), in *Collective Behavior*, edited by Ralph H. Turner and Lewis M. Killian (Englewood Cliffs, N.J.: Prentice-Hall, 1957), p. 169.

7. See V. O. Key, *Public Opinion and American Democracy* (New York: Alfred A. Knopf, 1962), Chapter 21; Hannah Arendt, *The Origins of Totalitarianism*, second enlarged edition (New York: Meridian Books, 1958), Chapter 10.

8. An essential teaching of psychoanalysis is that the private world is no more secure than the public. In fact, the terrors of private life stem in part from blocking (repressions) creative drives in the public world, employing "public" here in the sense of "outside."

one can retreat to "the privacy of one's own thoughts" and work out some rationalization for or refusal of the outside world, a variant on the "inner migration" often present in totalitarian situations.[9] In this way, private attitudes may provide an opportunity for the individual to adjust himself to the imperative demands made by public action, thus coming to some peace with the powers around him.

Political events are assimilated into the personality, with its objective background of heredity, environment and development, its present subjective strivings, and its future aspirations. These events, if noticed at all, may in some way be reconciled by the individual with the urgencies of his own personality. How he does this or refuses to do it varies from person to person, but the process of settlement with the world of action and risk appears universal. By conscious resolve and unconscious urge, the individual comes to terms with the imperatives of public disclosure. In Herman Finer's words, "the mind of every man and woman is truly pregnant with a state."[10] But this resolution is filled with unresolved tensions.

Sometimes reconciliation between private and public becomes mandatory. All law, for instance, demands resolution of private and public; litigants must end their retreat into privacy and "come out of hiding." This applies, not only to parties-at-law, but to other persons in a court situation such as jurors. Jurors have a calling to serve in public in the sense that they must act and reveal themselves to indirect others with whom they ordinarily share no relationships. In fact, they personify the anonymous public they represent. Sometimes individual jurors find it impossible to reconcile their private attitudes with the demands of their public place, that is, with their role as jurors, for example, in criminal cases involving capital punishment, and then they have the right to disqualify themselves.

All law, "repressive" and "restitutive," to employ Durkheim's classification (in *The Division of Labor in Society*), is

9. See Raymond A. Bauer, *et al.*, *How the Soviet System Works* (New York: Vintage Books, 1960), pp. 74, 122, 169, 191.

10. *The Theory and Practice of Modern Government*, revised edition (New York: Henry Holt, 1949), p. 9.

public in the sense that it requires individuals to leave their private sanctuaries and appear publicly by accepting the symbolic terms imposed by outsiders. For this reason, one of the outstanding problems in the development of jurisprudence has been public trial; star chambers, military courts, legislative committees, administrative procedures, kangaroo courts, and small-town justices of the peace, while occupying legal jurisdictions and operating essentially as trial courts, strain somewhat the notion of law as mandatory public disclosure of private persons. For the latter ideal to operate, not only actors but also their settings must possess public symbolism.

## Political Symbols: A General Introduction

Before discussing the congruence of public and private, a discussion reserved until the final chapter, it is necessary to examine more closely how private attitude is formed in the first place. It will be taken for granted that neither "private" nor "public" exists in any clearly defined form in tangible spaces, so that one can, just by walking through the revolving doors of a government office building enter the public sphere, or conversely, by falling asleep finally escape to one's private warren. Rather the opposite is true: persons employed by the United States Department of Interior no doubt deal with business affecting the authoritative disposition of sanctions ordering their society (that is, they are governmental officials), but they also make a living as officials, which constitutes a very private enterprise; on the other hand, public business (the outcome of an election, for example) may cause many a sleepless night for those who worry about such things.

Private and public, like the words "organism" and "environment," are morphological expressions, denoting symbolic, not tangible, dimensions in space and time.[11] In other words, public and private constitute expressions, as do all linguistic conven-

11. Andras Angyal, *Foundations for a Science of Personality* (New York: The Commonwealth Fund, 1941), pp. 92–94. See Murray Edelman, *The Symbolic Uses of Politics* (Urbana: University of Illinois Press, 1964).

tions, involving "the power of envisagement" and the "burden of understanding" appropriate to man the *animal symbolicum*.[12] Approaching matters this way, there does exist a distinction between private and public which broadly parallels that between organism and environment, with "public" a special kind of environment and "private" its juxtaposition in the organism, but this distinction by no means has tangible evidence at all times. Hence, we speak of the organism as tending in the *direction of autonomy* or *independence* and the environment in the *direction of heteronomy*, but both form together a single whole, the "biosphere."[13]

Private and public parallel this distinction *on the level of governmental affairs* where deliberate institutions and policies of authority and sanction operate to order a particular environment, institutions, and policies which may be contrasted to the tendencies of individual persons away from such ordering in the direction of autonomy, but private and public together constitute the "polity" (for want of a better word in modern vocabularies where Aristotle's *polis* no longer conveys meaning). Politics and its symbols represent the activities people pursue in governing this polity and the tensions between private and public such governance entails.

Government goes well beyond those ordinarily "formal" or typically "public" situations involving territorial governmental units. Likewise "public" means more than the "state." What concerns any given "clientele" is a "public" concern, be this concern union business, business business, church business, and whatever else. There are widening publics, of course, the widest usually a territorial state. But the latter polity is by no means always the "most inclusive," nor the only one possessing sanctions or even a monopoly of physical force, if one examines the

12. Ernst Cassirer, *Philosophie der symbolischen Formen*, 3 volumes (1929) selection in *Theories of Society, Foundations of Modern Sociological Theory*, 2 volumes, edited by Talcott Parsons, *et al.* (New York: The Free Press of Glencoe, Illinois, 1961) II, 1004–1008; Cassirer, *An Essay on Man* (Garden City, N.Y.: Doubleday Anchor Books, 1944), p. 44; Langer, *op. cit.*, p. 34.

13. Angyal, *op. cit.*, p. 100.

doctrines and structures of the Roman Catholic church or the activities of employers and employees during labor unrest.

In all cases, *outsiders* usually view the internal affairs of any polity as "private" or "domestic," at least in communities where pluralistic polities have traditional standing, though the interests and realms of outsiders are shifting ones indeed. Thus, Chester Barnard (in his *Functions of the Executive*, 1938) shows how the customer clientele for any firm functions as an integral part of the business itself: similarly, the international community operates in certain instances as the clientele of a given nation so that the latter's private business ("domestic affairs") becomes the business of outsiders too.

It seems wiser, therefore, to speak of "public situations" and "governmental situations," recognizing "situation" to be a "symbol situation" or a symbolic space constantly changing its shape and size.[14] We have already discussed political nature and will turn to symbolic space momentarily.

Political tensions are perceived symbolically, which is to say the space of politics has symbolic borders and contents for various participants, and hence the places and occasions for examining such tensions are found in the symbolic systems of citizens.[15] Since perceptions pertain to active, not passive people busily organizing their lives (for organizational activity appears to be the principle of life itself and it continues without cease[16]), it follows that envisaging and understanding the distinctions between private and public vary from person to person (and from political theorist to political theorist?), with perhaps broad though not unanimous agreements among various groupings of human beings.

At any rate, our discussion presumes the existence of symbolic spaces and times called public and private which vary from

14. See C. K. Ogden and I. A. Richards, *The Meaning of Meaning* (1923) (New York: Harvest Books, 1963), pp. 205–206, 209 f.

15. In terms of this discussion, the numerous controversies surrounding the tangible existence of a "public interest" seem futile.

16. Ludwig von Bertalanffy, *Problems of Life, an Evaluation of Modern Biological Thought* (New York: John Wiley, 1952) (originally published in German, *Das Biologische Weltbild, Die Stellung des Lebens in Natur und Wissenschaft*, 1949).

person to person and environment to environment. Political symbols—defining "political" as we did during our discussion of
"political nature" in Chapter Two—form a part of the symbolic
repertoire possessed by private persons, with such persons
usually expressing themselves in conventional political symbols
(though meanings may vary). So we are concerned in this
chapter with the relation between private attitude and the dynamics of symbolization in political affairs, a concern which
involves some distinction between political symbols and the activity of symbolizing.

To begin with, we shall inventory the general role performed
by political symbols—ignoring temporarily the process of symbolization itself—as that means by which a series of gaps are
filled by representational links, for symbolism may be roughly
defined as "A" represents "B."[17] These gaps can be called "data
gaps" for want of better terminology. First, there exists the
break between political data or referents and the perceiving
subject.[18] Second is the gap between what Whitehead called
"presentational immediacy" and "casual efficacy"—immediate
perception and deeper-lying past causes.[19] Third, is the chasm
between data and setting, what Kenneth Burke terms the question of "scene" or "circumference" (a specialized problem connected with scene).[20] "A word extends its meaning when it
passes from a narrow circle to a wider one; it restricts it when it
passes from a wider circle to a narrower one," explains R.
Meringer.[21]

In all three instances, the really basic problem concerns active

17. Angyal, *op. cit.*, p. 57.
18. *Ibid.*
19. *Symbolism, Its Meaning and Effect* (1927) (New York: Capricorn Books, 1959), pp. 49–53, hereafter cited as *Symbolism*.
20. *A Grammar of Motives* (1945) in *A Grammar of Motives and A
Rhetoric of Motives* (one volume) (Cleveland and New York: Meridian
Books, 1962), (copyright © by Prentice-Hall, Inc.), pp. 86–87. Hereafter *A Grammar of Motives* in this edition.
21. In "Wörter und Sachen (III)," *Indogermanische Forschungen*,
XVIII (1905–06), 204–296, at 232, quoted by Antoine Meillet, "How
Words Change Their Meanings," in *Theories of Society*, edited by T.
Parsons, *et al.*, II, 1013–1018, at 1015. See also Ricoeur's idea of "circles
of truth" in *History and Truth*, pp. 189–190.

perception, perception where the percipient produces "output" vis-à-vis his data as well as output in his final actions based on his perceptions of this data. Hence, by examining the general role of political symbols, we meet that old *Verboten*, "meaning," and it is to the processes by which meaning is formulated that we next direct our attention.

This discussion presumes a correlation between meaning and experience, thus conforming to the famous redefinition (actually more a re-evaluation) of meaning by Ogden and Richards in their *Meaning of Meaning* (1923). Though the writers more often followed in this chapter have modified Ogden and Richards in various respects, the basic reinterpretation endures: we must substitute for meaning a more adequate expression such as "language transaction" or "communication," where symbols are used "in such a way that acts of reference occur in a hearer which are similar in all relevant respects to those which are symbolized by them in the speaker." The problem then becomes one for communication theory and involves the delimitation and analysis of "psychological contexts" or "symbol situations."[22]

Speaking in terms more relevant to this essay, there is a symbolic activity which bridges the gaps noted above, the outcome of which can be conveniently, if somewhat imprecisely, called "meaning," and the dynamics of which can be variously labeled "symbolic reference" (Whitehead),[23] "symbolization" (Voegelin),[24] "symbolization" or "symbolic transformation" (Langer),[25] "symbolic process" or "symbolic thought" (Cassirer),[26] "symbolism" (Sapir),[27] "symbolic organization" (Par-

22. See footnote 14, this chapter, and Karl Deutsch, *The Nerves of Government* (New York: The Free Press of Glencoe, Ill., 1963).

23. *Symbolism*, pp. 18–19.

24. *Order and History*, three volumes (completed) (Baton Rouge: Louisiana State University Press, 1956), Volume I, Introduction.

25. *Op. cit.*, pp. 32 f.

26. *Philosophie der symbolischen Formen*, three volumes (Berlin: Bruno Cassirer, 1929), Volume III, Part 2, Chapter 5 ("Symbolische Prägnanz"); *An Essay on Man*, p. 58.

27. "Symbolism" from *Encyclopaedia of the Social Sciences*, in *Theories of Society*, edited by T. Parsons, *et al.*, II, 1018–1020, at 1018.

sons, *et al.*),[28] and "mentation" (Angyal),[29] to name only a few descriptions and theories.

Distinguished by its clear, highly suggestive terms, the neatest formulation concerning the dynamics of meaning is Kenneth Burke's statement that, "The relations of any one individual to the public medium can be understood only by examining the 'clusters' or 'equations' in his particular 'psychic economy.' "[30] While written by a foremost critic and applied by him to literary criticism, this statement has important ramifications for political analysis as well: the activity of symbolizing creates the equations necessary to bridge our data gaps and arrange economically the political world (as well as other worlds) around us.

The remainder of this chapter deals with the economy of creating, arranging, and maintaining political symbols in the private imagination.

Turning to the economy of creating, arranging, and maintaining political symbols through equations bridging gaps between data and perception, it seems apparent that,

Men seek for vocabularies that will be faithful *reflections* of reality. To this end, they must develop vocabularies that are *selections* of reality. And any selection of reality must, in certain circumstances function as a *deflection* of reality.[31]

In politics, the primary agency for such reflection, selection, and deflection is language and the action of government so intricately connected with language. Produced by the only animal capable of linguistic power and the concepts built on such power, all of man's activities are implicated in speaking, and surely politics, with its emphasis on conflict, consent, and polity,

28. Talcott Parsons, Robert F. Bales, and Edward A. Shils, *Working Papers in the Theory of Action*, Glencoe, Ill.: The Free Press, 1953), Chapter 2. For another theory by a modern sociologist from a somewhat different point of view, see Arnold M. Rose, "A Systematic Summary of Symbolic Interaction Theory," in *Human Behavior and Social Processes, An Interactionist Approach*, (London: Routledge & Kegan Paul, 1962), Chapter 1.
29. *Op. cit.*, p. 57.
30. *A Grammar of Motives*, p. 114.
31. *Ibid.*, p. 59.

contributes richly to our varieties of meaning and in turn is affected by this variety.[32] As a corollary to the assumption of symbolic economy, there seems no simple way out of the question of thought and action. Rather, the two are both instrumental in public affairs. George Herbert Mead phrased this most succinctly when he wrote,

language does not simply symbolize a situation or object which is already there in advance; it makes possible the existence or the appearance of that situation or object, for it is a part of the mechanism whereby that situation or object is created.[33]

The point to remember here is that any action denotes an intention, and intention means thought has entered the picture.[34] Surely politics encloses a realm of action *and* speech.[35]

Symbolic economy really subsumes three problems, compressed into one system: there are certain components of the human mind's experience which "elicit consciousness, beliefs, emotions, and usages, respecting other components of its experience. The former set of components are the 'symbols,' and the latter set constitute the 'meaning' of the symbols."[36] In other words three variables present themselves: experience (symbols), perception (meaning), and a system linking experience and perception. As noted in Chapter Three, "experience," as used by social scientists generally, provides an economical expression of greater precision than "existence" but also limits our perceptual space unduly. In the place of the more fashion-

32. Ralph Linton, *The Study of Man, An Introduction* (New York: D. Appleton-Century Co., 1936), Chapter 6; Max F. Müller, *The Science of Language*, 2 volumes (London: Longmans, Green & Co., 1891), I, 520–527.

33. *Mind, Self and Society*, edited by Charles W. Morris (Chicago: The University of Chicago Press, 1934) (copyright © 1934 by the University of Chicago), p. 78; Herbert Blumer, "Society as Symbolic Interaction" in *Human Behavior and Social Processes*, Chapter 9; Anselm Strauss, *Mirrors and Masks, the Search for Identity* (New York: The Free Press of Glencoe, Illinois, 1959), Chapter 1.

34. Stuart Hampshire, *Thought and Action* (London: Chatto and Windus, 1959), Chapter 2.

35. Hannah Arendt, *The Human Condition*, (Chicago: The University of Chicago Press, 1958), Chapter V; Edelman, *op. cit.*

36. Whitehead, *Symbolism*, p. 8.

able "experience," therefore, let us substitute "existence," and mean by the latter term the hypothetical periphery surrounding empirical phenomena, that is, the boundaries or "ground" for sense experience (Planck's "element of mystery").

In the system of linkage, an obvious transition is made from symbols to meanings, in which each retains a certain autonomy relative to the other. Thus, no symbol need be exhausted by any one meaning, and meaning can hardly be contained by symbolic exactitude short of using mathematical or some other restrictive logic. In Whitehead's words,

In analysis of the total activity involved in perception of the symbolic reference must be referred to the percipient. Such symbolic reference requires something in common between symbol and meaning which can be expressed without reference to the perfected percipient; but it also requires some activity of the percipient which can be considered without recourse either to the particular symbol or its particular meaning.[37]

Hence, an analytic distinction can be drawn between "symbol" and "symbolization" and the following two sections will discuss each part of the distinction. But first a few words are necessary concerning two general (and rather obvious) problems arising from the use and abuse of symbols in politics.

First, it remains imperative for science that the process of symbolization be separated from symbolic referent. As the eminent historian of science, George Sarton, once stated,

It is only after centuries of apparently sterile but necessary quarrels and after the final establishment of the experimental method and attitude that we have slowly learned to consider words as symbols, which, as far as scientific purposes are concerned, would be usefully replaced by arbitrary signs having no signification but the one explicitly defined. The distinction between names and things is now so deeply rooted in the mind of scientifically trained men that they would find it difficult to understand how they could ever be confused, if they did not detect examples of such confusion almost every day in their own environment.[38]

37. *Ibid.*, p. 9.
38. *Introduction to the History of Science*, 3 volumes (Baltimore: Williams & Wilkins, 1927), Carnegie Institution of Washington Publication Number 376, I, 7.

This complaint raises a specter of "the tyranny of words" (Stuart Chase) or the despotism of our "symbolic accessories" (Whitehead). Symbols achieve lives of their own and this separates them somewhat from the lives of their makers, particularly in the realm of ordinary discourse. While scientists might readily agree with Percy W. Bridgman's claim that scientific truths depend upon the operations of nature's tormentors,[39] politicians and ordinary citizens, including frequently these same scientists acting as citizens, may not hold such manipulative views of the polity and its symbols.

We constantly speak of "constitutional limits," "separation of powers," "federalism," and "due process," just as the Soviets employ shibboleths of "class conflict," "higher communism," and "democratic centralism," and our usages conjure up tangible arrangements, experiential truths where in fact symbols exist along with structures. Plainly, many actors in both the United States and the Soviet Union think they are limited by certain symbolic expressions, though in reality the structures of such limitations have different meanings from participant to participant. We immediately jump to the erroneous conclusion that this demonstrates a disparity between thought and action, not to mention devious chicane, because participants may say one thing and do another.

Actually, political participants are not so simply "saying" and "doing"; rather, they are *saying* two different things to themselves—"say this" and "do that." Sometimes the two "sayings" involve different messages such as, "Speak softly, but carry a big stick." Other times the message to action is hypothetical and deceptive: "Act as if you wanted peace, but circum-

39. *The Logic of Modern Physics* (New York: Macmillan, 1927), p. 5; Heisenberg, *op. cit.*, pp. 38–39; Albert Einstein, "The Fundaments of Theoretical Physics," Feigl and Brodbeck, *op. cit.*, pp. 253–261. But Einstein refuses to abandon "actually and forever, the idea of direct representation of physical reality in space and time," though presently "we are quite without any deterministic theory directly describing the events themselves and in consonance with the facts" (pp. 261, 260). Durkheim saw the scientist in the role of nature's tormentor—see his *Montesquieu et Rousseau, précursors de la sociologie*, p. 96.

stances nevertheless have weight too." On occasion the impetus is hypothetical without any trace of deception; for example, "I must act as if peace were possible, even though all portents indicate otherwise, for the act may have some influence."
The first problem, then, involves movement of symbols away from their users. Conceived in space and time, symbols become historical, traditional, and cultural.[40] Language itself is symbolism and has frequently been cited by Idealists as one reason why society transcends the individual.[41] Transcendence can be only a manner of speaking, but it may also carry more emotional overtones (as for the Idealists), because symbols enhance the meaning of things, lending emotional reinforcement to supposedly "objective" facts. Any situation is presumably "objective" in the sense that it contains raw material perceived by the mind, which in turn, however, acts as a curved mirror reflecting the object in more or less distorted pictures.[42] Whitehead observed that "the life of humanity can easily be overwhelmed by its symbolic accessories,"[43] though obviously he was speaking too generally since such "overwhelming" varies from culture to culture.[44] Whitehead further noted that the impulse to make symbols—"mankind must always be masquerading"—constitutes no idle masquerade.

40. This corresponds to Georg Simmel's concern about the opposition between *life* and *form* in civilization. See his essay, *Der Konflikt der Modernen Kultur*, 2nd edition, 1921, discussed by Fritz Pappenheim, *The Alienation of Modern Man* (New York: Monthly Review Press, 1959), Chapter 1.
41. Whitehead, *Symbolism*, p. 62. For instance, F. H. Bradley averred that the child "learns, or already perhaps has learned, to speak, and here he appropriates the common heritage of his race; the tongue that he makes his own is his country's language, it is (or it should be) the same that others speak, and it carries into his mind the ideas and sentiments of the race (over this I need not stay), and stamps them indelibly." "My Station and Its Duties" in *Ethical Studies* (Selected Essays) (New York: The Library of Liberal Arts, 1951), pp. 108–109.
42. Angyal, *op. cit.*, p. 76.
43. *Symbolism*, p. 61.
44. See Margaret Mead, "Public Opinion Mechanisms among Primitive People," *Public Opinion Quarterly* (1937), No. 3, pp. 5–16. It also varies within cultures from one subculture to another.

The function of these elements is to be definite, manageable, reproducible, and also to be charged with their own emotional efficacity: symbolic transference invests their correlative meanings with some or all of these attributes of the symbols, and thereby lifts the meanings into an intensity of definite effectiveness—as elements in knowledge, emotion, and purpose—an effectiveness which the meanings may, or may not, deserve on their own account. The object of symbolism is the enhancement of the importance of what is symbolized.[45]

The statement, "The object of symbolism is the enhancement of the importance of what is symbolized," readily indicates why symbols can become tyrannical in their autonomous tendencies. Needless to say, the sloppiness of human thinking gives aid and comfort to symbolific autonomy, but when Sarton laments the plight of even scientific men *as scientists*, a condition to which Bridgman attributed the shock of Einstein's revelatory discoveries,[46] then the matter is not simply either the sloppiness of our language or the carelessness of our thinking, as George Orwell once opined.[47] It is tempting and comforting for educated men to adopt the younger Plato's view of the "common herd," a view later amended after experience taught him lessons about the "better" people,[48] than to recognize that man is the symbolizing animal par excellence yet ironically becomes hopelessly ensnared in his own symbolic devices. "In mental processes," to draw once again on Andras Angyal's wisdom, "there is a kind of fusion between symbol and referent. The object is not only meant, but also experienced, in the perception."[49]

Examples of such symbolic autonomy could be multiplied indefinitely. In his book entitled *Untersuchungen über die Grundfragen des Sprachlebens* (1885) Philip Wegener recog-

45. *Symbolism*, pp. 62–63.

46. *Op. cit.*, Chapter I.

47. In his "Politics and the English Language" (1946), in *The Orwell Reader* (New York: Harvest Books, n.d.), pp. 355–366, at 355. Orwell was referring directly to politics, though he applied the sentiment more universally as well.

48. Compare the hierarchies of wisdom and pleasure in the *Republic* and *Philebus* after reading Plato's intervening *Seventh Epistle*.

49. *Op. cit.*, p. 67.

nized two general principles of linguistic development: *emendation* (syntactical evolution) and *metaphor* (source of generality). Evolving through these two means, language reaches out to embace many exigencies and develops through increased practicality an autonomy of its own.[50] Other symbolisms, such as mathematics, music, myth, and ritual, develop their own logics. While such symbolic expansion has aided man in controlling and ordering his environment and has proved instrumental in the astonishing advances made by modern science, this imperialism exacts its price. Not only are atoms and elements phrased in symbolic terms which deny us immediate experience with these phenomena, but moral life is also negotiated in symbols. In either case "immediacy" is mediated by symbolic transactions. And Langer, for one, sees such morality as a mixed blessing at best, whatever euphoria might be generated about the progress of the abstract sciences.

Because our moral life is negotiated so largely by symbols, it is more oppressive than the morality of animals . . . we control each other's merely incipient behavior with fantasies of force. We employ sanctions, threaten vague penalties, and try to forestall offences by merely exhibiting the symbols of the consequences.[51]

While the only symbolic animal, man is by no means freer than the beasts of the field, though his symbolizing fantasies allow him to think so (just as other such fantasies impose restraint). On the contrary, imprisoned by symbols, men are more like machines than they care to think: amenable to symbolic manipulation, they can be "programmed" as computers are, for cybernetics and computer technology have proven extremely adaptable to "human" situations.[52] Whitehead counseled,

50. Langer, *op. cit.*, pp. 121–127.
51. *Ibid.*, p. 241. On moral symbols as a linguistic problem, see Richard M. Hare, *The Language of Morals* (London: Oxford University Press, 1952).
52. Norbert Wiener, *The Human Use of Human Beings, Cybernetics and Society* (Boston: Houghton Mifflin, 1950), particularly Chapters 3–5; *Cybernetics* (1948); also, Karl Deutsch, *The Nerves of Government* (New York: The Free Press of Glencoe, Illinois, 1963), Part II.

The life of humanity can easily be overwhelmed by its symbolic accessories. A continuous process of pruning, and of adaptation to a future ever requiring new forms of expression, is a necessary function of every society. The successful adaptation of old symbols to changes of social structure is the final mark of wisdom in sociological statesmanship. Also an occasional revolution in symbolism is required.[53]

While promising the wonders of science fiction, however, the programming potentials of human symbols constantly encounter man's "vulgar folly." Meaning's diversity presents the second problem of symbol-making. "We require," says Whitehead, "both the advantages of social preservation, and the contrary stimulus of heterogeneity derived from freedom. The society is to run smoothly amidst the divergencies of its individuals."[54] On strictly utilitarian grounds there should remain plenty of room for divergent modes of symbolization in order to accommodate the human organism's thrust outward toward autonomy.[55] "National life has to face the disruptive elements introduced by these extreme claims for individual idiosyncrasies," Whitehead asserted during a hiatus of nationalistic sentiment in the twentieth-century world.[56]

But such divergency occurs not only within individual communities: symbolism in language, myth, and ritual produces many varieties of human cultures while simultaneously nourishing the philosophic hope, based on the vague notion that diverse symbolisms can somehow be uniformly programmed, that someday a harmony of all cultures can exist. George Herbert Mead, an ardent cosmopolitan in the spirit of Herder two centuries earlier, expressed his conviction that increased "national-mind-

53. *Symbolism*, p. 61.
54. *Ibid.*, p. 65.
55. What Alan Barth has called "the utility of freedom," *The Loyalty of Free Men* (New York: Viking Press, 1951), Chapter 10. See also Christian Bay, *The Structure of Freedom* (Stanford: Stanford University Press, 1958), pp. 95–100; Bertrand Russell, *Authority and the Individual* (New York: Simon and Schuster, 1949), Chapter 3; and of course, John Stuart Mill's *On Liberty*.
56. *Symbolism*, p. 65.

edness," that is, closer identification between the individual's interests and those of his community, would lead to greater security for the self and to increased "international-mindedness."[57] "Civilization is not," he wrote in 1929, "an affair of reasonableness; it is an affair of social organization. The selfhood of a community depends upon such an organization that common goods do become the ends of the individuals of the community."[58] Assuming civilization "is an affair of social organization," and defining social organization in terms of symbols and interactional meanings,[59] Mead was no doubt thinking of the unifying potentials proffered by symbolic programming.

Some efforts to explore the subtleties of meaning on the international scale have been undertaken by experts in "psycholinguistics" under the leadership of Charles E. Osgood.[60] Also, a spate of national character studies has attempted, from differing perspectives and points of view, to ascertain the variations and uniformities within international society. But on the surface it appears that man's symbolific efforts, by their very proliferation and protean forms, both divide and unite us in this common symbolic undertaking. Indeed, human beings even sacrifice their lives for symbolic political entities where linguistic confusions abound. How comforting for the thousands buried at Gettysburg to find that symbol and referent in "federalism" must not be confused! Or how interesting for the millions of casualties and victims in Hitler's Germany that they fell prey to such evocative symbols as "humanity" (*Menschheit*) which were manipulated in order to indict the Jews (who were *die Parasiten der Menschheit*)![61]

57. This was Herder's thesis one hundred-fifty years earlier.

58. "National-Mindedness and International-Mindedness," *International Journal of Ethics*, XXXIX (July 1929), 385–407, at 407.

59. *Mind, Self and Society*, pp. 253–260.

60. See *Psycholinguistics: A Survey of Theory and Research Problems*, edited by Charles E. Osgood (Baltimore: Waverly Press, 1954); Charles E. Osgood, in collaboration with George J. Suci and Percy H. Tannebaum, *The Measurement of Meaning* (Urbana: University of Illinois Press, 1957), *passim*.

61. *Der Nationalsozialismus Dokumente 1933–1945*, edited by Walther Hofer (Frankfurt a.M.: Fischer Bucherei, 1957), p. 281.

Naturally, no one *wants* to make these "mistakes" again, which is probably untrue, of course. We make *these* mistakes because we are human, involved in the flux of history, where we, alone among the animals, enjoy the pleasures and vicissitudes of both guilt and innocence. As Hegel so presciently observed, we are guilty because we are historical (he could have added "and symbolic").[62] But this does not excuse the hideous excesses of the Nazi regime, because "excess" itself furnishes the one baseline which remains for judging human conduct in a world of symbolic relativity, a baseline established upon some men's stubborn insistence that experiential reality and standards of thought must exist.[63] Arendt notes of Adolf Eichmann that while he was an ordinary man and any ordinary man *could* have done what he did in the "Jewish question" (the strength of totalitarianism relies on "normal" people), the fact remains that Eichmann did it.[64]

Experiential reality and standards of thought exist and persist because community as well as chaos can be founded on language. But when two or more individuals cannot attach the same value to vocal combinations and then use these combinations for communicating ideas, language becomes nothing but sound and fury, or "polemic and insult" as Camus characterized our age. It does not follow from the old saw, "We are all guilty," that anything is excusable. Yet this tortuous question has never been finally resolved, and in literature—a mirror for everyone—the issue has driven at least one character, Ivan Karamzov, insane. The moral world deals with specific cases and specific judgments in situations of social and political interaction. Hence, one cannot ignore the presence of evil in human affairs, for to ignore it would make evil "banal," in Arendt's words, but would not exorcise its presence. Yet to avow evil's existence one must do so symbolically as an historical person

62. *The Philosophy of History* (1822), in *The Philosophy of Hegel*, edited by Carl J. Friedrich (New York: Modern Library, 1953), p. 19.

63. Arendt, *The Origins of Totalitarianism*, p. 474.

64. Arendt, *Eichmann in Jerusalem* (New York: The Viking Press, 1963), pp. 254–256.

conscious of the hard work that a community of moral limits requires.[65]

"Meaning is not a quality, but a *function* of a term . . . in its total relation to the other terms about it," Susanne Langer states.[66] "Symbols are not proxy for their objects, but are vehicles for the conception of objects. . . . In talking *about* things we have conceptions of them, not the things themselves; and *it is the conceptions, not the things, that symbols* directly 'mean.' "[67] Herein lies the basis for both the autonomy (and possible tyranny) of symbols and the diverse uses to which such symbols are put. Does this condemn men to a world of symbolic and moral relativity? Does it in the political field? Obviously it does, with one important qualification. Through symbols, contingencies are envisaged in time and space; man's "power of envisagement" is denied the other animals. With this power, however, comes what Langer calls "the burden of understanding." Picture, in other words, a universe where every person, from nuclear physicist to illiterate,

lives not only in a place, but in Space; not only at a time, but in History. So he must conceive a world and a law of the world, a pattern of life, and a way of meeting death. All these things he knows and he had to make some adaptation to their reality.[68]

Langer agrees with Whitehead that "the essence of freedom is the practicability of purpose." Yet mankind "has chiefly suffered from the frustration of its prevalent purposes, even such

65. On "polemic and insult" see Albert Camus, "Le témoin de la liberté" (1948), *Actuelles, chroniques 1944–1948* (Paris: Gallimard, 1950), p. 258. On language, communication, and community John Dewey, *Experience and Nature*, second edition (1929) (New York: Dover Publications, 1958), Chapter 5; Linton, *op. cit.*, p. 83; G. H. Mead, *Mind, Self and Society*, pp. 138, 149; Whitehead, *Symbolism*, p. 68. On society and morality, Dorothy Emmet, *Rules, Roles and Relations* (London: Macmillan, 1966).

66. *Op. cit.*, p. 56.

67. *Ibid.*, p. 61.

68. *Ibid.*, p. 241. See also Peter Winch, *The Idea of a Social Science* (London: Routledge & Kegan Paul, 1958), Chapter 5.

as belong to the very definition of its species."[69] Adapting realistically seems the only answer, but Langer is too consistent to believe that such adaptation need be only in the direction of more and better science and other discursive knowledge. Even if it is true that "speech becomes increasingly discursive, practical, prosaic,"[70] how does one understand the modern "Wotanism" (C. G. Jung's expression) of Nazi Germany? Niceties in linguistic analysis or symbolic logic (in its more conventional modes) might explain the multiple usages of "humanity" but hardly be able to judge the qualitative transformations symbols undergo in the grips of political rhetoric and related practices.

Langer's answer, phrased in terms of a greatly amended semanticism, seems entirely consistent with her theory of all-pervasive symbolism, including both discursive and presentational forms. Answering this hypothetical query about relativism, she also supplies political theorists with a leading proposition for what might be termed a "theory of symbolic relativity": her theory of mind is based upon the symbolific function and its morphology of significance. In other words, significances change and can be plotted morphologically in a single system, because the force which governs the vast and mythical symbols of Race, Unity, Manifest Destiny, and Humanity, is the same force which quietly philosophizes in the cloisters at Oxford, Harvard, and Berkeley: "the force which governs [the age of unreason] is still the force of *mind*, the impulse toward symbolic formulation, expression, and understanding of experience."[71]

A relativity theory both condemns and frees men. Those who understand this paradoxical epistemology (and axiology) are condemned, like Camus' Sisyphus, "to ceaselessly rolling a rock to the top of a mountain, whence the stone would fall back of its

69. Alfred North Whitehead, *Adventures of Ideas* (New York: Macmillan Co., 1933), p. 84; Langer, *op. cit.*, p. 244.

70. *Ibid.*, p. 126.

71. *Ibid.*, p. 246. See also Lewis Mumford, "The Revolt of the Demons" (Review of C. G. Jung's *Memories, Dreams, Reflections*, Pantheon), *The New Yorker*, XL (May 23, 1964), 155–185. Though united in a single system, differences between types of symbols are quite significant, of course—see the reference to Quine's epistemology in footnote 27, Chapter 4, above.

own weight."[72] But in this absurdity, continues Camus, there also resides a kind of freedom.

I leave Sisyphus at the foot of the mountain! One always finds one's burden again. But Sisyphus teaches the higher fidelity that negates the gods and raises rocks. He too concludes that all is well. This universe henceforth without master seems to him neither sterile nor futile. Each atom of that stone, each mineral flake of that night-filled mountain, in itself forms a world. The struggle itself toward the heights is enough to fill a man's heart. One must imagine Sisyphus happy.[73]

It is not the task of political analysis to depict "history without events . . . the dead monotony of sameness, unfolded in time . . ."[74] The analyst must "detect this unexpected *new* with all its implications in any given period and to bring out the full power of its significance. . . . History is a story which has many beginnings but no end. . . ." Arendt's plea is for the "understanding heart" of Solomon, "understanding" equivalent to "imagination," which is "concerned with the particular darkness of the human heart and the peculiar density which surround everything that is real." Imagination means "distancing" things which are too close, and "bridging the abyss" to things far removed. Arendt concludes that to be at home on this earth, "even at the price of being at home in this century," men must take part in "the interminable dialogue with its essence"; that is, men must engage in understanding or imagination.[75]

A thorough understanding of symbolism which refuses to narrow our perceptual circumference to "what we know" under

72. Camus' celebrated notion of "absurdity" and "rebellion." See *The Myth of Sisyphus and Other Essays*, translated by Justin O'Brien (New York: Vintage Books, 1958), p. 88; see also, Camus, *The Rebel*, translated by Anthony Bower (New York: Vintage Books, 1956), pp. 271–277. Richard Wollheim notes the significance of "absurdity" and "rebellion" for political theory—"The Political Philosophy of Existentialism," *Cambridge Journal*, VII (October 1953), 3–19.

73. *The Myth of Sisyphus*, p. 91.

74. Hannah Arendt, "Understanding and Politics," *Partisan Review*, XX (July–August 1953), 377–392, at 389.

75. *Ibid.*, 392. Or men must become "engaged" in understanding and imagination.

some disputed theory of knowledge or learning will enhance the
political theorist's comprehension of politics. Regarding citizenship, such interest will facilitate understanding of those symbolic engagements between members and their political order
which comprise the citizen's role.

### Types of Political Symbols

Before discussing how symbols are internalized by participants as working hypotheses for their political actions, it might
prove instructive to classify political symbols. Such a classification aids, in the first place, in keeping symbolic referents and
symbolization logically separate and, second, encourages the
appreciation of symbolism's complexity in political life. Every
symbol need not be manifest to have importance and relevance
for individuals. Freud's dream analysis establishes a distinction
between "manifest" and "latent" content in dreams and in
"other psychopathological structures."[76] Parallels to Freud's
work appear in sociology—Robert K. Merton, George Herbert
Mead, Emile Durkheim, William Graham Sumner, Robert M.
MacIver, W. I. Thomas, Florian Znaniecki, to name a few.[77]
Symbols are not always apparent and in many instances require
the interpretation of trained analysts in political studies as
elsewhere.[78]

The following analysis leans toward the philosophical in its
approach, though adopting a classification of symbols modeled
after the work of an anthropologist, Edward Sapir, and a psychologist, Andras Angyal, a philosophical approach which expands experience to existence and seems most fruitful for under-

76. Sigmund Freud, *On Dreams*, translated by James Strachey; Copyright © 1952 by W. W. Norton & Company, Inc., New York; pp. 27,
94.

77. See Robert K. Merton, *Social Theory and Social Structure*, revised
edition (Glencoe, Ill.: The Free Press, 1957), pp. 60 ff.

78. For example, Harold D. Lasswell, Nathan Leites and Associates,
*The Language of Politics* (New York: George W. Stewart, 1949); and
Thurman Arnold, *The Symbols of Government* (New Haven: Yale
University Press, 1935); Jeremy Bentham, *A Handbook of Political
Fallacies* (1824); Edelman, *op. cit.*

standing political symbols. While Freud surely pioneered the study of symbols, both he and Jung tended to employ symbolism for interpreting unconscious and abnormal phenomena only, as "forms of indirect representation" which "must not be immediately intelligible."[79] Such an approach restricts symbolic activity to areas of action where forms of indirect representation are not immediately intelligible, confining its attention to phenomena latent with psychopathological significance, such as dreams, where actors (for example, "dreamers") are, by nature, "themselves unaware of the meaning of the symbols they use. . . ."[80] For interpretations, patients go to their psychoanalysts.

Our discussion relies on a theory which broadens symbolific activity to all realms of life, from the most discursive enterprise to the most presentational, from highly conscious enlightenment to the depths of the unconscious. This seems to fit the facts of political life more accurately than views which identify only the abnormal or mythical or ideological with symbolism, and contrast "symbolic" behavior to "real" behavior. Such realism seemingly follows Whitehead's statement that "Hard-headed men want facts and not symbols,"[81] but fails to heed his further observation that "Symbolism is no mere idle fancy or corrupt degeneration: it is inherent in the very texture of human life."[82]

Those who "realistically" separate thought and action are wholly unrealistic, for action itself is symbolic. When viewed by others it becomes *perceived* action, which means that it is interpreted by active percipients who convert what they see into their

79. *On Dreams*, p. 107. To quote in full: "There is only one method by which a dream which expresses erotic wishes can succeed in appearing innocently nonsexual in its manifest contest. The material of the sexual ideas must not be represented as such, but must be replaced in the content of the dream by hints, allusions and similar forms of indirect representation, that which is employed in dreams must not be immediately intelligible. The modes of representation which fulfill these conditions are so usually described as 'symbols' of the things which they represent."

80. *Ibid.*

81. *Symbolism*, p. 60.

82. *Ibid.*, pp. 61–62.

own coinage. Antitheses between "ideas" and "phenomena" are sheer illusion, therefore. Again we return to Kierkegaard's warnings against *objective* madness, which should be placed in the same bracket with *subjective* madness. We are consigned forever to a world of images: our task is to perfect our images of nature, not to find "nature itself." True, we still remain in a world of 'images,' " Cassirer stated,

> but these are not images which reproduce a self-subsistent world of "things"; they are image-worlds whose principle and origin are to be sought in an autonomous creation of the spirit. Through them alone we see what we call "reality," and in them alone we possess it: for the highest objective truth that is accessible to the spirit is ultimately the form of its own activity.[83]

A symbolic analysis that puts emphasis on symbolism's universally functional character in all regions of the mind from the most enlightened to most hideous holds promise for the study of politics. Adopting the approach of Cassirer and Langer, one is better able to see the manifold ways in which individual citizens are "involved" in politics around themselves. Through symbols, linguistic and otherwise, citizens translate any environment into their own environment, which explains why symbolism stands in the center of citizenship's dimension of private attitude. In sociological parlance, citizens "internalize" their political "system."[84] This functional quality inherent in all symbols gives them a certain flexibility, though symbols also tend toward an autonomy away from the user as they become artifacts characteristic of a culture.

We have noted the economical function of symbols: paraphrasing Edward Sapir, symbolism covers many apparently dissimilar modes of behavior with more or less elaborate signs pointing to ideas and actions of great complexity or consequence. For Sapir, all symbols share two generic characteristics,

83. From *Philosophie der symbolischen Formen*, selection in *Theories of Society*, edited by T. Parsons, *et al.*, II, 1007.

84. See Talcott Parsons, *et al.*, *Working Papers in the Theory of Action*, pp. 39 ff; and G. Almond and S. Verba, *The Civic Culture, Political Attitudes and Democracy in Five Nations* (Princeton: Princeton University Press, 1963), *passim.*

substituting for "some more closely intermediating form of behavior" and expressing "a condensation of energy" whose actual significance stands out of all proportion to the triviality of its form. Again, the economical value of symbols appears in Sapir's twofold classification of "referential symbolism" (agreed upon *devices* for reference, for example, telegraph codes and flags) and "condensation symbolism" ("a highly condensed form of substitutive *behavior* for direct expression allowing for the ready release of emotional tension in conscious and unconscious form"). In actual behavior both types blend together.[85] Similar to Sapir's classification, though not so elaborate, is Angyal's division between symbols which constitute "an abbreviation of the primary objects" and those which represent "something remotely related to the object."[86] Note again the accent on economy in both types, and on an abbreviated *device* in one symbol type, and something more diffuse and substitutive in other type.

In this connection Edmund Burke, by no means a psychologist (even by the eighteenth-century standards of Bentham, Diderot, Helvetius, Rousseau, and others), devoted some attention to "such things as affect us in various manners, according to their natural powers" and those "associations made at that early season, which we find it very hard afterwards to distinguish from natural effects."[87] And Freud, of course, established a similar classification for psychopathological phenomena in his interpretation of dreams:

There are dreams which come almost without any displacement. These are the ones which make sense and are intelligible, such for instance, as those which we have recognized as undisguised wishful dreams. On the other hand, there are dreams in which not a single piece of the dream thoughts has retained its own psychical value, or in which everything that is essential in the dream thoughts has been

85. Sapir, "Symbolism," *op. cit.*, p. 1019.
86. *Op. cit.*, p. 57.
87. *A Philosophical Enquiry into the Origin of Our Ideas of the Sublime and Beautiful*, second edition (1757), Part II, in *The Works and Correspondence of Edmund Burke*, 8 volumes (London: Francis and John Rivington, 1852), II, 649.

replaced by something trivial. And we can find a complete series of transitional cases between these two extremes.[88]

Here we shall combine Sapir's and Angyal's approaches and apply the idea of symbolic representation to political things as viewed from the citizen's standpoint. Those symbols which constitute "abbreviations" of primary objects will be "symbols of instrumental reference," and those which represent "something remotely related to the object" and simultaneously involve some behavior which is itself representational will be "symbols of condensed affect." Needless to say, these two types express analytic opposites, with actual blending quite common. Our distinction rests on a difference between instruments and acts where in one case the symbol is a *device* or *instrument* which evokes some kind of response, cognitive and/or affective, while in the other case, *behavior* itself is symbolic. "Old Glory" represents a totemic device, whereas the soldier's salute or that "chill up and down my spine every time Old Glory passes" are affective responses. Pictures are symbols, but so are acts and feelings by those who view them.

*Symbols of Instrumental Reference.* All manifest governmental symbols, including the highly developed language of politics, are pregnant with meaning, even though specific usages may change from context to context. Such symbols provide instrumental reference, comprising more or less agreed upon devices for representation and no doubt developing later in the history of mankind than "condensation" symbols.[89] The flag supplies a prototype for this kind of symbol, though to the extent that it prompts ceremony it is more than a convenient insignia and carries emotional overtones, blending into condensed affect as well.[90] However, the very sight of a flag conjures an immediate

88. *On Dreams*, p. 53.
89. Sapir, "Symbolism," *op. cit.*, p. 1019.
90. Clearly, the flag of National Socialism provided a device for conjuring meaning. In Hitler's words, "*A Symbol it really* is! In *red* we see the social idea of the movement, in *white* the nationalist idea, in the *swastika* the mission of the struggle for the victory of the Aryan man." Quoted in William L. Shirer, *The Rise and Fall of the Third Reich* (New York: Simon and Schuster, 1960), p. 44.

identification accomplished through cultural conditioning. Many other political symbols have instrumental value. Walter Bagehot's discussion of the five functions of English monarchy in the mid-nineteenth century demonstrated the instrumentalism implicit in royalty's symbolic richness. "The best reason why Monarchy is a strong government," Bagehot wrote, "is that it is an intelligible government. . . . It is often said that men are ruled by their imaginations; but it would be truer to say that they are governed by the weakness of the imagination."[91] He continued,

> The characteristic of the English Monarchy is that it retains the feelings by which the heroic kings governed their rude age, and has added the feelings by which the constitutions of later Greece ruled in more refined ages. . . . The Greek legislator had not to combine in his polity men like the laborers of Somersetshire, and men like Mr. Grote. He had not to deal with a community in which primitive barbarism lay as a recognized basis to acquired civilization. WE HAVE. We have no slaves to keep down by special terrors and independent legislation. But we have whole classes unable to comprehend the idea of a constitution—unable to feel the least attachment to impersonal laws. . . . A Republic has only difficult ideas in government; a Constitutional Monarchy has an easy idea too; it has a comprehensible element for the vacant many, as well as complex laws and notions for the inquiring few.

On the premise that a "royal family sweetens politics by the seasonable addition of nice and pretty events," Bagehot outlined the five functions of monarchy in Great Britain. First, "royalty is a government in which the attention of the nation is concentrated on one person doing interesting actions." Second, it strengthens English government with the durability of religion. Third, the monarch heads society ("society" defined as "the union of people for amusement and conversation").[92] Fourth, the Crown epitomizes English morality. Finally, monarchy acts as a disguise for transfers and upheavals of political power. Through all these functions runs the common symbol of unity.

91. *The English Constitution* (Washington and London: M. Walter Dunne Universal Classics Library, 1901), p. 26.
92. Previous citations, *ibid.*, pp. 29–37.

By remaining "aloof and solitary" from ordinary political hum-
drum, English royalty

seems to order, but it never seems to struggle. It is commonly hidden
like a mystery, and sometimes paraded like a pageant, but in neither
case is it contentious. The nation is divided into parties, but the
Crown is of no party. Its apparent separation from business is that
which removes it both from the enmities and from desecration,
which preserves its mystery, which enables it to combine the affection of conflicting parties—to be a visible symbol of unity to those
still so imperfectly educated as to need a symbol.[93]

Aside from his persistent identification of symbolism with
imperfect education—a mistake often made even by contemporary political scientists, as if their language were not a symbolism—Bagehot allowed his "political realism" to get the better of
him. His contention that "a Republic has only difficult ideas in
government" does not mean that in a Republic everyone appreci-
ates this difficulty. On the contrary, precisely because republican
forms—notably in the United States and France, the two oldest
republics—have no ready-made "easy idea" like monarchy, easy
ideas must be artificially created. There will always be those
who need "symbols" in Bagehot's sense, that is, "those still so
imperfectly educated as to need a symbol." But alas, all mankind seems imperfectly educated. Political leadership in the
early history of the United States faced this problem and
immediately set about raising the Constitution itself into such an
"easy idea."[94]

In another connection, but instructive here, one writer has
contrasted Luther and Calvin on a similar point: Luther resolved
the question of freedom and authority in religion in the direction
of freedom, but "the burden of freedom, save as a Paul or a

93. *Ibid.*, p. 35. Harold J. Laski was obviously influenced by Bagehot's analysis of "the metaphysics of limited monarchy" when he wrote:
"An active King, whose opinions were a matter of public concern, is
unthinkable within the framework of the British constitution." *Parliamen-
tary Government in England* (New York: Viking Press, 1947), p. 333.

94. See Arendt, *On Revolution* (London: Faber and Faber, 1963),
pp. 198 f; and Max Lerner, *Ideas for the Ice Age* (New York: Viking
Press, 1941), pp. 241–242; Wolin, *op. cit.*, p. 294, note 11.

Luther understands it, is too much."[95] Calvin, a practical man and the founder of a political state as well as a reformist denomination, confronted this fact of life realistically and his *Institutes of the Christian Religion* abound in legal terminology (he was a lawyer by training) and order the universe with the same dedication one finds in Aquinas' *Summa Theologica*.

A more general criticism can be leveled at Bagehot. If language, even in its most discursive forms, is symbolic, then even the more educated and perceptive need and use symbols. Not only the "easy idea" is symbolic; "complex laws and notions for the inquiring few" are too. Symbolic forms, omnipresent in all activities involving the mind, of which politics and citizenship surely present outstanding examples, remain as essential for historians and political analysts such as Grote and Bagehot, as for the "laborers of Somersetshire," even though the logical orders and rationative levels of these essential symbols may vary. "Ideas" enable us to handle situations more easily, so that what Bagehot called an "easy idea" seems redundant. The words "monarch," "constitution," "republic" and "politician" find expression in both Bagehot's writings and the laborers' conversations and perform the same shorthand function that any idea performs, but their meanings change with the relational context or placement of these words.

What appears most important here is that these expressions *conjure* meanings and do not simply *stand for* reality; in other words, political shorthand *evokes* as well as *substitutes*, and occurs even when the shorthand appears as so many "x's" and "y's" in place of verbal political expressions. In the United States, the Constitution's image (and invariably we capitalize "Constitution" just as we capitalize "God") provides much the same meaningful symbolism as the Royal Family, though specific meanings will vary widely from a constitutional lawyer (and among various constitutional lawyers) to a Daughter of the American Revolution (and among various Daughters of the American Revolution).

95. See J. S. Whale, *The Protestant Tradition* (Cambridge: Cambridge University Press, 1959), paperbound, p. 123.

Nor must one forget the "incantatory effects" of all words as symbols, "inviting men to make themselves over in the image of their imagery,"[96] whereby political scientists become political scientists when specific symbol-patterns, adopted in graduate school and perfected over the years, guide their research, and DARs become DARs when their self-image conforms to their incantations.

If one alleges a single "accurate" or "correct" meaning for a particular political word, then one must carefully state in what context one places this word.[97] Political science has reasonably clear definitions for "constitution" and "constitutionalism," yet scholars haggle over these terms. Similarly, the laws and conventions of modern citizenship are reasonably clear from nation to nation, yet we continue to discuss citizenship and its meanings.[98] While still meaningful, in other contexts political symbols are nevertheless charged with different valences than they are when used by political scientists. The academic analyst is perplexed by the fact that while what he writes within the confines of his own community makes a good deal of sense, and even seems self-evident, outside this circle his audience rapidly diminishes.[99]

96. Kenneth Burke, *Grammar of Motives*, p. 123.
97. See Burke on "Ways of Placement," *ibid.*, Part I.
98. See T. D. Weldon, *The Vocabulary of Politics* (London: Penguin Books, 1953), pp. 19, 45–83.
99. The great danger of intellectual frustration with lack of communication can lead to intellectual withdrawal. See Julien Benda, "De quelques Traits du Monde actuel," *Nouvelle Nouvelle Revue Française* (March 1953), 411–430. A good case study in intellectual frustration and retreat (or advance?) into jargon occurs in French "Existentialism." According to Sartre, the Existentialist credo is, "if I am given this world with its injustices, it is not so that I might contemplate them coldly, but that I might animate them with my indignation, that I might disclose them and create them with their nature as injustices, that is, as abuses to the suppressed." *What Is Literature?* p. 62. But in the *same* book, as he wrote Part IV, "Situation de l'écrivain en 1947," Sartre feared the "present" revolution was about to be "botched-up." Too many novels were already appearing about what he called "sad and stolen holidays" (those novels of Françoise Sagan, for example). Toward the end of this book Sartre fears that French writers have readers, but no important (that is,

Sometimes the scholar, despairing of this communicative limitation, will branch out, expand his energies in more "popular" directions, perhaps committing what Julian Benda called *"la trahison des clerqs"* to become an ideologist.[100] The use one makes of symbols depends upon one's location or situation—one's "symbol situation" (Ogden and Richards) or "placement" (Kenneth Burke)—in political time and space, as does the relationship of those symbols with others in a particular context.[101] Even the use of manifest symbols, where a particular symbol is instrumental, will be situation-bound, although the situation need not be determined for the actor by outside forces.[102]

Interactions between social situations and individual decision-makers create an almost inexhaustible complexity in the world of meaning and reality.[103] Beneath this surface complexity, in every phase of life including the political, move a limited number of meaningful symbols with their own almost inexhaustible variety of meanings. Even monistic reduction to a single

crucial decision-making leaders in public affairs—a power elite) public which could exert influence (*ibid.*, pp. 248–249). René Char—*before liberation*—nourished similar fears about a decline in French civic zeal with the advent of peace. See Arendt's discussion of Char in *On Revolution*, p. 284 ff. For a concise, interesting review of the springtime of French existentialism and its more recent maturity see the entire issue of *Yale French Studies* (Winter 1955–56); also Thomas Molnar, *The Decline of the Intellectual* (Cleveland and New York: Meridian Books, 1961), pp. 305–311.

100. Julien Benda, *The Betrayal of the Intellectuals*, translated by Richard Aldington (Boston: Beacon Press, 1955); and Molnar, *op. cit.*, Chapters 9–10, for comparison of American and European intellectuals today.

101. See the UNESCO survey on "democracy" conducted during 1948–49, and published in *Democracy in a World of Tensions*, edited by Richard McKeon (Chicago: University of Chicago Press, 1951), *passim.*

102. There is no contradiction in asserting that an individual's choice of symbols is limited by his situation, since he may choose his situation to some extent. Nevertheless, citizenship, unlike many situations, is seldom chosen deliberately, nor are its obligations actively sought by most persons.

103. Hampshire, *op. cit.*, pp. 20–22.

"God" or "Unmoved Mover" might still involve an infinity of meanings based upon individual experiences, though presumably an Aristotelian Unmoved Mover transcends experience entirely.

Many political symbols, however, are not so contentious, with most participants in particular situations using them in more or less the same way. Unquestioning usage—such as the American allegiance to "democracy"—gives many political symbols remarkable durability. Other symbols seem stable, but remain latent with variegated meanings as they represent areas of controversy among contending individuals and between struggling groups not yet evident in open warfare. The current belief held by many Americans that their nation has solved the problem of class conflict is contradicted by work alienation evident among both blue-collar and white-collar workers, to say nothing of racial conflict related to economic impoverishment of Negroes. "A nation without class struggle" comprises an elaborate symbol, however, which functions to hide latent conflict.

Similarly, what W. J. Cash (in his *Mind of the South*, 1941) called the "proto-Dorian myth" of white supremacy in the southern United States, serves to sublimate the innervating guilt that region unconsciously feels for its exploitative racial politics in general and its sexual exploitation of Negroes in particular. In any culture there exists both conservation and change, certain areas where a culture focuses its attention and others it deliberately ignores. Applying his theory that "the great variation in form is to be found in the aspect of a culture that is focal to the interests of a people" (and conversely that conservation remains strongest where interest is discouraged), the anthropologist Melville Herskovits writes:

> In modern American life, the focussing of the culture on technology and the associated phases of business activity needed to promote technological change is evident to anyone who will give the matter a moment's thought. We can see this in our readiness to accept technological changes, when contrasted to resistance to changes in economic theory—even though this is a field closely related to technology—or in social institutions or in religion. The lad who tinkers with a broken-down automobile until he has a workable

vehicle, or plays with a set of chemicals is prepared to welcome
"improvements" when he grows up. In this, he is merely responding
to a deep-seated enculturative drive. But nothing comparable exists
outside the focal aspect; it is in these other phases that our cultural
conservatism is most manifest.[104]

E. E. Evans-Pritchard observes of primitive societies.

Political values are relative and . . . the political system is an
equilibrium between opposed tendencies toward fission and fusion,
between the tendency of all groups to segment, and the tendency of
all groups to combine with segments of the same order.[105]

He describes this state as an "ordered society," an "acephalous
kinship state," lacking the niceties of legal institutions and
developed leadership.[106] Yet even with regular institutions and
developed leadership, political society is not much beyond an-
archy and avarice. Montesquieu discovered in all polities—both
advanced and backward—a latent discontent existing beneath
apparent order:

[when] virtue is banished, ambition invades the minds of those who
are disposed to receive it, and avarice possesses the whole community. The objects of their desires are changed; what they were fond
of before has become indifferent; they were free while under the
restraint of laws, but they would fain now be free to act against the

104. *Man and His Works* (New York: Alfred A. Knopf, 1951),
pp. 549–550. It is interesting that we are now thinking in terms of
"space law," necessitated by recent technological advances. Few doubt the
need for such law. But the legislative assemblies of most American states
still refuse to abolish an ancient and retaliatory practice like capital
punishment. We assume here that every culture asks the same basic
questions but answers will differ thus configuring that culture uniquely.
See Clyde Kluckhohn, "Dominant and Variant Value Orientations," in
*Personality in Nature, Society, and Culture*, edited by Clyde Kluckhohn
and H. A. Murray, second edition (New York: Alfred A. Knopf, 1953),
p. 346; "Universal Categories of Culture," in *Anthropology Today*, edited
by Sol Tax, *et al.* (Chicago: University of Chicago Press, 1953),
pp. 507–523; John R. Seeley, *et al.*, *Crestwood Heights, a Study of the
Culture of Suburban Life* (New York: Basic Books, 1956), p. 5.
105. *The Neur* (London: Oxford University Press, 1940),
pp. 143–144, 147.
106. *Ibid.*, p. 181.

law; and as each citizen is like a slave who has run away from his master, that which was a maxim of equity he calls rigor; that which was a rule of action he styles constraint; and to persecution he gives the name of fear. Frugality, and not the thirst of gain, now passes for avarice. Formerly the wealth of individuals constituted the public treasure; but now it has become the patrimony of private persons. The members of the commonwealth riot on the public spoils and its strength is only the power of a few, and the license of many.[107]

Under the exigencies of war, for instance, words even tend "to change their ordinary meanings and to take that which [is] now given them," as Thucydides observed poignantly of the Greek world during the Peloponnesian War.[108]

*Symbols of Condensed Affect.* Political symbols of condensed affect are not characterized by a "device," such as a flag, though incantations of totemic import may circulate round a flag, but by substitutive "behavior," "allowing for the ready release of emotional tension in conscious and unconscious form."[109] One such example of condensation symbolism operating through its economy to incapsulate many ramifications is *proskynēsis* or prostration before rulers, practiced in some places to this day and common throughout the great Oriental empires and satrapies. We shall discuss *proskynēsis* momentarily.

Sapir noted that condensation symbols probably preceded referential types in time, and that condensation symbols provide much more emotional immediacy than do referential devices. Language, which is referential symbolism when found in dictionaries but can involve emotional experience when placed in such contexts as political speeches, may have originated in substitutive cries for some emotion. At least in terms of the progres-

107. *The Spirit of the Laws*, Book III, Chapter 3, edited and translated by Nugent (London: Bonn's Standard Library, 1878), two volumes, I, 22.

108. Thucydides, *The Peloponnesian War*, Crawley translation (New York: Modern Library, 1951), p. 189. On today's "moral dilemma" involved in the exercise of power by another democracy, the United States, see George F. Kennan, *Russia and the West under Lenin and Stalin* (Boston: Atlantic-Little, Brown, 1960), pp. 397–398.

109. Sapir, "Symbolism," *loc. cit.*, p. 1019. See T. Parsons, *et al.*, *Working Papers in the Theory of Action*, p. 54, on "symbolic action."

sive organization and refinement of language, mankind experiences increased distance from the original context of an event and encounters that "emotional denudation" which so frequently accompanies progressively more discursive forms of thought. Such was Goethe's gravamen against Newton's mathematical optics, for example; for Goethe, Newton's mechanistic theory destroyed direct experience with color.

The origins of language and institutions which thrive on language, such as the state, have been lost, and we must resort partly to myth, partly to reason, in order to reconstruct what happened. Hence, myths regarding the foundation of states— including social contract symbols and Freud's "primal crime"—constitute attempts to describe and explain, in our overly rationalized language, an original context of events which certain theorists are convinced must have transpired in the dark and less discursive past. Locke and Rousseau seemed to be saying that words *to the effect* of the contract theory should have occurred at the founding of political authority. In actuality, the original expressions were probably somewhat less discursive, "Ugh, ugh, okraw," for example, but *to the same effect* as Locke and Rousseau envisaged.

Probably one of the most interesting symbols of condensed affect was the great oriental symbol of total submission, prostration (*proskynēsis*), almost universally practiced in Asian empires before the twentieth century and introduced into the Hellenistic Empire of Alexander.[110] Under Alexander's direction *proskynēsis* began for the Greeks at Bactra in 329–328 B.C., but according to Sir Ernest Barker, "he encountered difficulties, and had to abandon the attempt."[111] His chief opponent was Aristotle's nephew, Callisthenes, ordinarily a trusted information chief, who was executed for his opposition. *Proskynēsis* signified for the Persians a simple, mandatory act of denigrative obeisance, a symbol which acted out with superbly economical expression severely hierarchical political relationships.

110. Karl Wittfogel, *Oriental Despotism* (New Haven: Yale University Press, 1957), p. 152 ff.
111. *From Alexander to Constantine* (Oxford: Clarendon Press, 1956), p. 11.

While the Greeks, as loyal citizens, obeyed their leaders, they did so from a sense of obligation free from that prostrative symbolism reserved for the lordship of gods only. For Persians, prostration functioned as a device indicating complete subjection, since the act itself physically placed the person performing it in a nearly prone position. Still, prostration stood for a whole political system, and this condensation value of *proskynēsis* was not missed by the Greeks. Alexander's introduction of such a practice in honor of himself invited ridicule, for it appeared to the Greeks that he wanted to assume the position of a god. His actual intention was probably to introduce this as an imitation of formal Persian court etiquette which he greatly admired.[112] After all, the Greeks had no experience with emperors. They were used to a freer climate and in the democratic city states the good citizen was expected to display four major qualities: military courage, religious devotion, civic responsibility, and balanced judgment. But,

neither the Homeric age nor the classical period considered unquestioning obedience a virtue in a free man, except when he served in the army. Total submission was the duty—and the bitter fate—of the slave. The good citizen acted in accordance with the laws of his community; but no absolute political authorities controlled him absolutely.[113]

Perhaps Callisthenes, who according to Arrian made vocal objection to Alexander's plan for *proskynēsis* at Bactra, was only politely voicing a traditional Greek antipathy towards unquestioning obedience when he said:

Where men are concerned, salutation takes the form of a kiss; but deity has its seat in some upper region and may not be so much as touched, and for this reason accordingly it and it only is honoured by the act of prostration. . . . It is not proper, therefore, to confuse these things, or to raise men to an excessive state, by exaggerating their honours, and to reduce the gods, in consequence, to unseemly humiliation, by giving them no more honours than men. . . .[114]

112. *Ibid.*, p. 12.
113. Wittfogel, *op. cit.*, p. 149.
114. From Arrian, *Anabasis Alexandri*, quoted in Barker, *op. cit.*, p. 13.

Hence, while *proskynēsis* meant to the Greeks abject submissiveness, even further meanings could be attributed. Concomitant with total submissiveness in "Oriental despotism"[115] was the use of religious symbols by rulers in order to give sanctity to their own power. The earlier Greeks apparently recognized this typical "caesaro-papism" so evident later in the Near East (including the Byzantine Empire ruled by their successors), and themselves made sharp distinctions between governments of men and rule by the gods. Callisthenes' fear that *proskynēsis* would raise some men "to an excessive state" reflected a traditional Greek belief that human *hubris* proves dangerous both to men and to their communities. True community meant the friendship of equals, something hardly possible under the Alexandrine scheme where all were equal to be sure, but equally enslaved to a deified Caesar.[116]

## Political Symbolization

Symbolization involves the active appropriation of environmental phenomena by individual actors. Through political symbolization any political environment becomes the individual's own: the general materials available for private attitude become a particular private attitude. Whether the description of this process is Langer's "symbolic transformation," Cassirer's "symbolic process," or Whitehead's "symbolic reference," the accent focuses on the mind's search for meaning, or "mentation," as Angyal calls it. Political symbolization constitutes that constant "becoming" of politics in the individual's own private world, a dynamic process not readily apparent to outside observation. Indicative of symbolization's recondite character is the wealth of descriptive and explanatory studies on how private attitude is constructed by the individual and what factors influence this construction.[117]

115. Wittfogel's designation—see work cited of same title.
116. Running throughout Alexis de Tocqueville's work is this consistent theme of despotic equality or what has been termed "totalitarian democracy" or "Caesaristic democracy."
117. The classic study remains George Herbert Mead's *Mind, Self and Society*, Part III, "The Self." In some respects, political symbolization

Political symbolization is, therefore, the process by which individual actors internalize the political world around them. This world, involving as it does both discursive and presentational symbolic forms, encourages individual symbol-making. Political symbolization represents a form of manufacture: the citizen appropriates some symbol or symbols from outside himself, retreats into his privacy with its characteristic cares and woes, and modifies this symbol for his own use. Unusual metamorphosis may take place.[118]

But private attitude is not yet public opinion. Individual symbolific reaction to political phenomena does not necessarily guarantee an unsolicited public response to those particular phenomena. On the contrary, if opinion, as a "demand or expectation controvertible in a group," is by nature "public,"[119] then public opinion must not be confused with the isolated meanderings of private attitude. Defined in action terms, public opinion is some opinion expressed aloud in a group which recognizes that person's demand to be controvertible vis-à-vis that group. Here thought, language, and action are one. But the individual still retains his private store of thoughts which, while they may motivate him to public activity, remain his own private and political linguistic (hence symbolic) inventions, or perhaps his own favorite hallucinations.[120] Sometimes hallucinatory action results from such hallucinations.

---

and the construction of private attitude is similar to Walter Lippmann's "stereotypes." See Walter Lippmann, *Public Opinion* (1922) (New York: Macmillan, 1961), pp. 253–275.

118. Every political society takes precautions against extreme individual aberrations, for instance, by means of public education. But there exists no foolproof protection against aberrant individuals.

119. Harold D. Lasswell and Abraham Kaplan, *Power and Society* (New Haven: Yale University Press, 1950), p. 38.

120. Stuart Chase, observing his cat, Hobie Baker, ruminates: "Hobie can never learn to talk. He can learn to respond to my talk, as he responds to other signs. . . . He can utter cries indicating pain, pleasure, excitement. He can announce that he wants to go out of doors. . . . But he cannot master words and language. This in some respects is fortunate for Hobie, for he will not suffer from the hallucinations provoked by bad language. He will remain a realist all his life. . . . He is certainly able to think after a fashion, interpreting signs in the light of past experience,

Political symbolization is more private than opinion. "Meaning" best describes such symbolization. We shall follow Langer's advice here that meaning has no specific quality but can only be ascertained adequately (and accurately) in relational terms: "its essence lies in the realm of logic, where one does not deal with qualities, but only with relations." But rather than pass meaning over lightly as a "relation," we can speak more precisely by viewing it as "a *function* of a term."

Langer defines a "function" as "a *pattern* viewed with reference to one special term round which it centers; this pattern emerges when we look at the given term *in its total relation to the other terms about it.*" To illustrate this, she uses music. The base note of a chord is sometimes employed to express the chord as a whole by merely indicating numerically what other notes are in the chord. Hence, in old organ music the chord in G-Major, A, C, D, F#, might be expressed A, 6, 4, 3, and read, "The A-chord with the sixth, the fourth, and the third notes above A." The chord is treated as "a *pattern surrounding and including* A. It is expressed as a function of A." Likewise, the meaning of a term is a function resting on a pattern in which the term itself holds the key-position. Langer notes that a musician examining the harmony of chord A, C, D, F# would make reference to the note around which the chord is built harmonically, thus, "the second inversion of the seventh-chord on the dominant in the key of G."[121] For the student of harmony, the whole pattern centers around D, not A.

---

deliberately deciding his course of action, the survival value of which is high." *The Tyranny of Words* (New York: Harcourt, Brace & World, Inc., 1938), p. 46. Note the accent on response and realism in Chase's observations. Langer, on the other hand, commenting on Hobie Baker, says, "A cat with a 'stalking instinct,' or other special equipment, who could never learn to use that asset properly, but was forever stalking chairs or elephants, would scarcely rise in animal estate by virtue of his talent. Men who can use symbols to facilitate their practical response, but use them constantly to confuse and inhibit, warp and misadapt their actions *and gain no other end by their symbolic devices*, have no prospect of inheriting the earth." *Op. cit.*, p. 41.

121. Previous citations, *op. cit.*, p. 56.

It was noted earlier how this theory of meaning opens what
seems a Pandora's box of relativity, where the proclamations of
a Goebbels on humanity and mankind receive equal weight with
the discourses of enlightened men of the eighteenth century on
the same subject. Logically speaking, if meaning is functional,
any political premise no matter how absurd will do.[122] Depending on particular situations, however, different weight will be
given to different meanings. Meaning varies with its placement
and the clientele in that situation. We take for granted that
politics comprises a clash of conflicting symbolisms and possibly
even different processes of symbolization, so that Nazism would
inevitably find opposition (without evaluating the quality of this
opposition). By saying that Nazism has equal weight, we are
saying that every political symbolism *must be taken seriously*
because on the logical level of meaning they all share equally.
Kenneth Burke has expressed this very neatly.

So, one could, if he wished, maintain that all theology, metaphysics, philosophy, criticism, poetry, drama, fiction, political exhortation, historical interpretation, and personal statements about
the lovable and the hateful—one could if he wanted to be as drastically thorough as some of out positivists now seem to want to be—
maintain that every bit of this is nonsense. Yet those words of nonsense would themselves be real words, involving real tactics, having
real demonstrable relationships, and demonstrably affecting relationships. And as such, a study of their opportunities, necessities, and
embarrassments would be central to the study of human motives.

The design on a piece of primitive pottery may be wholly symbolic
or allegorical. But a drawing that accurately reproduces this design
in a scientific treatise would not be symbolic or allegorical, but realistic. And similarly, even when statements about the *nature of the
world* are abstractly metaphysical, statements about the *nature of
these statements* can be as empirical as the statement, "This is
Mr. Smith," made when introducing Mr. Smith in the accepted
manner.[123]

122. See Hannah Arendt, "History and Immortality," *Partisan Review*
(Winter 1957), 11–35.
123. *Grammar of Motives*, pp. 57–58. On knowledge as seeing and
living see also Kenneth Boulding, *The Image* (Ann Arbor: University of
Michigan Press, 1956).

The present argument goes even beyond Burke's "circumference" to argue that the copied designs in the scientific treatise convey a "realism" which functions symbolically for the scientific observer. Indeed, the occasion of "seeing" itself is symbolic. Pandora's relativist lid seldom opens completely (though it did during Europe's disillusionment following 1914), because cultures rank their experts in various fields. Generally, the historian is the ultimate source for truths regarding the past in Western civilization, but historians compete with each other about the "truth." Elsewhere, priests or astrologers or old men may be trusted repositories for age-old wisdom. So likewise are the truths of nature, the economy, the polity and so on guarded by various cultural groups. One great danger of so-called "mass society" is the breaking down of standards based on this "truth competence" of various groups, with resulting confusion and lack of direction. Note that it is not so much that trained historians lose their credentials and we therefore lose "solid truth," as it is that "all is possible" without social organization. Does it make that much difference whether astrologers or social scientists chart the future course of society and explain its present dilemmas, so long as some group possesses generally recognized competence to do so? Presumably men always search for final truth, but in the process relative truths require group stability in order to persist.

For the above reasons, extremist groups which call themselves "conservative" in mass society, but challenge the hierarchy of present social truths to substitute an "old-fashioned" hierarchy, are not conservative at all but radical. As David Riesman has noted of contemporary American society, even cultures tending toward massification attempt to conserve themselves by ordering truths. Extremist groups which arise in mass society, while advocating a "return to the past," are not promoting a regression to the days of structured society ruled by the "wealthy few," but are rather harkening back to their own reconstructed past which never existed and must therefore be utopian or radical (for example, the myth of rugged individualism in an American past dominated by a Hamiltonian subsidized economy).

Mass society's dynamics, based on industrial rationalization, can never turn backward but must constantly press onward. This means that extremist schemes, while ostensibly conservative, really aim at molding the future (which is the only direction mass societies know), but in some form other than that ordinarily dictated by the consumer-oriented dynamics of modern industrialism; particularly important will be the substitution of "old-fashioned" irrationality (called "individualism" and "thrift" by the new American Right) in place of more rationalization. But new industrial forces, typified by modernized military machines, bureaucracies public and private, well-organized police with the best available communications, and oligopolistic (if not monopolistic) combines in communications, manufacturing, and commerce, will be in charge of this old-fashioned irrationality, since any political program relies for its mobilization in mass society on "administration," which calls into play all the typical industrial forces noted above.

Indeed, every politician in every culture in every age depends on the prevailing technology; how much more so do political leaders in modern societies ruled by bewildering technologies controlled not by individuals but rationalized collectivities. If any political program relies on the mercy of future-directed forces of massification, then even "conservative" programs will seem liberal in the Darwinian and Wilsonian sense of moving forward ceaselessly, particularly when these programs aim, as they have in the British Conservative Party since Disraeli, to please the "masses" as well as the "elite."

But a program which is more than conservative, that is, one which goes beyond preserving existing hierarchies of values which will change anyway in mass society, and attempts instead to implement something "old-fashioned," turns out to be utopian and radical. Mass societies move forward inexorably and programs ostensibly aiming at regression are the most shocking of all, if and when they materialize in the future, since if one cultural law holds true for modern societies it is that the future moves out of the past at an astonishing rate. Historical change has been accelerated, both in units of time and in the quality of historical periods.

The most bizarre of all futures under such conditions would be that future which attempts to install regression as a policy. Nazi Germany proved the most awesome example of this in our time, juxtaposing a Gothic Nuremburg to a streamlined *Wehrmacht* through actual policies and in the brilliant propagandistic efforts made possible by an advanced communications technology during the 1930s. Erich Fromm, in his most famous book, *The Escape from Freedom* (1941), once aptly labeled this German effort an escape to *Ersatzgemeinschaft*.

The analogy drawn from music by Langer illustrates the logical parity of symbolic systems: logically, all views of what is the fundamental note of the chord, A, C, D, F# are equally meaningful. But in the specific situation of the harmonist, D, not A, is the "dominant" and will so appear in his work. Likewise, two assertions, one by an observer at 33 degrees North Latitude that was the Big Dipper and its companion, the North Star, dominate the evening sky, and the other by an observer at 33 degrees South Latitude that the Southern Cross is dominant, are both correct and meaningful. But those living and navigating in southern latitudes will find only the Southern Cross has significance for them, since obviously the Big Dipper cannot be seen there at all. At most, the Big Dipper has academic interest for these southerners.

Such rough analogies hold true in political life as well. A distinction must be made, of course, between "meaning" in the logical sense of what a certain symbol "means" in terms of inference, and the psychological problem of what a person "means" by his use of a particular symbol. But these two kinds of meaning "are distinguished and at the same time related to each other, by the general principle of viewing meaning as a function, not a property of terms."[124]

We have already noted that public opinion is related to action situations. Since we have also observed that action and behavior (that is, stimulus-response) do not necessarily denote the same thing, it follows that qualifications must be appended to Walter Lippmann's oversimplified "triangular relationship between the scene of action, the human picture of that scene, and the human

124. Langer, *op. cit.*, p. 32.

response to that picture working itself out upon the scene of action."[125] At the very least, Kenneth Burke's five-fold classification among act, scene, agent, agency, and purpose in dramatism ("What is involved, when we say what people are doing and why they are doing it?") seems elementary.[126] Although thought and action obviously interact, the very creativity of action, with its "new men and new beginnings" (Arendt) means that "public opinion" about "private meanings" may not be a "response" to the private picture, but a creative act based upon the individual's private pattern of political symbolization and meaning. Opinion is not only a "response to," but "an act based upon" a political world already symbolized in the actor's mind.

The idea that private pictures are more than responses is recognized by some public opinion analysts.[127] Hence, we learn from an American political scientist, Robert E. Lane, that American workers are basically happy with their television and commodity-ridden society, while a leading American radical, Harvey Swados, informs us that assembly-line workers at any rate, but apparently their white-collar brethren as well, really feel trapped and conform to the proletarian image of alienated persons. Significantly, Lane's book is entitled, *Political Ideology*, supposedly a "scientific" description and evaluation based on psychoanalytic "listening with a third ear" (Reik), while Swados' entitles his collection of essays, *A Radical's America*. Actually, *both* books are restricted by the authors' political values, though only Swados makes this clear.[128]

Political symbolization and its fabrication of meaning form part of symbolization in all aspects of life. The central theme of symbolization, to reiterate once again, is human response "as a constructive, not a passive thing."[129] According to this wider

125. Lippmann, *Public Opinion*, pp. 16–17.

126. *Grammar of Motives*, p. xvii.

127. See any reader in public opinion and propaganda, particularly those sections devoted to the social-psychological determinants of public opinion. But the idea of "response" seems the usual approach.

128. See Robert E. Lane, *Political Ideology* (New York: Free Press of Glencoe, Ill., 1963), *passim*, and note, pp. 65–97; and Harvey Swados, *A Radical's America* (Boston: Atlantic–Little, Brown, 1962), Introduction.

129. Langer, *op. cit.*, p. 32.

theory, the brain acts as a giant transformer, using sense-data and fulfilling the human need to make symbols regardless of their utility.[130]

Symbolism is pre-rationative, but not pre-rational. It is the starting point of all intellection in the human sense, and is more general than thinking, fancying, or taking action. For the brain is not merely a great transmitter, a super-switchboard; it is better likened to a great transformer. The current experience that passes through it undergoes a change of character, not through the agency of the sense by which the perception entered, but by virtue of a primary use which is made of it immediately: it is sucked into the stream of symbols which constitutes a human mind.[131]

Hence, the human brain, "constantly [carries] on a process of symbolic transformation of more or less spontaneous ideas." Langer theorizes that "all registered experience tends to terminate in action, *the sheer expression of ideas.*" In early life this is *"verbal play"* (the "lalling-impulse"), while later it is in the form of *"communication."* Obviously, language or speech form an integral part of "expressive acts," as do gesture, song, and sacrifice. Symbolization is not *the* essential act of thought but an act "essential to thought and prior to it." Hence, symbolization "is the essential act of mind; and mind takes in more than what is commonly called thought."[132] Langer's description of how young children learn to speak illustrates her theory of mind.

Young children learn to speak, after the fashion of Victor [the Savage of Aveyron], by constantly using words to bring things *into their minds*, not *into their hands*.[133]

Noting the previous distinction between "action" and "response," and Langer's own mixture of these two terms (symbolization is essentially constructive "human response," as well as "the essential act of mind"), it is possible to modify somewhat her conception of symbolization without drastically changing her ideas. Symbolization may be characterized as constructive

130. *Ibid.*, pp. 43–44; Cassirer, *An Essay on Man*, p. 44.
131. Langer, *op. cit.*, p. 46.
132. Previous citations, *ibid.*, pp. 45–52.
133. *Ibid.*, p. 109. See footnote 120, this chapter.

human response to sense-data, stored by the mind and perhaps articulated in action. Pursuing Arendt's notion of action, we will disagree with Langer's assertion that all registered experience tends "to terminate" in action. On the contrary, all previous sense-data, transformed by the mind and stored there, *begins* its new, transmuted life through action. For once symbolization reappears in the form of experiential activity, observed by both the individual actor and those around him, it marks a new beginning for more symbolization, and so on from action to symbolization to action, *ad infinitum*.

Action signals a "new beginning" in another way: the individual, whose mind symbolizes experiential data around himself and tailors this to fit his own pattern of existence, does not necessarily express or reveal his symbolization process through his activities. For various reasons he may dissimulate or conceal what he really thinks.[134] He may even foster another, fictitious and public symbolization to hide his real thoughts on certain matters. In the form of speech, gesture, and so forth, internal symbolization appears on the public stage, but not always that symbolizing an individual calls his own. Action's demands are public, whereas the imperatives of symbolization remain private in the sense that they are irrevocably the individual's "own," "true" responses to his situation expressed in relationship with himself.[135]

Contrary to Lippmann's simple model of human response to a private picture working itself out on the stage of action, the relation of the self with itself is not public at all. Only this relationship's end-product or some tentative byproduct may be public: and it is the individual who chooses when, where, and how to publicize himself. Men have been tortured so that public authorities might gain access to private knowledge, but often as

134. See Erving Goffman, *The Presentation of Self in Everyday Life* (Edinburgh: University of Edinburgh Social Science Research Centre, 1956), pp. 3–4.

135. It has been assumed throughout this study that human "relationships" *include* one's relations with oneself as well as with others. And further, that self-relations are relevant for political analysis. See Horney, *op. cit.*, pp. 155 f.; and Paul Tillich, *Love, Power and Justice*, p. 25.

not these authorities have found either nothing at all (the victim dies or is exonerated) or dissimulation (the victim lies). Referring to Oriental despotism, Karl Wittfogel notes,

> Living under the threat of total terror, the members of a hydraulic community [an agrarian society depending on large-scale irrigation projects, typically an Oriental empire] must shape their behavior accordingly. If they want to survive, they must not provoke the uncontrollable monster. To the demands of total authority common sense recommends one answer: obedience. And ideology stereotypes what common sense recommends. Under a despotic regime, obedience becomes the basis of good citizenship.[136]

Along with such total obedience comes total insecurity. The maxim of wise rulers is "Trust No One!"; of officials "Eternal Suspicion"; and of commoners, "Noninvolvement."[137] Another concomitant characteristic of Oriental despotism is "government by flogging"; that is, "the language of the whip" carries as much symbolism as *proskynēsis* in the traditional Oriental world. Torture operated in managerial, fiscal, and judicial procedures, and proved a ready and routine means for artificially stimulating private wills.[138] Under such circumstances, reliable expressions of private attitudes are apparently impossible.

These same considerations apply with regard to political symbolization. In terms of Langer's analysis the field of political symbolizing still must be explored, since she mentions only two epistemological theories presently studying symbolization: symbolic logic, and Freudian psychology. Actually, there are others, for example, the symbolic interactionist approach in sociology and social psychology, but much work remains. Freud's theory of personality, with its essentially pre-political ontogenetic and phylogenetic characteristics,[139] has perhaps only an indirect application to political problems, at least so far as symbolization is concerned. For instance, we touched on Freud's dream analysis at one point. Symbolic logic, on the other hand, relies directly on

136. *Op. cit.*, p. 149.
137. *Ibid.*, pp. 155–156.
138. *Ibid.*, pp. 143–147.
139. See Herbert Marcuse, *Eros and Civilization* (Boston: Beacon Press, 1955), p. 20.

mathematical orderings, the discipline of mathematics itself being more concerned with "symbolizing things" than with the making of "concepts."[140]

The use of "semantic differentials" and other tests in the psycholinguistic field has considerable interest, but the meanings explored usually are only tangential to political matters.[141] Surely the symbolic interactionist approach to societal phenomena portends well for political analysis, but so far little application has been made to political life.

Our aim here has been to assess some ways political meaning is conceived in personal life. This by no means denies that internal symbolization of politics has no intimate connections with the developmental history of persons. On the contrary, that is the whole meaning of symbolization in the first place. Our concern through these first five chapters has been, however, to examine ways of making definitions of developmental history more flexible, to add wider circumferences or "dimensions" to the study of self, implicated in the swirl of politics. We have noted how "experience" might be broadened to "existence"; how politics must be widened to account for the numerous polities within which citizenship is exercised and how political and public need not be synonymous though they are frequently confused in our symbolisms; how the distinction between private and public has imprecise limits because both private and public are symbolic expressions not always tangible and visible to the naked eye, but in spite of their imprecision they possess "real" limits if one accepts reality as itself symbolic; and how symbolization involves the brain as transformer not merely transmitter,

140. Langer, *op. cit.*, p. 28. And the paradox: "We can hardly sweep away *all* references to thinking without logic losing its original practical application: if this is the price of making logic mathematical, we shall be forced to pose the Kantian-sounding problem, 'Is mathematical logic at all *possible?*'" Stephen Toulmin, *The Uses of Argument* (Cambridge: Cambridge University Press, 1958), p. 6.

141. See Charles E. Osgood, *et al.*, *The Measurement of Meaning*; and a criticism of Osgood's earlier work in the psychology of meaning by Floyd Allport, *Theories of Perception and the Concept of Structure* (New York: John Wiley, 1955), pp. 570–571.

with all such transforming implies for citizenship or full membership in the polity.

In short, we have followed Kenneth Burke's dictum that "to *define* or *determine* a thing, is to mark its boundaries,"[142] as we examined those wider circumferences beyond more traditional political areas. With these considerations in mind, we approach this essay's final question. Given the imprecision, the symbolic abundance in citizenship's domain, what kind of composite sketch—for sketch it will have to be—can be drawn of the contemporary citizen as he acts within the jurisdiction of public order and, by his activity there, affects this jurisdiction? To this "asymptotic" participant, in what might be termed the diverse "symbolic placements" or manifold "symbol situations" of political life, we now turn.

142. *Grammar of Motives*, p. 24.

# VI The Congruence between Citizen and Public Audience: Action and Order

CITIZENSHIP, as membership in political society, provides a fertile ground for internal symbolizing. Celebrating his home city, Thebes, Pindar exclaimed: "For sacred songs a foundation of gold hath now been laid. Come! let us now build beauty of words, varied and vocal, thus making Thebes, which is already famous, still more splendid in streets belonging to gods as well as men."[1] Through such attitudinal symbolization—often as ecstatic as Pindar's—each individual participates in community life with varying style and intensity. Voting, party activity, and the like, while elementary to political life, are only outward signs of such political symbolizing—the visible iceberg so to speak. Private attitudes worked out through intricate, personalized symbol patterns complete the range of political life. Concentrating on political symbolism and the process of symbolization,

1. *The Odes of Pindar*, second, revised edition, translated by Sir John Sandys (Cambridge, Mass., and London: The Loeb Classical Library, Harvard University Press, and William Heinemann, 1957), p. 607; see also Cicero, *De Legibus* II, 2, 5.

Chapter Five explored this side of citizen action in some detail.
   Being members of a body politic, citizens share the potential
political energy of that polity. They are not only subject to
"powers" in the sense of those "authorities" found in Paul's
letter to the Romans,[2] but also obligated to "powers" suggesting
"mysteries" and hence psychological and even metaphysical
subjugation (if Hegel can be trusted) as well as formal subjection.[3] When one incorporates, interprets, interpenetrates any
part of a polity's dilemmas, enthusiasms, and symbols, one
becomes politically involved. Citizen and state confront each
other on various levels of consciousness and unconsciousness
with uneasy truces drawn between individuals and these powers.
Presumably the famous social contract theories dealt with this
question of political encounter.
   Citizenship provides the only station or situation in life where
this confrontation regularly occurs. Few have the opportunity to
rule men, but nearly every man is a citizen. In the latter role he
automatically enters into a relationship with politics, whether he
likes it or not. He probably understands very little about this
relationship—no one knows everything about politics, though
this hardly excuses ignorance—but some sort of *modus vivendi*
based on a particular level of political development takes place.
Fear, hatred, ignorance, superstition, as well as profound civic
knowledge, may form the basis for this relationship.
   Characteristically, polities strive for levels and styles of relationships fitting every possible competence. As an example, in
the United States there is the politics of the New York *Times*

2. The general usage of "powers that be" is in the sense of "authorities." For instance, the famous passage from Rom. 13:1 reads "powers"
in the King James Version of the *New Testament*, but "authorities" in its
Revised Standard Version.
3. See Jung's essay, "The Phenomenology of the Spirit in Fairy
Tales," in *Psyche and Symbol*, edited by Violet S. de Laszlo (Garden
City, N.Y.: Doubleday Anchor Books, 1958), pp. 61–112. He suggests
an interesting application of the "magic world of the hunter" or "Wotanism" to political life, in this case, to National Socialism. On metaphysical
subjection see G. W. F. Hegel, *Philosophy of Right and Law*, paragraph
268; and Ernst Cassirer, *The Myth of the State* (1946) (Garden City,
N.Y.: Doubleday Anchor Books, 1955), Chapter XVII.

reader, the politics of the New York *Daily News* reader, the politics of the nonreader, and so on. In a sense there exist many "political classes" based on the qualities of political relationships between various citizens and public order. What the college political science professor often means when he suggests that his students read the New York *Times* for information, is not only "You can get the full story, or a more complete and accurate version there," though this is what he most often says openly, but also, and perhaps primarily, though he seldom articulates this, "Come, join my political class, but one of our ceremonial rites is reading the New York *Times*."

It has been fundamental to the argument so far developed, that private attitude, molded by political symbolization, continues at all times rather than as an occasional process. The process endures, not because it is political (no collective act is continuous—we breathe by ourselves), but because it is symbolic. Heeding Cassirer's important insight once again, man is an *animal symbolicum*, rather than an *animal rationale*.[4] The spaces in which he finds himself, including political space, are symbolic ones, adjusted to, if not fashioned by, his own symbolizing as he constantly converts potential energy from outside into currents of his own. Repeating Langer's argument,

the brain is not merely a great transmitter, a super-switchboard; it is better likened to a great transformer. The current of experience that passes through it undergoes a change of character, not through the agency of the sense by which perception entered, but by virtue of a primary use which is made of it immediately: it is sucked into the stream of symbols which constitutes a human mind.[5]

Through symbolization the individual citizen makes his own private truce with the demands of political and public action around himself. This *modus vivendi* is always tentative: how quickly the law-abiding citizen turns into a member of an angry

4. Ernst Cassirer, *An Essay on Man* (Garden City, N.Y.: Doubleday Anchor Books, 1944), p. 44; Susanne K. Langer, *Philosophy in a New Key* (New York, 1958), pp. 43, 45.

5. Langer, *op. cit.*, p. 46. See also Sigmund Freud, "Formulations Regarding the Two Principles in Mental Functioning" (1911), in *Collected Papers*, IV, 13–21; and "Negation" (1925), *ibid.*, IV, 181–185.

mob![6] The citizen role furnishes, by virtue of its general nature, a rather sketchy specification of rights and duties. But even more important, political life in its modern dress presents such an overwhelming picture that any role-playing within its confines will have only nebulous limits. People no longer share intimate knowledge of politics, and in most modern nations individuals appear largely—if never entirely—on their own resources concerning accommodation and adjustment to political powers. Their bases for interpreting politics vary widely, and how they interpret political matters usually concerns only themselves. It is significant that where this generalization does not hold true—in the so-called totalitarian states—governments carefully monopolize all symbol-making media. "Thought control"—conscious and unconscious—assumes top priority in totalitarian systems, because internal symbolization, if left to individual, nonofficial community members, could not guarantee perfect synchronization between citizen purpose and leader purpose. "In the Soviet Union," Alex Inkeles and Raymond A. Bauer note, "it is a cardinal point of policy to structure the individual's life situation so that such choice situations occur as seldom as possible."[7] "Choice situations" are linked to internal symbolization, the latter at least partly controlled by manipulating decision alternatives found in any given situation.

Under more ordinary conditions of social life—and this can be said for most nondemocratic systems as well as democracies—there exists an uneasy truce, an imperfect union, between citizen and state. Or to recast this in another idiom, there persists imperfect "congruence" between the demands of public action and the symbolization of political things in private attitudes.[8]

6. See Robert C. Myers, "Anti-Communist Mob Action; A Case Study," R. K. Turner and L. M. Killian, *op. cit.*, pp. 113–116; Gustave LeBon, *The Crowd* (London: E. Benn, 1952), Chapter 2.

7. *The Soviet Citizen* (Cambridge: Harvard University Press, 1959), p. 283.

8. For somewhat different notions of "congruence" see the discussion by Gabriel Almond and Sidney Verba, *The Civic Culture, Political Attitudes and Democracy in Five Nations* (Princeton: Princeton University Press, 1963), pp. 32–36; on American politics only, V. O. Key, *Public Opinion and American Democracy*, (New York: Alfred A. Knopf,

Private and public coexist in tension and never quite fall together. Through internal symbolizing the single person interprets the political sights and sounds around him. And he may or may not act in the arena of politics. One thing seems certain: the individual symbolizer is always *in* the political arena because he constantly adjusts, perhaps at a very low level of consciousness and information, his life style to political nature, but this same person is not always *of* the political community he ostensibly serves and shares with others.

Surely external conditioning must be acknowledged, but normally such influence has less than total impact. For the sake of more precision, therefore, the meeting between public and private can be designated "congruency," but as this confrontation often lacks complete identity of aims, the relationship between public and private involves tension. Such enduring tensile congruence we shall call "asymptotic congruence" or "not-falling-together," a congruence characteristic of general citizen action. Note our earlier view that such tension characterizes politics in general and citizenship most of all. This means that politics is synonymous with the asymptotic congruence between public and private considerations which characterize the citizen's role; that is, the citizen epitomizes "political man" as indeed the Greeks, who invented the word "citizen," called him.

The primary role in this tension-filled space is the citizen's—that social person involved voluntarily and involuntarily in political things. Here we assume that normal behavior includes "anomic" or "normless" conduct, if the expression "anomie" itself makes any sense in politics at all, since no clear standard of what fully lawful behavior involves now exists, and further doubt persists whether citizen conduct would ever voluntarily conform or could be made to conform to such a standard should it materialize. Recall our earlier discussion of "political classes." Aside from the obvious practical significances, this tensility has relevance to political theory as a technical endeavor.

---

1961) p. 423. On the feeling of "incongruity" in personal identity (both with oneself and society) see Helen Merrell Lynd, *On Shame and the Search for Identity* (New York: Science Editions, 1961), p. 37 ff.

By grasping such imperfect, asymptotic congruence between individual and state, the analyst meets the vital requirements of conceptualizing, generalizing, and symbolizing relations between individual political actors. A. J. Ayer, no political theorist himself, nevertheless pictures adequately these requirements:

in the field of political philosophy, one will probably not be able to translate statements on the political level into statements about individual persons: for although what is said about a State, for example, is to be verified only by the behaviour of certain individuals, such a statement is usually indefinite in a way that prevents any particular set of statements about the behaviour of individuals from being exactly equivalent to it. Nevertheless, here again it is possible to indicate what types of relations must obtain between individual persons for the political statements in question to be true: so that even if no actual definitions are obtained, the meaning of the political statements is appropriately clarified.[9]

One ordinarily intuits *asymptōtos* when one refuses to bracket human beings with the rest of the zoological world, but rather contrasts man's "vulgar folly" (Dostoyevsky) to the anthill and beehive. The asymptotic relation of each individual to the world around him is the product of man's primary need for symbolization. Because of this basic drive man performs both more and less than optimally: he may deliberately sacrifice even minimal "satisficing" behavior[10] for foolishly unrealistic conduct.

A need to symbolize for the sheer sake of symbolizing manifests itself in action, too. For when one expresses one's symbolization to others merely for the sake of expression, perhaps even ignoring who the others are, one engages in action and interaction. Individuals publicize their symbolization and, becoming engaged, disclose themselves in the only way they can. Typically, this public stage comprises a political one, because it most

9. *Language, Truth and Logic*, 1946 edition (New York: Dover Publications, Inc., n.d.), p. 24. Reprinted by permission of the publisher.
10. On "satisficing" behavior, as contrasted to "optimal" or "maximal" behavior, see Herbert A. Simon, *Models of Man: Social and Rational* (New York: John Wiley, 1957), Chapter 15, "Rational Choice and the Structure of the Environment"; and the new introduction to the second edition of his *Administrative Behavior* (New York: Macmillan, 1957).

often provides a wider, more tension-filled environment for individual and group action than most other social situations. Political action may become a genuinely creative vocation—almost professional in its structure if not in its rewards—offering a vast area for exercise of individual and group powers. Typically, personal contact occurs in all professions, but the wider field of anonymous "others" contributes to an occupational status, rather more than does a personal status such as family member.

Being a doctor means having personal contacts with patients and with a wider realm of professional others, including a context of mandatory ethical procedures: there exists both a substantial and more abstract role of doctor. While intimate relations bar much latitudinarianism, more abstract roles encourage creativity and liberality. Politics provides the most abstract of all action roles, because its area of anonymity encompasses more ground, not only in terms of rulers, but also those ruled. Since politics furnishes the broadest field of action within a given geographical area, it has the most anonymous relationships. This is especially true of the citizen role, because citizens, as citizens, have the fewest personal political contacts of all that play political roles. As the broadest of political statuses, citizenship is characterized by the most anonymity among actors.

The conception of asymptotic congruence employed in this discussion grew mostly from studying various existentialist philosophies (none of which use the word "asymptotic"). Indicative, however, of the various languages which political theory confronts in its attempt to plumb the true complexity of political life is a sociological use of the word "asymptotic" by the social theorist Talcott Parsons, a follower of Durkheim, Pareto, and Weber,[11] who examines the individual's mature and normal "asymptotic" adjustment to social life.[12] Interested in regularities of social structure, Parsons uses the word to depict deviation from a normative pattern; his is a probabilistic usage. Modern psychology has so penetrated the world of social studies that

11. Parsons, *The Structure of Social Action*, (Glencoe, Ill.: The Free Press, 1949), Part II, Chapters 5–12; Part III, Chapters 14–17.
12. "Psychoanalysis and the Social Structure," *Psychoanalytic Quarterly*, XIX (July 1950), 371–384, at 379.

Parsons, a leading sociological theorist, must maintain some tension between "personality system" and "social system," and his notion of asymptotic congruence represents this concern. Parsons by no means appears content with such tensility, as evidenced in his attempt to rationalize the abherrant person into social structure. Here he follows Durkheim, not Freud,[13] but tension nevertheless characterizes Parsons's general theory of action.

Conflict and resulting asymptotic adjustment of individuals and groups to the polity around them may be expressed in idioms other than sociological ones. We have already noted in Chapter Four the possibility of political vocabularies that express purpose and vocation rather than function. In some ways, all three ranges complement one another, identifying different aspects of the same central problem of describing and explaining the obvious multidimensionality of political action and the activities of the citizenry in given political orders. For example, asymptotic tension, caused by an individual's *potentia* or need to create freely his self-image, a need which conflicts with the same need in others, has been treated very well by contemporary philosophers, poets, novelists, and theologians, though it has been a pressing problem in political space at least since the seventeenth century and Hobbes.

For Heidegger and Jaspers, philosophy must overcome its contemporary, puerile separations of empirical and metaphysical in order to confront factual questions about the alienation and anguish experienced by modern men. The ultimate problems in German existential philosophy, therefore, consist in combinations of empirical, ethical, and metaphysical reasoning. Thomas Langan comments on Heidegger's disregard for the proper technical boundaries.

In fact, the phenomenological consideration of the human essence as self-constitutive freedom, we are beginning to see, cuts across the traditional division between ontology and ethics. This is a sign, as Heidegger sees it, that the phenomenological analysis is more funda-

13. See also, Parsons, "The Superego and the Theory of Social Systems," 15–25.

mental than the objective categorical analysis of the traditional metaphysics. The discoveries of the *Existentiale* are, if you will, both ontological and ethical, since the grasp of the ontological structure of an essence—a free essence, grasped not as an object to be contemplated, but as a challenge to be lived.[14]

In other words, questions about existence and being, when posed about men as they live in the real world, no longer present abstract problems only, but mix with the issues and dilemmas of daily conduct—ethics. According to Heidegger, the authentic man awaits each instant a revelation about the ground of his being, but needless to say the paths to authenticity are narrow and confusing and require considerable mental application if not spiritual anguish. Through care over death, surely the most basic of human predicaments, men thirst for these revelations of being, indeed they "need" such revelations for their past, present, and future commitments.

Authentic persons do not necessarily include, therefore, philosophic and scientific elites (who actually run greater danger of inauthenticity), but those who worship Being (*Sein*) at the temporal horizons of their own finitude (*Dasein*).[15] The authentic find themselves in the stuff of things (*Seienden*), of ordinary life rather than in transcendent absolutes, but, by confronting death (an essentially human mundane confrontation), they surpass these material things and concentrate on that which surrounds the material world, namely, negation or "no-thing."[16] By experiencing Nothing (Death) and caring (*Sorge*) about that experience so passionately that one "needs" it, any man can be

14. Langan, *The Meaning of Heidegger* (New York: Columbia University Press, 1959), p. 40. See also Kierkegaard: "The infinite merit of the Socratic position was precisely to accentuate the fact that the knower is an existing individual, and that the task of existing is his essential task." *Concluding Unscientific Postscript*, translated by David Swenson, completed and edited by Walter Lowrie (Princeton: Princeton University Press and the American-Scandinavian Foundation, 1941), p. 185.

15. See Kierkegaard's penetrating essay, "Of the Difference Between a Genius and Apostle" (1847).

16. Martin Heidegger, *Kant und das Problem der Metaphysik* (Bonn: Fred Cohen, 1929), p. 71; Langan, *op. cit.*, p. 73.

authentic and hence philosophic in the true sense of the word—a lover of ultimate wisdom (though such a group itself is necessarily select, according to Heidegger).[17]

For political theory, the preceding discussion has considerable relevance, because such concern over death always remains asymptotic to ordinary collective life.[18] In a way it forces persons out from the madding crowd, fosters alienative and anomic conduct, and perhaps explains, at a depth most political analysts have no concern about fathoming, something about citizen action. One American commentator on existential philosophy remarks about Tolstoy's "Ivan Ilyich" that "the reality of death is precisely that it sunders Ivan Ilyich from all other human beings. . . ."[19] Heidegger argues that *Sorge* comes "before" (*vor*) all segmented temporal activity, including political action.

Care, as a primordial structural totality, lies "before" ["vor"] every factical "attitude" and "situation" of Dasein [the given, primordial structure of my Being-in-the-world], and it does so existentially *a priori;* this means that it always lies *in* them. So this phenomenon by no means expresses a priority of the "practical" attitude over the theoretical. When we ascertain something present-at-hand by merely beholding it, this activity has the character of care just as much as

17. "The formally existential totality of Dasein's ontological structural whole must therefore be grasped in the following structure: the Being of Dasein means ahead-of-itself-Being-already-in-(the-world) as Being-alongside (entities encountered within-the-world). This Being fills in the signification of the term *"care"* [*Sorge*], which is used in a purely ontologico-existential manner. From this signification every tendency of Being which one might have in mind ontically, such as worry [*Besorgnis*] or carefreeness [*Sorglosigkeit*], is ruled out." Martin Heidegger, *Being and Time*, translated by John Macquarrie and Edward Robinson (London: SCM Press, 1962), p. 237.

18. Ingmar Bergman has illustrated this theme brilliantly in the opening dream scene of his film, "Wild Strawberries," and then continues it in subsequent sequences. See *Four Screenplays of Ingmar Bergman*, translated by Lars Malmstrom and David Kushner (New York: Simon and Schuster, 1960), pp. 170–173.

19. "The reality of death is precisely that it sunders Ivan Ilyich from all other human beings, returns him to the absolute solitude of his own individual self, and destroys the fabric of society and family in which he had lost himself." Barrett, *op. cit.*, p. 127.

does a "political action" or taking a rest and enjoying oneself. "Theory" and "practice" are possibilities of Being for an entity whose Being must be defined as "care."[20]

Plainly, "is" and "ought" are jumbled in Heidegger's scheme. While life's empirical realities are essential to the authentication of self, we only know the "thingness" of empirical calculations after we understand ourselves as no-thing, that is, by ethically transcending and hence objectifying our world of things. This notion of individual authenticity—literally, of putting the self on the margin of things—differs radically from that held by social science, where the authentic individual appears as he who drinks deeply from the common heritage through almost insouciant interaction with others. (This is an overstatement for purposes of contrast only: the interactionism of Mead and Goffman hardly views human relationships carelessly.) Meaningful knowledge is public knowledge according to this latter view, because the most important educative processes occur in membership situations conductive to "socialization" or "integration" into given cultures.

Existential philosophy stresses exactly the opposite: the paths to authenticity appear as ethical freedom from all things, including social artifacts. Accordingly, neither fact nor value provides escape to absolute transcendence, but instead all existence appears factitious, the product of individual creation and personal style. Heidegger's interpretation of Kant, therefore, lays particular emphasis on Kant as the prophet of man's metaphysical finitude, because Kant's philosophical revolution questioned the possibility of the objectivizing encounter with the things-that-are.[21] A finite horizon serves as both fact and value, and the question of separating the two, since both are limited by the "things of the world," appears a dead issue.

A more fundamental existential problem concerns the true status of individual existence among Kant's things-in-them-

20. *Being and Time*, p. 238; also Thomas Langan, *op. cit.*, pp. 28–41. Though "care" is ontologically "earlier" than the phenomena of ordinary life, one can, "within certain limits," *describe* these phenomena without having "the full ontological horizon visible."

21. Langan, *op. cit.*, Chapter 2.

selves, which by their very illusiveness, sustain a mystery and tension in empirical social and psychological life. The mystery for which men seek answers surrounds them in mundane affairs; they need seek no further, but it is precisely this commonplace mystery which is most difficult to understand and appropriate. Authenticity's problem is to engage oneself in this mysterious, invariably ambiguous situation, and make drift, incertitude, and finitude virtues rather than vices.

Among the most awesome ambiguities (or even "absurdities," according to Camus) we find collective—including political—relationships. Proper, authentic responses to such ambiguities, however, are those which befit rational men, not scared animals. Hence, a new tension appears between rational man and his mysterious empirical surroundings with a resulting ethic that constitutes revolt against finitude, yet a revolt which knows it can never win ultimately and therefore can never finalize societal and political arrangements as if incertitude had been banished forever. All this truly constitutes a metaphysics of profane finitude.

For Heidegger, the human condition presents a constant tension between "man's drifting from the mystery to the practicable and from one practicability to the next, always missing the mystery."[22] Freedom flows from this errancy or drifting, because men quest after truth which is nothing if not this freedom. Yet such freedom offers no real direction, no final goals, no absolutely fixed points for navigation. Always needing this mystery but never apprehending or controlling it completely, men wander in a lonely search of the distant finitude of their own personal horizons. Indeed, Heidegger characterizes human existence as "wandering in need" (*Das Dasein ist die Wendung in die Not*).[23] In the historical development of the West today's

22. Martin Heidegger, *Vom Wesen der Wahrheit*, second edition (Frankfurt: Vottorio Klostermann, 1949), p. 21, quoted in Langan, *op. cit.*, p. 137.

23. *Vom Wesen der Wahrheit*, p. 23, quoted in Langan, *op. cit.*, p. 138. It should be observed that Heidegger's *die Wendung in die Not* is progressive in the sense that every historical stage has its openness accompanied by error. Since error is "the stamp of Nothing in the heart

human beings are hardly any longer the "pilgrims" so familiar to John Bunyan's seventeenth-century England, but rather more like "outsiders," "strangers," "wanderers." Bunyan wrote beautifully in his *Pilgrim's Progress*,

> Christian no sooner leaves the world but meets
> Evangelist, who lovingly him greets
> With tidings of another; and doth show
> Him how to mount to that from this below.

In poignant contrast, the twentieth-century poet W. B. Yeats saw no such transcendence in his time:

> Now that my ladder's gone,
> I must lie down where all ladders start,
> In the foul rag-and-bone shop of my heart.[24]

A. E. Housman expressed a correlative theme when he queried,

> And how am I to face the odds
> Of man's bedevilment and God's?
> I, a stranger and afraid
> In a world I never made.[25]

Albert Camus averred his desire "to know whether I can live with what I know and with that alone,"[26] while Hannah Arendt notes,

---

of our finite revelation through time of the things-that-are," it follows that we shall not easily forget the mystery of Dasein but rather constantly strive after it. "As soon as man considers his homelessness, this homelessness ceases to be a misery; rather, correctly considered and rightly held to, it becomes the authentic exhortation calling the mortal to dwell." Quoted in Langan, *op. cit.*, p. 128. Homelessness, rather than the community of others, becomes the mark of authenticity.

24. William Butler Yeats, "The Circus Animals' Desertion" from "Last Poems" (1936–1939) in *The Collected Poems of W. B. Yeats* (New York: Macmillan, 1959), p. 336. Reprinted with permission of Macmillan; copyright © 1940 by Georgie Yeats.

25. From "The Laws of God, the Laws of man" from *The Collected Poems of A. E. Housman*. Copyright © 1950 by Barclays Bank, Ltd. Reprinted by permission of Holt, Rinehart and Winston, Inc. All of this twelfth poem is worth reading in connection with asymptotic congruence.

26. *The Myth of Sisyphus and Other Essays*, translated by Justin O'Brien (New York: Vintage Books, 1958) p. 30.

Modern man, when he lost the certainty of a world to come, was thrown back on himself and not upon this world; far from believing that the world might be potentially immortal, he was not even sure that it was real.[27]

The modern political phenomenon of "statelessness" after two world wars parallels the homelessness in Heidegger's philosophy and elsewhere and amply proves the changed nature of membership in temporal society.[28] A heightened concern over the problems of "identity" and "alienation" seems obvious to any sensitive reader, and while considerable amounts of this literature belong to current popular culture itself, one cannot discount as mere faddism the serious work by social scientists, psychologists, novelists, essayists, and others, including theologians. For many oppressed peoples living under tyrannous political regimes, no hope remains of pilgrimage to a fixed, free destination, or if they still harbor such hopes these function as means of alienation from main currents in their society.

But political regimes are not the only oppressive instruments of the modern world. In any event, the idea of pilgrimage is very old-fashioned and has been replaced in the literature created by contemporary intellectual elites by the idea of permanent wandering, homelessness, and rootlessness (*Wendung*). Politically speaking, this lack of roots, this vagabondage, has great significance, both from the philosophical standpoint and as a matter of

27. *The Human Condition*, (Garden City, N.Y.: Doubleday Anchor Books, 1959), p. 292. The inclusion of Heidegger here is based only on the way he has captured a contemporary mood of errancy. He co-operated with the Nazis, but this is surely not traceable to his views on philosophical wandering. Or better put, whatever the relations between his existentialism and his personal political decisions, there is no necessary causal connection between Heidegger's philosophy and the moral decisions of *others*. Nazism represented a crisis in political community as much as a movement in formal philosophy.

28. Hannah Arendt, *The Origins of Totalitarianism*, second enlarged edition (New York: Meredian Books, 1958), pp. 267–290; Jaspers, *Reason and Anti-Reason in Our Time*, p. 61; Jane P. C. Carey, "Some Aspects of Statelessness Since World War I," *American Political Science Review*, XL (February 1946), 113–123; Chief Justice Warren in *Perez* v. *Brownell*, 356 U.S. 64 (1958), and in *Trop* v. *Dulles*, 356 U.S. 101–103 (1958).

practical citizenship. More than ever men are assailed by their own finitude, by their dead gods and dead souls, and they have no capabilities, save those of myth and illusion, with which to meet their assailants. Many are going somewhere, but nowhere in particular. There seems to be a kind of animalistic urge just to "go, go, go," in the words of one of Jack Kerouac's vagabonds.[29]

That there should be widespread anxiety on the part of social scientists, psychologists, and others (all of whom share in the *Wendung* themselves and may even encourage it) over these developments is not surprising. *Wendung* (literally "wending") finds expression in the shibboleths of "alienation," "anomie," "disorganization," to name only a few of the well-known diagnoses. Current literature—fact and fiction—alternately worries about and celebrates a sense of errancy, truancy, wandering, and, most ominously, helplessness, in the face of such trends.

Symptomatic of this helplessness is Yeats's observation about our broken ladders. Yet without ladders utopian thinking is impossible, which means that we have no intellectual leverage or appropriate vision with which to surpass our present difficulties and rationally devise new solutions.[30] Perhaps equally tragic, the past, as well as the future, has disappeared as a meaningful temporal dimension. Universally men search for roots and hope for community. Simone Weil summarized this rootlessness poignantly.

To be rooted is perhaps the most important and least recognized need of the human soul. . . . A human being has roots by virtue of his real, active and natural participation in the life of a community which preserves in living shape certain particular treasures of the past and certain particular expectations for the future. . . . Every human being needs to have multiple roots. It is necessary for him to draw wellnigh the whole of his moral, intellectual and spiritual life by way of the environment of which he forms a natural part.[31]

29. In his novel *On the Road* (1955).

30. See Judith Skhlar, *After Utopia* (Princeton: Princeton University Press, 1957).

31. *The Need for Roots*, translated by A. F. Wills (London: Routledge and Kegan Paul, 1952), p. 41. See also Philip Selznick's discussion of the "stalinoid" personality in *The Organization Weapon* (New York: McGraw-Hill, RAND, 1952), Chapter 7.

Much modern literature and philosophy understands this contemporary *Wendung* more as the typical modern "style" and hence a positive challenge for social philosophy rather than a curse or disease. *Wendung* still presents distressing problems to this point of view, as it does for functional analysis, but problems of a different order. If restlessness, rootlessness, and the flattening of life-spaces to finite dimensions are seen in relation to social structure, the relationships can be labeled "anomic," "alienative," "marginal," and the corresponding cures will deal with "organization" and "reconstruction." On the other hand, if *asymptōtos* appears normal to the contemporary human situation (and probably to past situations as well), then other kinds of language seem called for.

Sharing in the full range of functional, purposive, and vocational relationships available to human existence, political life borders on metaphysical problems of errancy, as well as on the sociological disturbances of anomie. The asymptotic person, on the one hand an active deviant from social norms, also plays the role of lonely observer, bereft of any intimate community with others. This person has freedom, but freedom for what? Probably "free for nothing" in Sartre's words, which, if not an optimistic appraisal, does propose a challenge. Clemence, the leading character in Camus' *The Fall*, waxes euphoric over the flattened life space which, while grim, constitutes his own experience:

Isn't it the most beautiful negative landscape? . . . A soggy hell indeed! Everything horizontal, no relief; space is colorless, and life dead. Is it not universal obliteration, everlasting nothingness, made visible? No human beings, above all, no human beings! You and I alone facing the planet at last deserted![32]

32. *The Fall*, translated by Justin O'Brien (New York: Alfred A. Knopf, 1957), pp. 72–73. Camus was much influenced by Simone Weil—see John Cruickshank, *Albert Camus* (London: Oxford University Press, 1959), p. 17.

Robert Penn Warren, the distinguished American novelist and teacher, has also accented the world's flatness, nondimensionality, like taking a card out of a stereopticon and examining it without aid of that device. *Night Rider* (Boston: Houghton Mifflin, 1939), p. 161.

On the other hand, stands the inauthentic "renegade" or "true believer," he who rejects his fate of real finitude and dedicates himself to an unreal infinity, which because of its existential unreality must authoritatively suppress the voice of genuine inner allegiance if it wishes to flourish in the real world. As pictured by Camus, such brutal suppression symbolically occurs when the "Fetish" or "Master" initiates the "renegade" by tearing out the latter's tongue. Thus liberated from his voice, the outcast freely surrenders in order to serve malevolently his master's wishes.

I hated my people, the Fetish was there and from the depths of the hole in which I was I did more than pray to him, I believed in him and denied all I had believed up to then. Hail! he was strength and power, he could be destroyed but not converted, he stared over my head with his empty, rusty eyes. Hail! he was the master, the only lord, whose indisputable attribute was malice, there are no good masters. For the first time, as a result of offenses, my whole body crying out a single pain, I surrendered to him and approved his maleficent order. I adored in him the evil principle of the world. A prisoner of his kingdom—the sterile city carved out of a mountain of salt . . . I freely became its tortured, hate-filled citizen, I repudiated the long history that had been taught me.[33]

Although much research has examined ways in which families, businesses, labor unions, close acquaintances, and others affect the political behavior of individuals in general and the activity of citizens in particular, there has been little research or understanding of how the need to wander or to deviate—the need to reject every social group and "the long history that had been taught me" (Camus)—is acted out in political life.[34] Modern techniques of persuasion, such as "brainwashing," prey upon the rootlessness and errancy common to modern life. Such *Wen-*

33. *Exile and the Kingdom*, translated by Justin O'Brien (New York: Alfred A. Knopf, 1958), pp. 53–54 (the story entitled "The Renegade"); see also Eric Hoffer, *The True Believer* (New York: Harpers, 1951), Chapter 2.

34. See Robert E. Lane, *Political Life* (Glencoe, Ill.: The Free Press, 1959); and *Political Ideology* (New York: The Free Press of Glencoe, Ill., 1962), for a closer discussion of orthodox approaches to individual political behavior in social science research.

*dung* frequently connects to problems of personal egotism, and the two conspire together, making a life of common political involvements impossible.

These persuasive techniques also attempt to divide, conquer, and even convert isolated individuals to other causes. The fact that such persons harbor notions prejudicial to their fellow citizens and contrary to the general aims of their political society, surely assists in what Joost A. M. Meerloo has called "the rape of the mind."[35] In contrast, ancient Athens provided a special political area where a limited number of adult males possessed equal citizenship. Their most famous leader, Pericles, assumed that politics provided special opportunities worthy of dedicated endeavor, and, in turn, the standards of this political space—emphasizing a common good—would exercise beneficent influences on private life. Today, it is more often asserted that personal egotism must work itself out in political action, rather than the opposite, Periclean notion of good citizenship.

Perhaps an example of how estrangement from social and political structures can be treated from differing standpoints would best illustrate the complementary relationship social science and existential points of view enjoy in the analysis of modern citizenship. On the one hand is Leo Srole's scale for measuring anomie, the first really systematic attempt to measure this social phenomenon as an internal, psychological variable.[36] His inquiry presumes social structure, cultural tradition, and personality systems; in other words, his scale concentrates on structure and function.[37] Assume next an existential position with reference to the same subject—the normless individual—and note a significant shift in the theory of action involved. In the second instance, the individual is inauthentic

35. *The Rape of the Mind: The Psychology of Thought Control, Menticide and Brainwashing* (New York: World Publishing Co., 1956).

36. See Alan H. Roberts and Milton Rokeach, "Anomie, Authoritarianism, and Prejudice; a Replication," *American Journal of Sociology*, LXI (1956), 355–358; Leo Srole, *ibid.*, LXII (1956), 63–67.

37. Robert K. Merton, *Social Theory and Social Structure*, revised and enlarged edition (Glencoe, Ill.: The Free Press, 1957), pp. 161–164.

when bound too closely to society, and social allegiances are measured against the presumed necessity for self-fulfillment. Functionally speaking, anomie means social disease: vocationally (in terms of the creating person), anomie would have no such negative implications.

In other words, marginality has virtues as well as vices. The two sides of the coin here are *nomos* and *anomos*. Sociologists concern themselves with *nomos*-adjustment, convention, and inheritance. The existential view labels such integration into the "average Dasein" or the "marketplace" as unreal, inauthentic, bad faith, but, above all, as activity injurious to the actor. One must turn anomie to account as a challenge: anguish and suffering are hardly cured by re-socializing, but by de-socializing—extracting—oneself from alienative social structures.[38] Although it has a positive side, the existentialist hope for modern man, by paradoxically placing positive value on disinheritance, promises destruction, not reconstruction.[39]

Srole has devised five general attitudes intended to serve as indicators for anomie in individuals; these indicators refer to structural malfunctions. Following Merton's analysis of Srole's scale, these attitudes are as follows: "(1) the perception that community leaders are indifferent to one's needs; (2) the perception that little can be accomplished in the society which is seen as basically unpredictable and lacking order; (3) the perception that life-goals are receding rather than being realized; (4) a sense of futility; and (5) the conviction that one cannot count on personal associates for social and psychological support."[40]

Now revise slightly these attitudes: (1) the perception that community leaders are *hostile* to one's needs; (2) the perception that little can be done in a *predictable* and *ordered* society; (3)

38. Rollo May, *et al.*, *Existence, A New Dimension in Psychiatry and Psychology* (New York: Basic Books, 1958), p. 35; also Robert Lindner, *Must You Conform?* (New York: Grove Press Black Cat Edition, 1961), pp. 123–210.

39. Langan, *op. cit.*, pp. 143–144.

40. Merton, *op. cit.*, pp. 164–165.

the perception that life's *potential is blocked;* (4) a sense of *exasperation;* (5) a conviction that one cannot count on personal associates *to understand* one's social and psychological life. If these changes were made (with some further modification, particularly in the word "hostile" in the first attitude) then Srole's questionnaire shifts from its sociological focus and assumes an existential one—a change from structure and function to vocation and personal power (*potentia*). In fact, the scale would no longer measure attitudes within a structural setting complete with elaborate role-expectations, but attitudes in spite of conventional society. The guidelines shift from structural norms to individual aspirations. Mandatory under these circumstances is less, not more, integration.

Of course, the Srole scale originally expressed the negative connotations of functional anomie, the authentic person inheriting social impulse by keeping in tune with the harmony of his environment. Supplementing his biologic capabilities and often in spite of these capabilities, the individual learns adaptation to others around him by acquiring a second, social nature. In creative terms, however, authenticity often operates asocially and dysfunctionally. From the existential point of view, the change in Srole's scale suggests that social—and political— estrangement may not only involve behavioral deviance from existing norms, but a moral transvaluation of normative procedures. In other words, when assessing dysfunction the first question concerns the "functions of dysfunction" for individual persons.

Vocationally speaking, the individual self may be "in the world but not of it." Originally, the asymptotic personality was the Christian who heeded Paul's admonition, "Do not be conformed to this world."[41] A stranger, in the sense of a pilgrim with only transient moments on earth, the Christian pursued a supratemporal destination in the Kingdom of God, that secure community in heaven towering above and outside time, yet

41. "Do not be conformed to this world but be transformed by the renewal of your mind, that you may prove what is the will of God, what is good and acceptable and perfect." Rom. 12:2 (RSV).

ruling all time.[42] Christian lives filled themselves with this tension between the "already fulfilled" and the "not yet completed."[43] Illustrative was the gospel song, "I'm but a stranger
here, heaven is my home." Many other Christian hymns celebrated the controlling, supratemporal force guiding life toward
final culmination; for example, "Jesus Savior, pilot me/Over
life's tempestuous sea." The Christ was "pilot," "heavenly
bosom," "eternal rest," "rock of ages"; His church a "firm
foundation" and "mighty fortress." God's providence mani-
fested itself in the heavens and firmament, and sheltered those
saints marching toward the promised Zion, altogether an alienated band in a paradoxically Christianized West.

Under adversity—and for Christians each individual life
promised its share of woes—these saints looked more like tattered pilgrims than a mighty army. But whether tattered or
triumphant these believers had a fixed transcendent destination
toward which their path inevitably led them, if only they maintained their faith in the face of both defeat and victory. One can
expand this commentary beyond Christianity to include all the
world's major religions, for religious life without controlled
purpose and ultimate design seems a contradiction.[44]

42. Augustine's *The City of God* was dedicated to the theme, "My
God is everywhere present." I, xxviii.

43. See Oscar Cullmann, *The State in the New Testament* (London:
SCM Press, 1957), p. 6.

44. Freud's conception of the religious myth of a future life is suggestive. A life "beyond," says Freud, represents the triumph of the "reality-
principle" over the "pleasure-principle" by the postponement of pleasure
in this life. However, *science*, he continues, comes closest to a reality
which can subdue pleasure. See "Mental Functioning" (1911) in *Collected Papers*, IV, 18. This idea forms part of Freud's positivist conviction that civilization and history evolve toward more "reality-ego," as
opposed to sheer indulgence of the "pleasure-ego." It is "a strengthening
of the intellect, which is beginning to govern instinctual life, and an
internalization of the aggressive impulses with all its consequent advantages and perils." "Why War?" (1932) in *Collected Papers*, V, 286.
Freud holds that both Christianity and science are part of the same
tradition of freeing intellect from instinct. The price for such a tradition
of increasing rationality has been, in fact, so great that modern art and
literature have revolted against this tradition. ("Our time," wrote Max

Nietzsche's oft-quoted announcement in the nineteenth century that God was dead stated only the *ens Summum* of three centuries.[45] Previously, Hebraic-Christian thought had rationalized an innate sense of finitude, endemic in human affairs, by nurturing the complementary urge to be identified with something "beyond" earthly frailties and limitations.[46] Symbolically, the ancient Hebrew tabernacle, with its veiled Holy of Holies, furnished an inner sanctum beyond the material artifacts in the outer tent accessible only to priests.[47] The New Testament, with equal symbolic force, rent the veil and men came face-to-face with the Holy through the Holy acting as mediator, Jesus Christ.[48]

Nietzsche's rhetorical destruction of this intimacy, culminating several centuries of methodical doubt, left men with finitude only, or at least much of the Western intellectual community was so bereft. No longer could fixed destinations be taken for granted, nor would such well marked paths and reliable signposts to eternal life have the literary status they enjoyed in Dante's *Divine Comedy* or Bunyan's *Pilgrim's Progress*. Ambiguity quickly gained status in seventeenth-century Europe, including the greater and lesser literature of the English Revolution, and spread rapidly thereafter. Today, even in Christian literature (admittedly of the more cerebral sort), the stranger, instead of traveling through a familiar world with Luther's very

Scheler, "is the first in which man has become thoroughly and completely problematic to himself.") Freud, "Resistances to Psycho-Analysis" (1925), in *Collected Papers*, V, 170; Jung, in *Psyche and Symbol*, pp. 125–127; and Talcott Parsons, "Social Disintegration and Fascism," *Social Forces*, XXI (December 1942).

45. Nietzsche, "The Gay Science" (1882), Aphorism 125.

46. Reinhold Niebuhr, *The Nature and Destiny of Man*, two volumes (London: Nisbet and Co., 1941), Volume I, Chapter 6.

47. Exod. 26:33–35.

48. This event accompanies the high point in the drama of the Crucifixion, the death of Jesus, and is related in all three synoptic gospels. "And Jesus cried with a loud voice and yielded up his spirit. And behold, the curtain of the temple was torn in two, from top to bottom; and the earth shook, and the rocks were split. . . ." Matt. 27:50–51 (RSV). Also in Mark 15:37–38; Luke 23:45–46.

real devils "seeking to devour us," wanders and stumbles in Eliot's "Waste Land."

> What is that sound high in the air
> Murmur of maternal lamentation
> Who are those hooded hordes swarming
> Over endless plains, stumbling in cracked earth
> Ringed by the flat horizon only
> What is the city over the mountains
> Cracks and reforms and bursts in the violet air
> Falling towards
> Jerusalem Athens Alexandria
> Vienna London
> Unreal[49]

Errancy, rootlessness and wandering form central themes in much contemporary literature. Modern pilgrims seem deprived of destinations and controlling purposes, which means they are not pilgrims at all, but hobos, bums, waiting for that which will never come and which they will never see. Such an absurd world, lacking a transcendent way out of its perplexities, can scarcely claim immortality; on the contrary, it all seems grotesquely unreal. Heidegger's observation concerning "man's drifting from the mystery to the practicability to the next, always missing the mystery," finds powerful, earlier statement in Herman Melville's *Moby Dick*.

Why did the Persians hold the sea holy? Why did the Greeks give it a separate deity, and own brother of Jove? Surely all this is not without meaning. And still deeper the meaning of the story of Narcissus, who because he could not grasp the tormenting, wild image he was in the fountain, plunged into it and was drowned. But the same image, we ourselves see in all rivers and oceans. It is the image of the ungraspable phantom of life; and this is the key to it all.[50]

And what better observation for political analysts to recall than these two searching sentences from Fitzgerald's *Great Gatsby*?

49. From "The Waste Land" in *Collected Poems 1909–1962* by T. S. Eliot, copyright, 1936, by Harcourt, Brace & World, Inc.; copyright, © 1963, 1964 by T. S. Eliot. Reprinted by permission of the publisher.
50. *Moby Dick* (New York: Modern Library), 1944, p. 4.

Yet high over the city our line of yellow windows must have contributed their share of human secrecy to the casual watcher in the darkening streets, and I was him too, looking up and wondering. I was within and without, simultaneously enchanted and repelled by the inexhaustible variety of life.[51]

Everywhere there exists a world of inexhaustible variety, a world that engages men on their way to nowhere who scarcely seem aware of their errant condition. Yet such errancy debilitates orderly, communicative understanding within a more traditional conception of society. An idealist, transcendent vision of political order becomes increasingly grotesque in its implementation. The very irrelevance and antipathy of contemporary errancy to the demands by some for a political order within a stable, normative social structure forces us to re-examine constantly the cherished stereotypes of "community" and "consensus," seemingly all the more cherished as they become more illusory and banal. While painful, the process and results of such re-examination will probably show that a "life of common involvements" includes our common confusions and contradictions as well as our mutual identities, and that only by recognizing and accommodating such ambiguities can a peaceful community persist among real men in the mid–twentieth century. Such political lessons do the expanded theories of social science and existentialism outline for modern citizenship.

51. F. Scott Fitzgerald, *The Great Gatsby* (New York: Charles Scribner's Sons, 1953), p. 36. What Camus called "the absurd."

# Index

221